D0040874

STRAIGHT UP

HONEST, UNFILTERED,
AS-REAL-AS-I-CAN-PUT-IT
ADVICE FOR LIFE'S
BIGGEST CHALLENGES

TRENT SHELTON

WITH DAVID TIECHE

ZONDERVAN®

ZONDERVAN

Straight Up
Copyright © 2020 by Trent Shelton

Requests for information should be addressed to:
Zondervan, *3900 Sparks Dr. SE, Grand Rapids, Michigan 49546*

Hardcover ISBN 978-0-310-76560-8

Audio download ISBN 978-0-310-76554-7

Ebook ISBN 978-0-310-76528-8

Cover direction: Ron Huizinga
Interior design: Denise Froehlich

Printed in the United States of America

20 21 22 23 24 / LSC / 10 9 8 7 6 5 4 3 2 1

Contents

IV. STRAIGHT UP ABOUT YOUR ENVIRONMENT

V. STRAIGHT UP ABOUT FRIENDS

VI. STRAIGHT UP ABOUT PAIN + SUFFERING

VII. STRAIGHT UP ABOUT RELATIONSHIPS

VIII. STRAIGHT UP ABOUT HARD WORK

IX. STRAIGHT UP ABOUT CHANGE

X. STRAIGHT UP ABOUT FEAR

XI. STRAIGHT UP ABOUT YOUR HEART

XII. STRAIGHT UP ABOUT MAKING AN IMPACT

STRAIGHT UP

ABOUT REALITY

SINK OR SWIM

I stood at the starting line with a couple hundred other athletes, leaning forward like a coiled spring, waiting for the starter pistol to go off. I was in Fort Worth, Texas, for a Mud Run, a race that featured a couple miles of trail runs filled with military-style obstacles, ending in a short swim to the finish line.

A few weeks earlier, I'd embarrassed myself in front of friends and colleagues when I couldn't finish a Mud Run. I hadn't trained for that one, thinking my natural athleticism would carry me. But it was so much tougher than I'd anticipated, and I had to drop out.

But this time? This time, I was ready. I had trained like a beast. I was winning this thing.

Because I, Trent Shelton, was an elite athlete. I was a former NFL wide receiver, a former standout collegiate athlete. Since junior high, I'd been training with the top coaches in the nation to bring the machine of my body into its peak form.

This was going to be fun. A fun workout. I would run, swim, sweat, probably win the whole race, and then drink a Gatorade (Arctic Blitz, y'all!) to hydrate. Cakewalk.

The starter pistol went off, and so did the mass of humans. And that was the first moment during the race that my pride and ego got the best of me.

I bolted out to an early lead, running as though I was being chased by those demon dogs in *Stranger Things 2*. I had the lead. I was going to show everyone what happens when Trent Shelton, world-class athlete, trains for something. I was going to show them my dust.

The first issue was the terrain. I'd been practicing hard on trail runs, but all the courses I'd trained on were more or less flat. This course was hilly. Super hilly. "No matter," I said to myself, "just push through."

This was the second time my pride and ego got the best of me. I'd forgotten when you push through several times in a row, something happens to your body: it starts to get tired. One can only push through so many times.

But I was almost done.

The military-style climbing wall was the final obstacle. I ran up the wall, imagining I looked a little bit like Batman. I grabbed the top of the wall, pulled myself over, and stood at the top. From here, it was pretty easy. All I had to do was grab a zip line, zoom down the wire, drop into the lake, and swim a couple hundred yards to the shore, where the finish line—and my first-place trophy—awaited.

I took a second to breathe in, and my body complained loudly. I was tired. I mean, I'd pushed myself and I was *tired*. But I wanted that first-place finish.

I grabbed the zip line and flew through the air over the small lake. I hit the end of the line, let go, and dropped into the water.

As soon as my body hit the lake, I knew I was in trouble.

It was cold.

Not like, "Oh, it's a little chilly outside today, I think I'll put on a sweater" cold.

More like, "I think polar bears would die in this water" cold.

The sharpness of the cold water literally took my breath away. For a split second, all the muscles around my chest tightened in response to the temperature shock. I could almost feel the cold in my lungs as I tried to fill them with air.

"You gotta swim, dude," I said to myself, most obvious motivational speech in the history of humanity.

And so I did. Just one stroke after another. "Kick with your legs. Pull with your arms. Remember your form."

And I did this for a while. There was a marker buoy and some race marshals, who sat on the shore, making sure everyone was okay. They were looking for telltale signs that someone was in trouble and could get to them in a few seconds.

I should have listened to my body at that point. It was screaming at me in a way my body had never screamed at me. I played football in Texas and did two-a-days in the hot summer Waco sun, sweating until I felt like there was no liquid left in my body. I've gotten cramps in my calves that have been so painful, it felt like someone shot me in the leg. I know my body.

I should have paid attention to the warning signs.

But I didn't.

I kept swimming, pushing through the pain and discomfort. I didn't want to be that guy. The one who called out for help. I had embarrassed myself before, and I was NOT going to do that again.

"You've got this, Trent," I said to myself. "You've got this."

But I didn't. I didn't have it. I was lying to myself.

I was denying reality.

And about a minute later, reality caught up to me.

I literally could not swim anymore. I tried to make my legs kick. They would not move.

A pastor I knew once tried to explain Genesis 1 to me, how God created everything with a single word and a single thought. He said, "We actually know what this is like. There's one area in our lives where God has given us that level of control and power—and that's in our bodies. When you think, 'Arm, move,' your arm listens and moves. When you say, 'Thumb, up,' your thumb obeys." It's pretty incredible, if you think about it.

Which is why it was so deeply concerning when my body

stopped listening. It's a weird thing for you to tell your body to do something—to try to move your muscles or tell your arms or legs to move—and have no response. But that's what was happening to me.

I literally couldn't swim anymore.

And I was in the middle of a lake.

I don't know how deep it was. Maybe it was only twenty feet deep. Not that deep. But I'm not twenty feet tall, so that's deep enough for me to drown three times over.

I felt panic set in.

I tried to kick my legs, to tread water. They were done. Nothing left.

Adrenaline shot through me (because fear is funny that way). I started flapping my arms in the water, like I was a bird trying to fly away. I gasped for air.

And it was in that moment I knew I was in trouble.

Not "a little bit of trouble" like when you come home twenty-two minutes past your curfew and your mama's waiting for you.

Not "a little bit of trouble" like when your teacher says, "Okay, it's time for the unit test" and you didn't study.

Not "a little bit of trouble" like when you and your brother get caught eating Halloween candy for breakfast.

I was in trouble.

Big trouble.

Has this ever happened to you? Have you ever been in a situation and suddenly realized you were in trouble? Maybe not literally at risk of drowning in a lake. But I bet you've been in a situation where you felt overwhelmed. Unprepared. Unable to handle it.

We've all been there.

Maybe it's a math class you thought you could handle, but it turns out it's really complex, and everyone else seems to be getting it—it's clicking for them with light bulbs going on in their heads—but it's like staring at a foreign language for you. And you're just not getting it. You're in trouble.

Or maybe it's a situation with a friend. They text you late at night, asking to talk. But you're not up, so you awake to a string of texts that is deeply concerning. You see phrases like *I can't go on* and *I don't know what to do anymore* and maybe even *I don't even know if I want to live.* It weighs *heavy* on you. And you realize you have no idea how to help your friend. No idea what to say. You're in trouble.

Or maybe it's not about a friend. Maybe it's about you. Maybe you have a thing that's keeping you up at night. You worry about it constantly. It's the last thing you think about at night before you fall asleep, and the first worry that runs through your brain when your eyes snap open in the morning. It's a situation you just don't know how to solve. You're stuck, like a rabbit in a snare. And you don't know how to get out. You're in trouble.

Here's what that moment in the lake taught me:

Denying reality never helps.

Ever.

I was splashing at that point, flailing in the water like a drunk dolphin. I was not okay. And that's when I said it.

"Help," I said, as loud as I could.

And with that one word, I stopped denying reality.

I told the truth.

There was a safety guy from the race on the shore who heard me. Ironically, at this point, I wasn't really *that* far from the shore. He grabbed a floatation buoy and ran out as far as he could into the shallow water. He threw a floatation device attached to a gleaming white rope out to me. I don't really know how he threw that thing so far. Maybe he was an Olympic discus thrower or something. But suddenly, a floating red buoy was right in front of me. This man had trained for this moment. He was fully equipped to help me. He gave me everything I needed to make it out of that water safely.

But I had to call for help first.

And in that water, with the red buoy in front of me, I realized an important life lesson. Pretending that things aren't that bad or ignoring the clear warning signs that things are going sideways is almost always the surest way to get yourself into real trouble.

I have a good friend who is a recovering drug addict. He was deeply helped by a twelve-step program called Drug Addicts Anonymous that helps people get free from a life of addiction. He tells me all the time:

The first step of the twelve steps is to admit you're in trouble.

The language my friend uses is "I was powerless."

And I know it sounds strange, but I learned that lesson completely and fully in that moment in the middle of the lake.

I realized in that moment that if you refuse to accept the reality of your situation, it can really hurt you.

If you refuse to accept reality, it can really hurt you.

And if you're going under the water, it does no good to pretend things aren't really that bad.

Or that "you got this."

Because sometimes you don't.

Sometimes you're drowning.

But if you refuse to admit you're drowning, you really are in trouble.

Because—as my friend the former drug addict tells me all the time—the only way to get help is to admit you need help. And the only way to get out of a bad situation is to stop pretending that you're NOT in one.

So, I don't know why you're reading this book. Or what compelled you to pick it up. I don't know why you're reading these words right now.

But maybe you've been like me. Trying so hard, and exhausting yourself, trying to stay above the water. And if you're honest, you're not doing so well. If you're honest, life is hard right now. And you're doing your best, but it's just too much.

That's okay.

Admit it.

That's what this whole book is for.

That's why I wrote it. That's why I'm here.

Because denying reality never helps.

It's time to tell the truth.

Because if you don't, you just might drown.

REHAB TIME

Here are a few questions to help you think about this chapter and how it relates to you. Spend some time on these questions, and answer them as honestly as you can.

COACH PEP TALK

This chapter is about facing reality, but often we don't like to do this. We prefer to deny reality or pretend. It's not easy to force ourselves to think about these things in our lives, because it's painful. But as I learned, if you aren't honest, you might drown. And that's no good. So, try to be as honest as you can about the aches of your own heart.

QUESTION 1

In this chapter, I faced a situation that was pretty bad, but I didn't want to admit it was as bad as it was. Is there anything in your life right now that isn't going very well that you really wish were different?

The reality I've been avoiding/not facing honestly in my life is . . .

....
....
....
....
....
....
....
....

As you think about this problem, fill out this chart.

Things I **CANNOT** control in this situation	Things I **CAN** control in this situation

QUESTION 2

Looking at the column on the right, what is something you can do today or this week to start making progress on this problem?

The one thing I can do today/this week to make things better in my reality is . . .

....

....

....

....

....

....

....

GRAB THE BUOY

In the previous chapter, you'll remember I was trying to complete a race and dramatically underestimated how difficult the course was, how freezing cold the water was, and how tired my body was.

There I was, in the middle of the lake, when I was hit with what was essentially a full-body cramp. I didn't want to admit I was in trouble, but I quickly realized that pretending was no longer an option.

So I yelled out, "Help!"

Within seconds, a marshal from the race who was standing on the shore threw a floatation device attached to a gleaming white rope to me.

And I grabbed that buoy. I grabbed that buoy like it was my bae. I grabbed that buoy like my life depended on it.

Because, of course, it did.

And in the process of that situation, I learned a few things.

The man slowly pulled me toward the shore, and as he pulled me into shallow water, he came out to help me walk to dry land. As he grabbed my exhausted body and helped me walk, the man said a simple sentence to me I don't think I'll ever forget.

"What took you so long?" he asked.

I thought to myself, "What took *you* so long? I almost drowned out here."

But then I realized he was asking me, "Why did you wait until it was almost too late to call out for help? Why didn't you let me know the second you started struggling?"

What *had* taken me so long? I'll tell you why I didn't call out for help. It was because I didn't want anyone to know I needed help.

I thought that would make me look weak.

Or dumb.

I didn't want to expose the fact I didn't know what I was doing.

Also, I didn't want to reinforce the stereotype that black people can't swim and become a walking cliché. But mostly the other stuff.

Have you ever done this? Have you ever NOT asked for help when you clearly needed it because you didn't want to look foolish?

- You don't understand what's happening in class, but you don't raise your hand to ask the teacher for clarification.
- Your coach says to do something, but you have no idea what she's asking or even how to do it, so you just nod your head.
- You have a conflict with a friend, and you don't know how to make things right.

And in that moment, I realized something.

NOT ASKING FOR HELP IS FOOLISH

Like we talked about in the previous chapter, refusing to accept reality can cause you to drown, but not asking for help when you know you need it will result in the exact same thing.

But that's not the only thing I learned in the middle of the freezing cold lake that day. As I grabbed the buoy, and the race marshals literally pulled me from the deep water to the shore, I realized something else.

"I NEED HELP" IS A SUPER POWERFUL SENTENCE

I used to hate the word *help*. I did. I thought it meant I was weak. In my mind, when someone said the word *help*, I automatically related that to helplessness. And I didn't want to be helpless.

But you're not strong because of your strength. Being strong is about character. It's about not giving up when you lose, about admitting you're weak and trying to get better, and also, sometimes, being brave enough (which requires inner strength) to ask for help.

But we—as people—are embarrassed to ask for help. Be brave. Ask for help. Because when you do, and this is my next point . . .

GOOD PEOPLE WILL RESPOND

As I struggled to keep my head above the water and screamed out the word *help*, I wasn't paying attention to who was around me. But within seconds, someone was running *Baywatch*-style into the water to throw me a buoy. And then, seconds after that, I was being helped onto the shore. And seconds after that, some emergency medical personnel were checking my vitals to make sure I was okay. And someone else wrapped a blanket around my shivering frame.

This is very important for you to know: if you ask for help, good people will respond.

That's what good people do.

I recently saw an incredible documentary called *Won't You Be My Neighbor?* about Fred Rogers, who in the 1970s developed an educational show for kids called *Mister Rogers' Neighborhood*. Fred Rogers had an incredible knack for explaining difficult things in ways that helped kids. One of his most famous quotes is this:

> "When I was a boy and I would see scary things in the news, my mother would say to me, 'Look for the helpers. You will always find people who are helping.'"[1]

When bad things happen . . .

When tragedy hits . . .

When something scary occurs . . .

There will always be people running toward the chaos to help. There will.

When the Thai soccer team was trapped in the cave, the helpers rushed in.

After the Boston Marathon bombing, the helpers rushed in.

After the tragedy of September 11th, the helpers rushed in.

Now, I know there are some of you reading this who have been deeply hurt, and even betrayed, by adults who were supposed to run in and help—who SHOULD have rushed in to help you—and they did not. They didn't do their job. And I know that's deeply disappointing. And it's true. I'm not going to sugarcoat it. There *will* be adults who are paralyzed with fear, stuck on the sidelines. Or adults who are selfish and run away from difficult things to protect their own lives.

That is true.

BUT.

This is also true: there will always be people who run to help.

Also, I don't believe God leaves us in this world alone, just flailing about in the water as we slowly drown. I believe God puts people in our lives providentially to help us. God wants you to have big faith in Him (faith in His goodness and trustworthiness), and one of the ways He does this is to send people into your life to help you.

Always.

If you call out for help, there will always be people who run to help.

(And ideally, as you become an adult, you will become that person who rushes in to help others. That's one of the big goals of life, and a big sign of maturity.)

But for now:

If you're in a lake.

And you have a full-body cramp.

And you've called out for help.
Look around for the buoy.
And grab it.
Grab. The. Buoy.
You'd be a fool not to.

REHAB TIME

COACH PEP TALK

Just like I had to reach out for the buoy, you might have to reach out to someone for help. The best person is ideally a parent. They love you the most, and in a lot of situations they are likely the best people to talk to. If you're someone who just doesn't have parents you can rely on, try to find someone you trust and who believes in you. Take some time to fill this form out.

PERSON I KNOW WHO MIGHT BE ABLE TO REALLY HELP ME IN THIS SITUATION	WHAT I NEED FROM THEM

One of the best ways to reach out to someone is sending an email or text. Here's a template and sample note to help you with that email or text.

Dear So-And-So,
In one sentence, describe the situation.
Describe how you're stuck.
Describe what you need.
Request to meet.
Thank them.
Sign your name.

Dear Mr. Kenobi,

I have a tough situation in my life right now that I need help with. As you know, I live with my aunt and uncle on a moisture farm way out in the middle of nowhere. They want me to run the family business. It's not that I don't love my relatives, it's just that I want so much more than moisture. If I'm honest, I aspire to join the Rebellion, and maybe even become a star pilot and lead a strike force of X-wings against the evil Empire. But I feel trapped. I don't know what to do.

Would you be willing to meet with me, to give me advice and help me figure out what to do in this situation? I really respect you, and I sense you'd help me.

Let me know where and when works best for you.

Thank you.

Sincerely,

L. Skywalker

LESSON 03

WHAT IF THE END
ISN'T THE END?

I remember the exact moment I knew my NFL career was over.

I remember the exact place where my dream of playing football died, officially.

For almost two decades, football had been my life. I'd put on Pee Wee football pads when I was six years old. I'd started all four years of high school—in Texas, where football isn't a game, it's more like a local religion. I'd been recruited and given an athletic scholarship to a Division I school. I'd been invited to try out for three different NFL teams and made their rosters. Football was my life.

Until it wasn't.

In October of 2009, in the office of Washington's player personnel director inside the team's headquarters, I knew it was all over.

"We really like you," the personnel director said to me, being kind. "We love what you do. But it's a numbers game."

I cut the gentleman off. Not to be rude, but partly because I wanted to spare both him and me some time and embarrassment.

"I appreciate the opportunity," I said. "I really do."

I took out the official Redskins playbook they had given me when I arrived at camp and handed it to the man.

"If something opens up . . ." he began.

"Nothing's going to open up," I said. "It's okay. Again, I really appreciate the opportunity."

I walked out of the practice facility. And that was it. I had gotten cut. That was my last moment in the NFL. And in football.

Have you ever felt that way? Like something was ending? Like a door you'd hoped would open was not only slammed in your face, but locked? Like a dream you'd been carrying for so long was suddenly gone?

It can feel hopeless.

Really hopeless.

Some of you know *exactly* what I'm talking about. (And if you haven't experienced this yet, it is probably *going* to happen.)

But I think about that moment a lot. Because—and I'm being honest here—that moment was one of the best moments of my life.

Not at the time, of course. It was only raw pain then. But now? Now I see it very, very differently.

SOMETIMES IT TAKES CERTAIN THINGS FALLING APART TO HAVE BETTER THINGS FALL INTO PLACE

You see, that moment in October 2009 was the end of my childhood dream. But it was also the beginning of the second part of my life. That moment was painful, yes, but it was also the moment when a few very big things happened in my life.

> **I realized I'd been living for myself, and myself alone.** God used this moment to wake me up inside. I had been living a me-focused, selfish life. I knew going forward, I had to change things.
>
> **I realized that all the fame from football wasn't going to fill the void inside me.** I recognized football had been like a shiny gold idol, promising me lots of things but never delivering. I

thought if I made it into the NFL, then I'd be somebody, and the dull ache inside would go away. That's not how it worked.

I realized there was more to me than just football. For so many years, how I performed on the gridiron defined my identity. It wasn't just what I did—it was who I was. It was the only thing I was. If I did well on the field, I was good. If I did poorly, or made a mistake, I was bad. God used this moment to show me I had more to offer than just athleticism. I had a mind. A heart. Other talents. But even more than that, God showed me that He didn't love me because of my performance, but simply because I was His son.

That moment was the death of a dream. But it was also the birth of something new. I reconnected meaningfully with God. A few months earlier, I'd started posting videos, trying to be inspirational, to help people. They had gained popularity, and more than that, I loved doing them. Additionally, a few months earlier, my buddy had asked me to speak to his youth group, and though I was scared out of my mind, I'd done it. And it had gone well. And more than that, I enjoyed doing it. I now had time to do those things.

And as I look back on it now, here's the incredible thing: getting cut led to RehabTime, my organization that works to uplift people. It led to a job I love. It led to me meeting my wife. Having a son. Having a daughter.

So many good things were up ahead on the road. I just couldn't see them.

SOMETIMES, LIFE'S REJECTION IS REALLY JUST GOD'S REDIRECTION

Sometimes it takes losing what you're settling for to lead you to what you most need.

Think about it this way. When my son was in kindergarten, his entire class was learning about plants. So each child took a Styrofoam cup, filled it with dirt, and buried a small green bean seed under the potting soil.

But there was one kid in my son's class who really loved that bean seed. Her name was Kira.[1] She thought that bean seed was awesome. She carried it around (I think she thought it might have been magic, like the story of Jack and the Beanstalk). The teacher finally had to convince Kira to bury the seed, and that no, the seed was not afraid of the dark.

Kira placed the cup on the windowsill in the kitchen, where it could sit in the warm sun. And every night, she'd water that Styrofoam cup. Then one day, a little green shoot broke through the soil, with little tiny leaves. Like Baby Groot. Super cute.

And Kira started crying.

"Where did my bean go?" she said through big tears. "I want my bean back."

Kira's dad had to explain to her that the bean was gone, but the tiny plant was now there. The little bean had to go away so the tiny plant could grow. And that tiny plant would have to go away so that the bigger leafy plant could grow.

That's how life works.

The end of one thing doesn't mean the end. It often means the start of something else. Football had been my bean. It had to go away so something new could grow. Something . . .

New.

Beautiful.

Growing.

THE WORST DAY IN HISTORY

Let me remind you of the greatest slammed door in the history of the world. Imagine that moment, more than two thousand years ago, when a young teenager named John watched as Jesus of Nazareth was tortured by the Roman guards and hung on a cruel cross with nine-inch nails through His wrists. Imagine what would have been going through John's mind and heart as he tried to comfort Mary, the mother of Jesus, while she wept for her boy. What would John have been thinking?

It's ruined.

All of it.

They killed Him.

He was the best man I ever knew.

He taught with nothing but love.

I saw Him heal with His hands, with His words.

He was the Messiah.

God Himself.

And they killed Him. Like that. On a cross.

Truly, this is the worst day in human history.

That's what John would have thought. That's what everyone at the foot of that cross would have thought. And yet.

It was not the WORST day in human history.

It was the BEST day in human history.

John just didn't know what God was up to. And often, neither do we. So I want to remind you.

This door slamming is not the end.

This difficult chapter is not your whole story.

This stinging moment is not your whole life.

This situation is not your final destination.

When things fall apart, instead of thinking your life is falling apart, maybe ask yourself this faith-filled question: *What might God be up to? I bet it's for my own good.*

REHAB TIME

COACH PEP TALK

Being young is difficult, mainly because you haven't been alive that long. If you're fifteen, that means you have only fifteen years of life to look back on (and some of that, you hardly remember!). Which is why age has its benefits. In this activity, I'm going to have you chat with two people who are significantly older than you. They'll help and encourage you with their perspective.

ACTIVITY

Pick two people who are at least fifteen years older than you, and ask them these two questions. Make sure these are people you respect (and like!). Listen to their answers.

NAME OF PERSON	WHAT TO SAY
PERSON 1: _____ PERSON 2: _____	QUESTION 1: Can you tell me about a time when something happened to you that (at the time) you thought was very bad, but now, looking back on it, turned out to be very good for you? QUESTION 2: What did you learn from this situation?

What did you learn from this exercise?

....
....
....
....
....
....
....
....
....
....

II.

STRAIGHT UP

ABOUT
PAST
HURTS
+
EXCUSES

OWN YOUR PAST (BEFORE IT OWNS YOU)

Listen. You are not your past.

Too many of us break our own heart by staying stuck in our past. We allow the mistakes in our yesterday to ruin our tomorrow.

What you did is what you've done.

But don't think your mistakes disqualify you from living a good life. Don't let your mistakes keep you from being great.

A bad chapter doesn't mean you can't have a great story.

A bad quarter doesn't mean you can't have a great game.

So when you say things like, *"I can't bounce back from this,"* or *"I've made too many mistakes,"* that is defeatist self-talk.

There's more to you than what broke you. There's more to you than who left you. There's more to you than the mistakes you've made.

That's not your identity. You're more than that.

Your past should be like a bookmark of what God delivered you from and where God has brought you from.

So your life hasn't been perfect.

So what?

Congrats. You're human.

Maybe you've said this line to yourself: *I could never forgive myself.*

Let me break down what's going on when I hear people say that sentence out loud:

This is the language of shame. This statement is all sorts of messed up.

God forgives you. But you can't?

Speaking or even thinking that line means there is something inside of you that you feel is more important than what God thinks.

All these self-responses are really feelings of embarrassment or shame.

We try to be perfect for imperfect people, but you have to understand that nobody's perfect. I need you to understand this too:

Your pain is not special.

I don't mean to minimize or undermine your suffering. What I mean is that your pain is not unique to you. There are likely thousands of people who have failed in almost EXACTLY the same way you have.

When you talk about it, when you're honest about it, you realize you're not disconnected from the human race. Your mistakes, if you learn from them and move past them, connect you to other people.

It's powerful to see someone who has owned their own past, has made it through it, and is able to talk about it.

Let me give you a powerful example of someone who owned their past.

She was an African American, born to a teenage mother in rural Mississippi who lived in the poorest of circumstances. Her father left the family when she was little, and she and her single mother had to move to inner city Milwaukee.

There, things got even worse. She was raped by her older cousin and sexually abused multiple times by other relatives. She became pregnant at fourteen and was sent to a juvenile detention center, but didn't stay because there wasn't a bed for her when she arrived. She gave birth prematurely and the baby boy died.

A horrible start.

But this young woman didn't give up. She moved in with her father, a former US soldier and disciplinarian. He sensed that his daughter was smart, so he made her read a book and write a report every week. She did it, and rocketed up in school, where she became a star honors student.[1] She later said that her father saved her life.[2] He convinced her of something.

A bad chapter doesn't mean you can't have a great story.

She decided to go into journalism, graduated from college, and took a job as a TV reporter. She moved to Baltimore. This was her big break.

But there was a problem. She was too emotional. Too empathetic. She couldn't distance herself from the stories. When she encountered people who were struggling, she'd stop reporting and go get them some blankets.[3] She was always getting written up by her bosses for becoming too involved. She cried during interviews with people. She'd laugh too hard at people's jokes. Her bosses had finally had enough. "You're not a good reporter," they told her. "You're not cut out for it."

She got fired (well, technically, demoted).

Again, a new low.

But a bad chapter doesn't mean you can't have a great story.

She refused to let this failure define her. She knew she understood how to tell a good story. And she knew she was great at interacting with people. The news station had signed a contract with her, and to run out her contract, they shuffled her over to an afternoon show. They had her interview people.

And this is where she shined.

Something about her made people trust her. She talked openly about her background of poverty and abuse. Her vulnerability made people drop their guard. Her terrible childhood wasn't something she hid but talked about. And the people she interviewed felt safe. Almost as if whatever they were going through, this young woman would probably understand.

The talk show blew up. Audiences loved her. They loved her honesty. She moved to Chicago to start her own talk show. The producers titled it after her name.

The Oprah Winfrey Show.

Oh sure, Oprah is worth more than three billion dollars now. But that's not what's most valuable about her. I think she's so valuable because she shows that our past—no matter how terrible—doesn't disqualify us from being great.

So how can you own your past without it owning you?

TREAT YOURSELF THE SAME WAY YOU'D TREAT A GOOD FRIEND

A lot of people I meet have a lot of negative self-talk. When they mess up, or because they mess up, they say things to themselves like, "You're so stupid. You'll never be anything." Do you do this? It's crazy, if you think about it. I bet if your good friend messed up, you would NEVER say, "Man, Vanessa, you are a royal mess up. A complete failure." You'd never say that to others, so why in the world are you saying that to yourself? Change the way you talk to yourself. Be as kind to yourself as you would be to someone you love.

EXAMINE HOW YOUR DIFFICULT PAST HELPED YOU BECOME THE PERSON YOU ARE TODAY

A mistake isn't a mistake if you grow from it. Then it's a learning experience. And sometimes, the biggest mistakes or failures make the best teachers. I wouldn't be writing this book if I didn't have a past where I'd failed. My past failure to make it in the NFL created a positive situation where I had to hit rock bottom and figure out what life was about and what I was about. My mistakes gave me great pain, and that pain forced me to examine my own life. So what did you learn from that mistake or that tough season in your life? How did it change you for the better? What did you learn? What can you take with you going forward?

Look, your past happened.

It's time to move on.

The world needs the best you.

So get to it.

--------- REHAB TIME ---------

COACH PEP TALK

I need you to be kind to yourself when you're thinking about your own mistakes. But I also want you to realize that mistakes are often great life teachers. Examine your life, and answer this question: How did my past mistakes help me learn and grow?

YOUR STORY

The toughest thing I've been through is . . .

....
....
....

Here are two things I learned from that tough experience:

....
....
....

Complete this sentence: That difficult experience in my past turned me into a person who . . .

....
....
....

BURN SOME BRIDGES

People say, "Don't burn bridges."
　　I don't agree.

A bridge is a connection, most of the time between people but also between habits and activities. And sometimes—let's be real—you have no business having that bridge in your life, because you should NOT be connected to that person or that thing.

I want to be careful here, because burning a bridge is a serious thing.

The reason people say, "Don't burn bridges" is because once you burn it, it's gone. Gone. And rebuilding it takes a LONG time. And other bridges may get damaged along the way. You need to be exceedingly wise about this. You should not burn bridges because of a minor disagreement, for something petty that can be fixed. I always say that "Small disagreements should never kill powerful things."

So I want you to feel the importance and weight of this. Burning a bridge is a big deal and should be done with real thought.

But bridges that lead to destructive people and activities need to be burned.

There are certain people and activities that we cannot afford to have in our lives. A good question to ask is, "Where is this bridge consistently leading me?"

Is there a bridge that brings you to depression? To self-hatred? To pain? To thinking of yourself as less-than? To regret? To laziness? To bitterness? To abuse? To feelings of being useless or worthless?

That bridge cannot exist in your life. You can't allow that connection in your life.

Some bridges are meant to be burned because there are certain things in your life that you can't afford to go back to.

These bridges aren't dead ends. They're worse—they lead to death.

I know this very well. Immediately after college, when I was trying to make it into the pro game, I had a group of friends I had a strong bridge to. I spent A LOT of time with this crew partying, and by "a lot" I mean practically every night. I had a great time hanging with them, but I realized after a few months that this bridge was leading to only one thing: more partying.

Even though I had the realization, I kept heading to that bridge for a long time. Too long, in fact.

Eventually, it started becoming less fun. I'd wake up feeling terrible. This shouldn't be surprising, because drinking too much alcohol is basically like drinking poison that your kidneys have to filter out. But I was feeling terrible in other ways.

I was becoming the kind of person who was doing things—and valuing things—I didn't want to value. My priorities were off-balance, big time. Here I was, trying my hardest to make gains in one area of my life, and then doing things that were counterproductive to that goal the very next minute.

The bridge to this group of friends was consistently leading me to places that were not helping me.

I had to burn this bridge. I had to stop traveling across this bridge because it was taking me in the exact opposite direction I wanted to go.

And you see, that's the first key in burning bridges. For you to know if you should burn the bridge, you have to know where it leads.

And then you have to assess if it's the kind of place you WANT to go. So . . .

BE CLEAR ON WHERE YOU WANT YOUR LIFE TO GO

If you don't know where you want to go, then how are you supposed to know if you're getting there?

It's like that moment in *Alice's Adventures in Wonderland* where Alice approaches a fork in the road. She's lost. Suddenly, the bright, moon-shaped smile of the Cheshire Cat appears, and she asks him for directions.

> "Would you tell me, please, which way I ought to go from here?"
>
> "That depends a good deal on where you want to get to," said the Cat.
>
> "I don't much care where—" said Alice.
>
> "Then it doesn't matter which way you go," said the Cat.[1]

If you don't know where you're going—what you're trying to accomplish—then it makes it tough to know which road you should follow.

But once you know where you want to go, and you realize that a bridge is leading you in the opposite direction, then it's easier to get back on the right path.

Here's what I need you to know: You can keep these bridges in your life if you want to, but the bridges in your life need to match the ambitions of your dreams.

In my case, I knew that I wanted to be in the NFL. I had to focus. Drinking that much alcohol on the nightly wasn't going to help my body become a machine. Secondly, some things shifted in my life when my son Tristan was born. I realized I had to wake up and smell the responsibility. I had a new human being depending on me. I had to become the greatest me for his sake. I had to become a great father. And very few great fathers hang out at the club until two a.m. five days a week.

One of my mentors, Steve, is a great golfer. He has the silly pants and the red Tiger Woods Nike golf shirt. And he plays frequently. Golf is such a precise sport that you must play frequently to become and stay good. But he told me that when his kids were young—from about age two to about age eighteen—he hardly golfed at all. He gave it up.

Steve knew that the amount of time it would take to play golf weekly—four hours, or maybe more—would cut into the time he needed to spend with his boys and his wife. He knew that the money it would take to maintain his equipment was money his family needed for other things.

So he burned that bridge. And Steve kept the bridge to golf burned for sixteen years.

I asked him if that tough for him to do, since he has always loved golfing.

"Not really," he told me. "Inside every no is something that's a much bigger yes. I wasn't saying no to golf. I was saying yes to a loving family and connection with my sons."

(Man, I freaking love Steve.)

It's easier to burn the bridge if you have a big "yes" inside of you and it's clear the bridge isn't helping you get there.

HOW DO I CUT SOMEONE OFF?

I get that this is the most difficult part. I remember sitting down with that crew who partied—that crew I had been partying with for months and months. And I had to be straight up.

Look. This is my dream. There is where I want to go. I want to make it in the NFL, and I want to be a better man for my son. For me to move up, there are some things I must be willing to give up. Straight up.

If you're not willing to grow with me, then I will leave you here. Because I am going in this direction, with or without you. If you're not willing to change, then some things in our relationship will need to change.

We can't keep doing the same thing. Are you with me?

Now here was the difficult part. Some of my friends didn't get it. They didn't get it at all. They got mad at me, in fact. And they said some hurtful things to me that stung.

But.

I had a clear vision going forward.

I knew where I wanted to go. And I had seen the consistent effects of this bridge. And it did not lead to where I wanted to go.

So, what if they don't want to grow with you? If they don't want to come along? If they put you down because you're trying to do something positive in your life?

Well . . .

That might be proof you really need to burn that bridge.

By the way, not everyone in that crew reacted badly. There was one friend who basically said, "Oh, thank God you said something. I feel the same way." And he wasn't as far along in this decision as I was (after all, I'd been thinking about it for a while), but once he heard me say it, he knew that was what he wanted for his life too. So he walked across that bridge and burned it as well. And we started walking together to different bridges. To this day, he's a good friend and a close brother. He came with me. And I count his friendship in my life as a good gift from God.

The point is, there are some things and even some people you need to cut ties to.

You need to burn that bridge.

REHAB TIME

COACH PEP TALK

It's a serious thing to cut someone out of your life. Think hard on it. But sometimes it becomes crystal clear that you need to go in a direction that is the exact opposite of where someone else is headed. They're going down a path that's destructive for you. These questions are designed to help you unearth that.

QUESTION 1

This bigger question comes in three parts, which have to do with identifying people who you might want to cut out of your life. Think about them for a bit.

When I ask you, "Is there someone in your life who consistently makes you feel bad about yourself or your life?" does anyone come to mind?

....

When I ask you, "Is there someone in your friend group who is constantly trying to influence you in a negative way?" does anyone come to mind?

....

When I ask you, "Is there someone who is in your life who shouldn't be?" does anyone come to mind?

....

QUESTION 2

Being honest with yourself, is there any reason to keep this person in your life? Are they for you, and helping you become who you are trying to become?

....

....

....

....

QUESTION 3

What steps could you take to remove yourself from this person? How could you begin to burn the bridge to that person? What needs to change?

....

....

....

....

THE WORST PHRASE EVER

Well, that's easier said than done."
This is my *least* favorite sentence in the English language.
I hate it.

I hate it more than "Your dentist appointment is today." I hate it more than "Your account balance is low." I hate it more than "We're all out of ice cream."

I have heard this phrase more often than I care to remember. And every time it makes my blood boil.

Hear me on this: literally everything in life is easier said than done. Everything.

It's easier to say, "I'm getting dressed for school" than to actually get dressed. It's easier to say, "I'm going to make macaroni and cheese" than to cook it. It's easier to say, "I'm going to graduate from high school" than to do it. It is always easier to say something—to talk about a plan or a goal—than to actually accomplish it. This is a "duh" statement.

So why do people say it? In my own life, I think when I've said this phrase, it's usually meant one of three things.

"I don't have the skills to figure out how to tackle this plan, so it is pointless for me to try."

"Well, that's a goal that will require a very complex and difficult

plan, and while I could probably figure out how it could be done, I don't want to put forth the effort."

"I already figured out what achieving that goal will mean as far as time and work, and I am overwhelmed by that commitment, so I'll just emotionally shut down."

I think the reason I hate the phrase so much is because I used to say it all the time. Especially when I was younger, I would use this line when there was a challenge in front of me I knew was not going to be easy—one I knew would push me beyond my current limits.

I'd say it as a way to deflect, to make me feel good about a decision to not pursue what I knew in my heart I needed to do at the time.

You've probably said this too. This phrase "Well, that's easier said than done" is the number one excuse people write every time I post a video. By a long shot.

I get it. Most people just want that thing to magically happen in their life. They want the tough part to be done already. They want that big problem that's looming to be solved.

But that's not really the way life works.

In the words of the famous American poet Vanilla Ice, "If there was a problem, yo, I'll solve it."

GET IT DONE

When you say you're going to do something, and someone says to you, "Well, that's easier said than done," you need to ignore that mess. Just because they couldn't do it doesn't mean you can't do it. I realized a while ago that people tend to project their own fears and limitations on you. Their imagination isn't very big, and you start telling them things that their imaginations can't imagine, so they shut it down. Your dreams are too big for them.

I remember when I was young, whenever said I wanted to be in the NFL, people would respond:

"Only a tiny fraction of people make it."
"*No one* from this town's ever been in the pros."
"That's unrealistic, Trent."

Then, when I told folks I wanted to be a speaker:

"Trent, you aren't professional enough."
"You have too many tattoos."
"You use way too much slang."

There's always a reason why it's going to be tough. So instead of saying, "Well, that's easier said than done," I think this phrase is better:

"I'm going to get it done."

No matter how hard it may be . . . I'm going to get it done. No matter how difficult it may seem . . . I'm going to get it done. No matter how many obstacles are in my path . . . I'm going to get it done.

I'm going to get it done, because I have to get it done.

WORTH IT

Let me give you an inspiring example of what it means to refuse to give in to the phrase, "Well, that's easier said than done."

On May 25, 1961, then-president John F. Kennedy stood before Congress and said, "I believe that this nation should commit itself to achieving the goal, before this decade is out, of landing a man on the moon and returning him safely to the Earth."[1]

This was one of the most ambitious plans in human history. And let me tell you, there were critics. They said it was impossible. They said, "Well, that's easier said than done." And they were very right.

The Apollo moon landing project might very well have been the most difficult project ever faced by humans. Here's what it cost:

- Adjusted for inflation, the US spent $98 billion dollars.[2]
- At the program's peak, more than 400,000 people worked on the Apollo taskforce.[3]
- That's 400,000 people.
- Likely working 50 weeks a year.
- 40 hours a week (although many of the engineers said they were required to work at least 56 hours a week).
- For about 9 years straight.

How much hard work is that?

Building the Empire State building took 7 million man-hours.[4] Building the Panama Canal took 20 million man-hours.[5] Going to the moon took 5.23 *BILLION* man-hours.

That is a staggering amount of work. Staggering.

Imagine if these hardworking men and women had said, "Going to the moon? Well, that's easier said than done."

But they didn't. They said: **"I'm going to get it done."**

But it's not just about giant, history-making space journeys. This isn't about astronauts. This is about you. In your life, you will face something difficult that will require a great deal of work. It will be frightening. It will be overwhelming. People will say you can't do it, or that it's too difficult. You have to push through and say, "I'm going to get it done."

Losing weight and getting healthy is easier said than done. Put in the work. Your body is worth it.

Quitting smoking is easier said than done. Put in the work. Your lungs are worth it.

Graduating from college is easier said than done. Put in the work. Your career is worth it.

Being a good, loyal friend is easier said than done. Put in the work. Your friend is worth it.

Forgiving someone who has hurt you is easier said than done. Put in the work. Your emotional health is worth it.

Going to counseling to get healing is easier said than done. Put in the work. You are worth it.

Letting go of a toxic relationship is easier said than done. Put in the work. Your future happiness is worth it.

Stop letting that phrase "it's easier said than done" be an excuse. Stop using that excuse to not move forward. Stop using that excuse to not make the changes you need to make in your life.

Get after it. Do the hard work.

REHAB TIME

COACH PEP TALK

Giving up because something will likely be difficult is no reason to not do a thing. Nothing worth ANYTHING has ever been easy. We all have places in our lives where we're tempted to sneer and say, "Well, that's easier said than done." These questions are designed to help you see what those areas are for you . . . and help you change your perspective.

QUESTION 1

Is there some area of your life that, when you think about it, makes you feel overwhelmed with how difficult it will be, or how hard you'll have to work, or how much work it will require? What is that area?

....

....

....

QUESTION 2

Why is working hard for that thing worth it? What will you gain?

....

....

....

LESSON 07

COMPARISON IS DEATH

"Comparison is the death of joy."
MARK TWAIN

In my experience working with teens, by far the most common stress factors that pop up are school and grades.

This is not only my experience. It's backed up by data. According to a Pew Research study, when asked about what is stressing them out, the number one answer (by a wide margin) was school performance. In fact, 61 percent of teens said they feel a lot of pressure to get good grades. The next two major stress factors (to look good and to fit in socially) were at 29 percent and 28 percent respectively, less than half the percentage of grades.[1]

But if school stresses every teen to some degree, what happens to teenagers when you increase the expectations and pressure? New York University studied this exact trend, examining the stress levels of high school juniors enrolled in two highly selective private secondary schools in the Northeast. What they found was that the pressure was pretty intense.

Almost half (49 percent) of all students reported feeling a "great deal of stress" on a daily basis. And roughly 26 percent of these juniors reported symptoms of depression at what the researchers called a "clinically significant level."

That's a lot of stress.

So much stress, in fact, that Dr. Charles Cleland—one of the lead investigators on the study—said:

> Substance use for stress relief was a predominant theme in our interviews with students, over two-thirds of whom described substance use [drugs or alcohol] as both endemic to their social experience and as a method for managing stress.[2]

Wow.

But here's the thing: even if you're not a student at an elite Ivy League prep school in upstate New York, you know about the pressure to perform academically.

The realm of school is where *most* students spend *most* of their day, and every student is evaluated with a grade every few months, giving them an indication of how they're doing.

The bottom line is, grades are a measuring stick. Someone else is measuring you based on some criteria. And you get a piece of paper that tells you, objectively, some numbers on a scale of 1–100. Grades are tied to so many things, including:

- your sense of how well your present is going (How well did I do on that test? In that class?)
- your self-worth (If I do well in school, I'm okay, and if not, I'm not.)
- your identity (Am I a good student? A bad student? A mediocre student?)
- Your future (Will I be able to get into a good college?)
- and all sorts of other things.

I read an article about students who were a part of the international baccalaureate program (a pretty intense college-prep program offered in some high schools—think Advanced Placement classes for every subject).[3] They created their own hashtag: #ibprobs. Some of these posts were straight-up clever:

> "Laminate your index cards while studying. Not only does it prevent smearing but the teardrops actually roll right off."

But some of them weren't . . .

> "I don't even feel tired anymore, I just am tired. Like it's a part of me."

It's not just IB students who feel this way, though, is it? I have been around students across the country, from the West to the South to the Midwest and the East Coast, and every place I go, students are exhausted from the pressure.

I have a good friend who lives in the San Francisco Bay area—one of the most educated regions and wealthiest places in the US. It's the home of Stanford University and a whole slew of powerful, innovative tech companies. And its schools are some of the highest-performing in the nation. And that means that there's tremendous pressure put on every kid to academically perform. He told me that at his kid's junior high school, a large percentage of the 6th, 7th, and 8th graders take courses throughout the summer in math. The goal is to enter junior high at least a grade ahead in math.[4] He said that instead of taking a leisurely break filled with playing outside, going to the pool, watching movies, and going on long family summer vacations, these students spend several hours a day racing through math concepts to learn an entire grade level worth of skills in one summer.

He said in some circles, it's actually seen as *shameful* for a student to be in their actual grade in math.

I just shook my head. That's a lot of pressure to excel. To be at least a grade ahead in math. To be in as many advanced and honors courses as possible. To get perfect grades.

The problem is there are very, very, very, very few people who are THAT good at THAT many subjects in school. Most people are not equally good at every single subject. Most students are either gifted at math/science or English/language arts. But instead of school being a supportive place that helps kids find their sweet spot, a hypercompetitive culture begins to emerge where kids are expected to be perfect IN EVERY AREA.

And I worry about this.

I saw a Reddit conversation the other day saying this was the new grading scale:

A = Average
B = Below average
C = Can't have dinner
D = Don't come home
F = Find a new family[5]

Which was funny. Until it wasn't.

This kind of pressure creates unhealth. Students who begin spending hours and hours and hours on homework, doing their absolute best to ace their next test, and turning in a flawless research paper that took numerous hours of writing and rewriting. Students who cut out sleep in an effort to get better grades.

And for a lot of students, this pressure is too much. Because there comes a time when you look around and realize you can't keep up academically.

It's like that popular meme you might have seen floating around that says:

Everybody is a genius, but if you judge a fish by its ability to climb a tree, it will live its whole life believing that it is stupid.

What if you're a student who is a fish and being asked to climb trees? Or a kangaroo judged by your ability to fly?

What happens when you put a mule in a horse race? It will lose every time. No matter how hard it tries, it can't beat those graceful colts and filles who were built for speed. And, perhaps worst of all, the mule stops focusing on the fact that it is *just* as strong as a horse, if not more so. It stops seeing its own usefulness, its own gifts. It only sees what it's NOT, instead of what it is. This is why comparison robs your joy.

I know that you've felt that way. I know it. Everyone has.

If you were more athletic like so-and-so, just a bit stronger or faster, you'd get more playing time, and then you'd be okay.

If you were prettier, like so-and-so, or had her hair, then you'd feel okay about yourself, and then you'd be okay.

If you were better in math, like so-and-so in your class, then your GPA would be higher, and then you'd be okay.

If you were a little bit taller.

Or shorter.

Or had bigger muscles.

Or a smaller nose.

Or hair that was wavy.

Or hair that was straight.

Or could sing better.

Or jump higher.

Then you would be okay.

I know you think this way, because everyone does. But I'm telling you, it does no good to compare yourself to other people.

Should an elephant wish it were as light as a cat? Then it would lose its strength.

Should a dolphin wish it had feathers? Then it wouldn't be graceful in the water.

Should an eagle wish it had the strength of a rhino? It would be too heavy to soar.

Do you see? It DOES NO GOOD to compare. It not only makes you feel bad about yourself, but it causes you to lose sight of the very things that make you special and wonderful and unique.

COMPARISON IS DEATH.

Comparison will get you to fixate on a lie that screams because you're not like so-and-so, you aren't good enough.

And here's what I'm afraid of most (and it's a fear that is grounded in reality): that this comparison will lead people to believe awful things.[6, 7] That there will be a student—maybe you've even done this—who will compare themselves to everyone else around them and come to a terrible, terrible conclusion.

I'm no good.

I'll never be good.

And then, perhaps, the next, terrible, terrible thought.

It would be better for me to be dead than be who I am.

Dear heaven, that any young person would feel this way just breaks my heart.

COMPARISON SAYS TO GOD, "YOU MADE A MISTAKE."

And that's a lie.

Because God doesn't make mistakes.

Never let what you "aren't" dominate your thoughts, become your focus, or distract you from what you ARE.

Don't fall for the lie.

REHAB TIME

COACH PEP TALK

One way to get out of the trap of comparison is to shift your focus from what you ARE NOT to what you ARE. I want you to complete this activity by choosing at least three people from the list on the left and then texting them the script that's written on the right.

PEOPLE WHO KNOW ME WELL AND LIKE ME	WHAT TO ASK THEM
(circle three) MOM DAD GRANDMA GRANDPA TRUSTED ADULT COACH NEIGHBOR GOOD FRIEND 1 GOOD FRIEND 2 SIBLING RELATIVE FAVORITE AUNT FAVORITE UNCLE FAVORITE TEACHER YOUTH PASTOR/WORKER	**Text them this question** Hey, _____! I am doing an activity for a book I am reading. I am supposed to ask someone who knows me well the following questions. Could you please help me by texting back some answers? **QUESTION 1:** What do you think makes me unique? **QUESTION 2:** What do you think I am good at? **QUESTION 3:** What 2–3 adjectives come to mind when you think of me?

What did you learn from this exercise?

....

....

....

STRAIGHT TALK ABOUT FORGIVENESS

Let me be real with you.

Some of you are stuck. You're stuck with bitterness. Someone hurt you, and you're not forgiving them.

"They don't deserve to be forgiven," you say.

And that might be true.

But if you don't forgive them, you will die inside.

Forgiving someone doesn't excuse what the other person did to you. What it does is give you the power to free yourself and move on from what they did. You can physically move on from the person, but until you forgive them, it becomes emotionally impossible to move on from the pain.

It's even possible to be deeply wounded by someone who is no longer in your life at all. You literally may never see them, but they're still affecting your life in a negative way.

Why? Because the pain they gave you is still in your life.

That's baggage your heart cannot afford to carry.

Care enough about yourself and care enough about your FUTURE self to stop giving that person that much control.

Don't let someone who didn't care about you then hurt you now.

They might have ruined your past.

And they might be ruining your now.

DO NOT let them ruin your future.

Without forgiveness, I promise you this: your life will become a reflection of the pain they gave you.

So many times, we hold hate and anger in our hearts, thinking we're getting back at the person who created those feelings inside us. But holding that resentment in our hearts only burdens our lives, not theirs. In fact, I have so often seen that people who don't forgive turn into bitter and terrible people.

Stop giving power to the person who's made you feel powerless.

Free yourself.

Understand that they gave you pain because they themselves suffered. They could never do right by you because they were never right within themselves. Their addiction to their sin, or their brokenness or their selfishness, was stronger than their love for you (or anyone else, for that matter). Their battle wasn't with you, it was with their own addictions and brokenness.

When you understand that, you go from hating them and wishing the worst for them to feeling sorry for them and their condition.

That's how you know you're healing.

But you must let go of the hate. You have to move on from the resentment. You need to open your hand and let go of the bitterness.

Not for their sake.

But for yours.

Enough is enough.

NOT FORGIVING GETS YOU STUCK IN A MOMENT IN TIME

Life is always moving forward. And when you're deeply hurt, and you stay there and don't forgive, you basically are stuck in that moment of pain. And you can't move forward. It's like you're a donkey tied to a post, continually pulling a stone around a circular path that has become a deep, deep rut after so many journeys that go nowhere.

My friend Alicia was deeply betrayed by a guy she thought loved her. She caught him cheating on her and broke up with him. I was proud of her for that, but after about a year, I realized that she still wasn't over him. I know that breakups can be painful, but this seemed like too much. While she was talking to me and my wife, we realized she was still very hurt and very angry.

She shared that nearly every song on the radio reminded her of him. She kept thinking about that moment when she discovered his unfaithfulness. It kept coming up in her mind, and she couldn't move on from it.

NOT FORGIVING LOCKS YOU IN HOPELESSNESS

When you're stuck in pain, it feels like it's going to go on forever and will never end. But that's not true. Back to my friend Alicia. During our conversation, she pounded the table through her tears. "He ruined everything," she said.

"No," my wife shot out. "No, he did not. In fact, he only ruined one thing. He ruined his chance to be with you. He destroyed your relationship. But he didn't ruin you. Or your future."

Alicia was convinced that everything was ruined. She was giving this guy way too much power and dramatically overestimating his ability to influence her life.

Alicia was locked in a mindset of hopelessness. My wife—she's a firecracker—popped off a bunch of questions for Alicia to get her out of that mindset.

- What if there's another guy who is totally different?
- What if there's another guy who also has been hurt and vows to never experience that again?

- What if there's another guy whose character is based on loyalty and love?
- What if God is at work in this pain and you can't see it?
- What if God had you catch this jerk because otherwise you would have been trapped in a bad relationship?
- What if God views you like a beloved daughter, and there's no way He would allow you to be tethered for life to a man who would hurt you?
- What if God is up to something?

Alicia was trapped in her thinking.

NOT FORGIVING SEPARATES YOU FROM YOURSELF, OTHERS, AND GOD

I know grown adults who are still carrying around hurt and pain. And oftentimes, if they haven't done the hard work of forgiving other people, they start to turn into a person consumed by hatred. They turn into a person who's ugly on the inside.

Martin Luther King, Jr. understood this well. Facing the atrocities of segregation and violence against black people in the South took a toll on him and so many others. And King saw a propensity in himself to give into hatred in those moments, which he knew would cripple him. He once said, "We must develop and maintain the capacity to forgive. He who is devoid of the power to forgive is devoid of the power to love . . . There is some good in the worst of us and some evil in the best of us. When we discover this, we are less prone to hate our enemies."[1]

King knew that hatred corrupts people. I think this is why Jesus spoke so strongly about forgiveness, saying, "For if you forgive other people when they sin against you, your heavenly Father will also forgive you. But if you do not forgive others their sins, your Father will not forgive your sins" (Matthew 6:14–15). Jesus made this nonnegotiable. He understood that refusing to forgive destroys the very bridge that we need to get to God Himself, because we too are always in need of forgiveness.

This isn't academic for me. A while ago, there was a guy—a booking agent—I did business with. This dude did me dirty and stole money from me. I trusted him. I thought he was something he obviously was not, and he took advantage of my trust.

I was embarrassed. I was angry. I felt helpless to do anything. But then something even worse happened to me. That one experience with that one terrible, shady person made me not trust other people. I said, "I'm never going to do business with anyone again." I began to isolate myself, and in the process, I cut myself off from opportunities to meet great people. I was hurting myself.

In addition, I started going out of my way to make sure other people didn't work with this guy. I spread the word that he was a crook. I started to make my life mission to tear him down.

Well, as you might imagine, God refused to let me stay there. He did business on my heart. I realized this hatred was doing ABSOLUTELY nothing for my life. As long as I was focused on the person who cheated me, I couldn't move on. I couldn't concentrate on me or what I needed to do. And it was changing me into a person I didn't recognize and really didn't like.

I'm telling you: not forgiving someone will really hurt you.

So you need to forgive.

Don't you see? Forgiving is a gift that you give yourself. It's not easy. But it's critical.

Do the hard work.

Be brave.

Forgive who you need to forgive.

It all starts with you.

REHAB TIME

COACH PEP TALK

Discovering if you have a person you have not forgiven because they've hurt you is not always easy. But it's a necessary activity if you want to move forward. This activity is designed to help you identify what's going on inside you, and if you have areas of unforgiveness in your own heart.

STEP 1

Go through this list of questions and see if anyone comes to mind. If so, it's likely you're dealing with unforgiveness.

Do you hold a grudge against someone in your life who has hurt you in the past?

Do you get angry being around someone in your life, or even feel that way just thinking about them?

Do you keep a mental list of offenses someone has made against you?

Is there someone you tend to lash out at?

Is there some moment in your life where someone hurt you that you keep replaying in your head?

Is there someone you find yourself gossiping about?

STEP 2

If someone's name came to mind during step 1, then go to the next chapter, LESSON 09, and do the activity at the end.

HOW TO FORGIVE SOMEONE (EVEN IF THEY DON'T DESERVE IT)

I could never forgive them for what they've done."

I've heard so many people say this to me. And often, it's from a place of deep pain. But you need to understand something.

If you don't forgive, it will control you for the rest of your life. It can turn you into a person who has a lot of hate in their heart, and that poisonous root will grow and turn you into someone you don't even recognize.

Unforgiveness is death.

Forgiveness is letting go for your own sake.

The theologian Dallas Willard put it this way: "Forgiveness is like oxygen."[1]

I'd like to remind you what happens if you don't get any oxygen. You die.

That's how important it is.

But doing so is not easy. Forgiveness is very, very difficult. It takes a strong person to say, "I'm sorry." It takes an even stronger person to forgive. One of the world's greatest leaders, Mahatma Gandhi, once said, "The weak can never forgive. Forgiveness is the attribute of the strong."[2]

But before we go any further, you need to know what forgiveness truly is—and one way of discovering that is looking at what it is NOT.

WHAT FORGIVENESS IS NOT

FORGIVENESS IS NOT PRETENDING IT DIDN'T HAPPEN.

There are some people who think the best way to deal with things is to pretend like they didn't happen. They might even say something like, "Forgive and forget." But that's always sounded an awful lot like denial to me. Denial is denying reality. And it never works. Ever. If you want to move on, you have to face what really happened.

FORGIVENESS IS NOT PRETENDING YOU'RE NOT HURT.

Forgiveness is not minimizing the pain the other person caused. You don't have to say things like, "It's not that big of a deal" or "I'll be okay." What if it was a big deal? What if you're not okay? Then what? Don't go playing mental tricks on yourself. In fact, if you pretend it's not a big deal, and you try to forgive, nine times out of ten the bitterness will creep right back in. You can only deal with the pain you admit is there.

FORGIVENESS IS NOT TRUST.

Forgiveness is not the same thing as trust. In fact, just because you forgive someone doesn't mean that you should trust them. It's possible the person should not be in your life in the same way as before—or perhaps at all. Forgiveness is free. Trust is earned. Forgiveness is physically granted in an instant. Trust takes time to restore.

FORGIVENESS IS NOT RECONCILIATION.

Forgiveness is a one-way street. But reconciliation is a two-way street. This can't always happen. For example, if the other person refuses to admit they've even done anything wrong, reconciliation is simply not possible. Or maybe the person lost contact, or has died. Sometimes it's just not smart to try to reconcile because the other person is so toxic. The point is, forgiving someone is not the same as reconciling with them.

FORGIVENESS IS NOT A ONE-TIME THING.

Forgiveness is a choice that you make in the moment. But that doesn't mean it's a one-time thing internally. I can almost guarantee there will be a moment, when you're alone with your thoughts, where the anger and hurt will rise up again. You will think about what the other person did and just how much it hurt you. And the anger will rush back. In those moments, you will have to stop and forgive the other person. Again. Sometimes, it's a choice you have to make daily.

FORGIVENESS DOES NOT REQUIRE THE OTHER PERSON TO APOLOGIZE.

It's almost always easier to forgive a person if they admit they were wrong. But what happens if they don't? You still need to forgive them. Forgiveness is about you letting go of the desire to get revenge. It is about letting go of that pain and the hatred that's like a stone around your neck. Forgiveness is your journey.

FORGIVENESS IS NOT REALLY ABOUT THE OTHER PERSON AT ALL.

I once met a young man named Joey who wore dog tags around his neck. I always wondered why he did this, and one day, I asked him. He explained to me that his father was in the military, and when he was two years old and his younger brother was just a baby, his dad abandoned his family. "Just left us," Joey said. "Which is why I wear these—to remind me that I am NOTHING like my father." As he said this, Joey's voice shook with rage. I got a chance to talk with Joey and helped him realize that even though his dad was no longer in his life, this man was still hurting him and controlling him. Joey realized that not forgiving his father wasn't affecting his deadbeat dad, it was affecting *him*. He was the one carrying around all that pain.

Now that we know what forgiveness is NOT and can see what it IS, we need to move. So, what helps me forgive? Here are three things that help me forgive others.

WAYS TOWARD FORGIVENESS

I UNDERSTAND I'VE BEEN FORGIVEN.

I know myself. I know I am not perfect. In fact, I'm far from it. Now, I happen to be a spiritual person, so as I review my day and try to be honest before God, I realize I need to ask God for forgiveness every single day. There's not a day that goes by where I'm like, "I did nothing wrong today, God. I'm good." Not a single day. So if I expect forgiveness, I have to give forgiveness. Otherwise, I'm a hypocrite. This helps me forgive.

I UNDERSTAND THERE ARE CONSEQUENCES IF I DON'T FORGIVE.

We talked a lot about this in the previous chapter. Not forgiving means I'm allowing a situation to control so much of my life going forward. Not forgiving means I'm going to be mired in a negative mindset. Not forgiving means I'm going to let anger and bitterness have full run of parts of my heart. No good can come of this. There are real consequences if I don't forgive.

I UNDERSTAND THIS ISN'T ABOUT ME.

When someone has hurt you, it's usually because they themselves are hurt. People who are healed and happy and whole usually don't go around leaving emotional wreckage in their wake. It's highly likely that they're hurting. Maybe they were hurt, and they've never offered forgiveness to the people in their past, and that's changed them into someone they don't even want to be. Maybe hate's in their heart, and it's just leaked out onto you. When people don't know how to deal with their stuff, it often comes out in destructive ways.

It doesn't make it right. It doesn't make the things they did okay.

But it does make extending sympathy to them much easier. It makes it easier for me to forgive them.

I get that forgiveness is a private thing.

You don't have to have an audible conversation with someone. Oftentimes, I go on hikes in the middle of nowhere, and I think about these things and talk out loud about what's going on to no one (except God).

I've seen people write the names of people who have hurt them on a piece of paper and throw it into a fire as a way to say, "I am letting go of this."

I was at a camp once where we took small rocks and used a Sharpie to write the name of a person who had hurt us on each one, and then we threw the rocks into the lake. It was our way of saying, "I'm letting go of this."

There are some steps in the activity below that might help.

But whatever you do, start now.

Start today.

It's not optional.

REHAB TIME

COACH PEP TALK

Forgiving other people is hard work. Here's a step-by-step process that has helped me:

STEP 1: Be honest about your pain.

What was done? What was said? How did it impact you? How did it make you feel? How did this affect your life, and how is it still affecting your life?

STEP 2: Make a decision to forgive.

This is the hard part, because you won't feel like forgiving. That's okay. To forgive is to make a promise to not bring up the wrong with the person, or with others, or in your own thoughts. It's a promise not to dwell on the hurt, and to stop wishing harm on the perpetrator, wishing instead that God would work in their life and do good things in their life.

STEP 3: Choose empathy.

Empathy happens when you try to take on another person's perspective. Why do you think the other person did this to you? Put yourself in their shoes.

STEP 4: Ask God for help.

Remember that God forgives us. And that God commands us to forgive. Plus, God wouldn't ask you to do something you can't do without helping you. So ask for help.

STEP 5: Repeat as needed.

As we looked at before, forgiveness usually isn't a one-time thing. Every time the memories flood back, and you feel yourself getting upset, go through this process again. I promise, it does get easier.

LESSON 10

THE TWIN ASSASSINS OF BLAME + COMPLAIN

I'm going to be blunt with you.

The people who blame and complain are always people who aren't doing much in their life.

You want to stall your life? It's easy. Be a person who focuses on blaming and complaining. They are the twin assassins that will kill your life.

I call this the B/C mindset (blame/complain). It's a prison. It holds people in a jail cell of negativity and doesn't let them progress in life.

The B/C mindset is a trap because it makes you okay with things that aren't okay.

Blaming and complaining makes you feel good about doing nothing.

It's basically saying, "What's going wrong in life? Well, it's not on me." And as long as it's somebody else's fault, you never do anything. And things stay the same.

The B/C mindset actually short-circuits the only power you have in these situations, which is to take responsibility. I always say, "It all starts with you." As long as we're above ground, we have a chance to make a new beginning.

The only way to make change in your life is to make changes.
I know that sounds simplistic, but it's the truth.

The opposite of the B/C mindset is the A/C mindset: Accept and change. That is where you get power. The B/C mindset is weakness.

If you don't make changes, nothing will change. And you'll spend the rest of your life in a B/C mindset. And that's not going to help you.

I have not only seen this B/C mindset, but I have lived it. When I was trying out for the NFL and trying to make a squad and kept getting cut, let me tell you, it was NEVER my fault. It was everybody else's fault.

It was my coaches' fault for not helping me train better.

It was my parents' fault for not giving me the genetics to run faster.

It was my friends' fault for distracting me with fun and not pushing me to focus harder.

This is very common in sports. I've seen this a lot with other wide receivers I've played with who were having an off year. The blame game starts.

It's because of the quarterback.
It's because of the offensive coordinator.
It's because of the play calling.

Of course, their lackluster season wasn't because they didn't work hard on conditioning, or studying film, or memorizing the playbook. It was because of factors outside of them. It wasn't their fault.

Pointing fingers.

But here's the thing. Even if it is true—even if you are 100 percent right that your situation is someone else's fault—how is that helping you?

Blaming and complaining never help you move (even if you're right).

In my life, I've had my fair share of bad business relationships and failed projects. I bet you have too. Have you ever had a bad group project experience in high school? Man, I have. One time, I almost had my grade drop a whole letter grade in English class because my partner did absolutely no work, despite clear objectives being laid out by the teacher. I had to drag his lazy butt over the finish line just to eke out a C on the presentation. Ever been there? Man, that is frustrating.

But in some ways, it's worse in business, when both your money *and* your reputation are on the line. I've been a part of work projects that started to tank. Hard-core. And it absolutely was NOT my fault. I was doing my part of the group project. I had every right to blame the failure on the people around me (who weren't doing what they said they would do or couldn't follow through with what they said they would do). I had every right to blame. Every right to complain.

But then I thought, "Who was the person who entered into this agreement? Who let these people into my business life?"

And I realized the answer was *me*.

I had to switch to an A/C mindset. I had to ACCEPT the situation. And ACCEPT that I was partly to blame for letting those people into my life.

And then, after I accepted it, it was easy to see what came next. I knew I needed to make some CHANGES.

In some cases, I'd fire the person. Or I'd just quickly dissolve our partnership. Move on. I wrote down what I learned from the mistake. I made a list of things I needed to do in the future, homework I needed to do before choosing business partners. And that allowed me to charge ahead, looking for a new business venture partner who was good for me.

Suddenly, I wasn't stuck blaming and complaining. I was moving forward and making some changes.

So, here's how to move from the B/C to the A/C mindset.

STEP 1: FOCUS ON WHAT YOU CAN CONTROL

When life gets overwhelming, it's easy to focus on all the things swirling around us that we wish were different. But the honest truth is, sometimes we don't have any control over those factors, and focusing our attention on them only frustrates us. Instead, focus on ONE change you can control. One thing you have the power to change in your life. Otherwise, I'm telling you, it's going to be overwhelming, and you'll shut down emotionally. Make ONE change. It doesn't have to be major. It just has to move you forward.

STEP 2: FIND A MENTOR OR COACH

Find someone who is a few steps ahead of you, who has success doing what you're trying to do, and get some help. Now, it is great if you can talk to them in person. But you don't have to. For example, maybe your help comes from a book. A lot of my mentors and the people who have truly helped me gain understanding and perspective are long dead. But I read their books. In order for me to change, I need new information and some help. And people say, "Experience is the best teacher." And by that they mean, "The hard knocks of life have a way of teaching you better than anything else." And that's true. But you and I can ALSO learn from other people's pain and suffering. Their hard knocks. So get a coach.

STEP 3: GET IN AN ENVIRONMENT OF GROWTH

One of the best things you can do is to get into a group that supports you. When you get around other people who are trying to grow in the way you're trying to grow, that helps you get out of the B/C mindset and into the A/C mindset. You must put yourself into an environment where what you're trying to accomplish is NORMAL. An environment where it's something that other people around you are going for.

This is part of the power of everything from CrossFit gyms to high school marching bands to churches to AA meetings—each of these are filled with people united in direction, all going after the same thing. Not only will a group give you support, but just seeing the successes of the people around you will inspire you with hope that it will also happen for you.

I'm telling you, straight up.

Blaming and complaining are twin assassins.

Get them out of your life before they kill your future.

REHAB TIME

COACH PEP TALK

Blaming and complaining are pretty common, and if we're not intentional, we'll easily slip into these habits. This activity is meant to help you identify things you've been in a B/C mindset about, and help you switch to an A/C mindset.

QUESTION 1

Being honest with yourself, is there something that you've complained a lot about recently to your friends or the people around you? What is it? Perhaps there's something going on.

....
....
....

QUESTION 2

When you complain, what do you say?

....
....
....
....

QUESTION 3

Who do you tend to blame for this situation?

....

....

....

QUESTION 4

What is one step you can take (that you can control) to change your situation?

....

....

....

III.
STRAIGHT UP
ABOUT YOU

YOUR INTEGRITY IS WORTH MORE THAN $14.61

Listen.

Integrity is one of the few things in this life you can control.

There are lots of things in life you can't control. The weather. Traffic. The future. Other people's happiness. But this is the beautiful thing about your integrity. You have control over it.

You can control whether or not you're a person with integrity.

And honestly (I tell my son this all the time)—this is one of the best talents and most important traits a person can have. Because people *love* trustworthy people. They want to know, "Are you a person I can trust or not?" Because at our core, we all know we should avoid people we cannot trust.

So, the question before you in this life is this: Are you willing to stand up for what you stand for, even if it means that you're standing alone? That's integrity. That's what we need in this world.

There will be times when the people around you are doing the wrong thing. There will be times when the crowd will be doing the wrong thing. There will be times when your friends will be doing the wrong thing.

And you have the choice to be a person with integrity. Because you know the bigger picture.

In working with young people, I know SO MANY folks who were good kids, but they got caught up in the wrong crowd. And their friends started making the wrong decisions, and instead of standing up, they just went along with it.

Are you willing to stand up for something even if it means standing alone?

Because it's worth it in order to become a person others can trust.

Let me tell you a story. I know a guy named Alex who, during his time in college at UC Santa Barbara, worked at a little coffee shop on campus. Coffee shops are very important to college students. A customer once said to Alex, "Water is the most important element on earth, because it's used to make coffee."

Every day, Alex and his coworkers would tend to the caffeine needs of their fellow students. During finals week, they even developed a specialty drink they called "The Blitz"—which was an iced Frappuccino with four shots of espresso, a six-pack of Oreos, and a 5-Hour Energy shot blended together. I am not sure this drink is street legal. I developed diabetes and a heart murmur just thinking about it.

One day, Alex and a coworker named Ketan were working and began talking about life. Ketan said that he believed that all people were, at their core, basically evil. Alex said he didn't know about that. He'd seen that sometimes people, when given the chance, choose to do what's right.

Ketan then made a bet with Alex. "I will bet you, that given a choice to do what's right or what's wrong, people will choose to do the wrong thing," he said.

"How are you going to test that?" Alex asked.

"Watch this," Ketan said, and turned to a young woman who had just walked in.

"I'll take a large latte," she said.

"Okay, that will be $5.39," Ketan said.

The woman handed Ketan a $10 bill.

"Out of $20," Ketan said, pretending that he had misread the $10 bill in his hand. Ketan opened the cash register, pulled out $14.61 in change, and handed the incorrect amount of change to the woman.

He turned to look at Alex, who understood what Ketan was doing. It was a test.

Would the woman realize the barista had given her TOO MUCH change and give back the extra money? Or would she walk out of the store and pocket the money?

Are people basically evil?

Or basically good?

The woman looked at the change, looked at it again, took the change, put it in her pocket, grabbed her drink, and walked out of the door.

"See?" Ketan said, turning to Alex. "People are garbage. That woman right there just sold her integrity for the low-low price of $14.61."

That line stuck with Alex.

"She sold her integrity for $14.61."

That seemed like an awfully low amount to Alex.

Ketan then launched into a tirade, bringing up example after example of people being terrible to one another, lecturing Alex on his naïve views.

Moments later, the door opened, and the same woman came back in. She walked to the counter and approached Ketan.

"I was in here earlier, and you gave me too much change," the woman said. "I know it was an accident, and I know I technically didn't do anything wrong, but my conscience wouldn't leave me alone."

She put the extra $10 on the counter, and then put the remaining $4.61 of her change in the tip jar. Then she walked out.

Alex grinned at his coworker. "You were saying?" he said, smirking.

Now that episode in Alex's coffee shop reveals so much about us as people, doesn't it?

Here's what that episode in Alex's coffee shop shows me: that the answer to the question of "Are people good or bad?" is yes. Humans are walking contradictions sometimes.

In my own life, I know the right thing to do, and I don't want to do it. I know what's right but am stubborn and selfish. At times my conscience screams out at me.

Sometimes I listen.

Other times I don't.

I'm a mixed bag. Sometimes I do the right thing. Sometimes I don't.

The ability to choose is a beautiful gift from God, because we can choose to do the RIGHT thing. But it's also a terrible gift, because it means we also have the option to do the WRONG thing.

We have the ability to choose. To make our own decisions. This is real power that God's given us.

And like Spider-Man's Uncle Ben always said, "With great power comes great responsibility."[1]

Which is why I'm so inspired by the ending of this story. This young woman understood something vitally important, which reminds me of a Charles Marshall quote from *Shattering the Glass Slipper*:

"Integrity is doing the right thing, even when no one is watching."

She didn't know two baristas had a bet on her. In the quietness of her own heart and mind, she knew that keeping the money was wrong, and decided to do the brave thing and keep her integrity.

She used her power to choose to do what was RIGHT.

You and I have that same chance. And part of us will want to be selfish or lie or take things from other people.

But we can choose to do what's right.

Don't sell your integrity for $14.61.

Don't sell your integrity for any price.

Choose to do what's right, even if no one else is looking.

REHAB TIME

COACH PEP TALK

Sometimes we make the WRONG decision in life, and other times, we make the RIGHT decision. The woman in the coffee shop in this story did BOTH on the same day. I have found that it's sometimes helpful to think back both on the times you got it wrong AND the times you got it right to figure out what you can learn from those decisions. Because in the end, we want to get it RIGHT.

Time you made the WRONG decision	Time you made the RIGHT decision
What did you do?	What did you do?
What factors pushed you to make the wrong decision?	What factors pushed you to make the right decision?
What did you learn about yourself from this situation?	What did you learn about yourself from this situation?

QUESTION

Has there been a time recently when you've faced a tough choice and known what the right thing to do was, but didn't want to do it? How can you take a step to be brave and do the right thing the next time you need to make a difficult decision?

LESSON 12

STOP LIVING FOR
THE EXTERNAL

saw a shirt the other day that made me laugh. It said:

Be yourself.
Unless you can be Batman.
Then always be Batman.

I know it's funny, but it made me think. I see so many young people who say, "I just want to be myself," but in reality, they're always secretly wishing to be someone better or more glamorous.

Maybe this is because Instagram shows us so many people with picture-perfect lives, and it makes us feel bad about ours.

But this dysfunction isn't new.

I remember the first time I thought, subconsciously, "Hey, maybe I should try to pretend to be someone else so that people will like and accept me."

For most people, this moment probably happened in junior high. Or maybe freshman year of high school. Do you remember the first day of freshman year of high school?

How nervous you were? How you carefully picked out what you were going to wear?

And then, the biggest moment of all came.

Lunchtime.

And the crucial question. Who were you going to sit with?

Because this mattered. Lunchtime, the first day of high school, was like a giant watering hole on the Serengeti plain.

You have the wildebeest over here.

The lions over there.

The warthogs over there.

The elephants over there.

The giraffes over there.

And the antelope over there.

Which group do you belong in?

Which animal are you?

Because if you choose the wrong group, you'll get eaten. Antelope don't just go hang out with the lions, after all.

And in that moment, one dominant question rises up.

Where do I fit in?

This question is death.

Because when fitting in is the goal, you'll do whatever it takes to be accepted. You'll shape-shift. You'll change what you wear. You'll agree with things you're not even sure you agree with. You'll laugh at jokes you're not sure are funny. In short, you'll change your outside appearance (who you say you are) so that people will accept you. But this isn't the real you. It's all external.

STOP LIVING FOR THE EXTERNAL

Think about it like this: imagine you're a zebra. And you walk into that high school lunchroom, and you don't see any zebras around that watering hole. But you *have* to sit somewhere, so you put on an elephant mask with a fake trunk and start trumpeting and trying to drink water out of your nose.

And the elephants are like, "Aren't you a little small to be an elephant?" But hey, you fake it until you make it.

But deep down, you know you're not an elephant. There's nothing even vaguely elephant about you.

But the face that you present to the world says, "I'm an elephant!" And so people are confused. They start treating you like an elephant.

But you're not an elephant. You just created a reality that isn't true.

You can't be true to anybody else if you're not being true to yourself.

Don't try to be something you're not just to try to fit in. Don't paint a picture that isn't real. Because it's a form of lying, both to others and yourself. Honesty is the baseline for human relationships. And the only time you're really honest with others is when you're being real with yourself.

But there's another reason why you shouldn't do this. Because it won't get you what you really need.

In her book *Braving the Wilderness*, social scientist and researcher Brené Brown found that what people really want most is to belong. Belonging is when you are truly connected to other people.

"True belonging doesn't require you to change who you are," Brown writes. "It requires you to be who you are."[1]

So here are your options:

- Keep pretending you're an elephant when you're really a zebra. You'll be loved and accepted around the watering hole . . . but you won't be known. The whole thing will feel fake because you're pretending. This is shallow.
- Reveal you're a zebra and let the chips fall where they may. Some will reject you. You'll be known, but not loved. This is our biggest fear. And honestly, it's why we hide.
- Know your true friends will accept you. And then you'll get what you most need: to be fully known and fully loved.

So you need to do something. You need to have courage and be brave.

Stop pretending. Stop lying to yourself. Stop creating a perception that's far from your reality.

You can maybe fool everybody else, but I promise you this: you can never fool yourself.

Learn to be comfortable in your own skin. You should never sacrifice who you are just to please people. Don't change who you are just to be accepted.

The people who are happiest in life RISK REJECTION in order to be more honest about who they are.

So have the courage to show up. Be brave enough to let the world see who you are. And if they reject you, then they reject you. But at least you won't be lying to yourself and others.

And if you do that, you have the BEST CHANCE to be happy.

You want to learn the Elvish language from *The Lord of the Rings* so you can write secret notes to your friends? Do it.

You want to study all the secret Easter eggs hidden in each Pixar movie and form a giant conspiracy theory about how it's all the same universe? Knock yourself out.

You love running and want to see if you can match the pace of Eliud Kipchoge (the best distance runner in the history of mankind)?[2] Track your stats and geek out.

The point is, be yourself.

Because here's what could happen:

When you first looked around that watering hole and saw no other zebras, you felt alone.

But if you take off the elephant mask and show your zebra stripes, there's a good chance that another zebra will walk to the watering hole.

And they'll see you.

And they won't feel alone.

And you'll be like, "I get you."

So be you. Stay true to you.

Live it. Breathe it. Be it.

REHAB TIME

COACH PEP TALK

It's good to spend a little time thinking about who you are, what you are about, what you love and why. Fill out the form below and be as honest as you can.

BONUS POINTS: After you fill this out, text the questions back and forth with a good friend to share and compare answers. This will help you get to know them too.

THE ME MATRIX

What is something you're legitimately afraid of?	
What is something that makes you different than other people?	
What is your actual favorite movie?	
Write down five of the most awesome songs you've ever heard that you absolutely love.	
Besides your immediate family, who is your favorite relative? Why?	
What fictional character do you most identify with?	
If you got a tattoo tomorrow, what would it be and why?	
What's the most adventurous or daring thing you've ever done?	
What was your favorite vacation that you've ever taken and why?	
What is something in this world that upsets you/makes you mad?	
What's the best thing about you?	

LESSON 13

YOU WERE GIVEN
WORTH AT BIRTH

Imagine you're sitting at your favorite fast-food restaurant.

Did you pick one? Good.

Imagine yourself there, sitting on the brightly colored hard plastic chairs.

Someone comes by and puts a milkshake on the table where you're sitting.

"Here you go," they say as they set the cup down. "Here is a chocolate milkshake for you. It's delicious. It's creamy. And, oh yeah, I put some deadly poison in it."

Would you drink the poison milkshake?

No.

No, you would not.

Because poison has a way of ruining a perfectly good milkshake. And because although I'm frequently in the mood for a good milkshake, I'm INFREQUENTLY in the mood for death.

Sure, this is a silly illustration, but I want to point something out.

You'd never drink poison, but so often, we drink EMOTIONAL POISON.

Emotional poison is the lies that people say to us and about us.

Things that are not true. Things that tear us down. Things that do harm to our emotions and souls. Things that slowly kill us from the inside.

And we drink these in ALL THE TIME.

I knew a girl named Nina whose mother had a nickname for her. She called her "Oops" because Nina was an unplanned pregnancy. Nina's mother reminded her frequently that the reason her biological father left was because he didn't want to be a father. That the unplanned pregnancy—her life—had caused her dad to leave.

Now, I don't know what it's like to have a mother who constantly calls you a mistake—but I know what it did to Nina. It made her feel very unloved. Like her mother, if given a choice, would have chosen NOT to have a daughter.

Maybe something like that has happened to you. Someone has said something to you that hurt.

Tried to give you a poison milkshake.

Something like:

- You're not cool.
- You're not smart.
- You look funny.
- You're poor.
- You can't be my friend.
- You can't sit at this table.
- Nobody likes you.

Whatever it was, it made you feel like Nina. It made you feel a little bit worthless.

Listen. Straight up.

God gave you worth at birth.

Before anybody—and I mean ANYBODY—else had a say, God gave you value. God said you have value. And people who make you feel worthless are like fools standing over a one hundred-dollar bill saying, "This piece of paper is not worth anything!"

Fool. It says a hundred dollars right there. Multiple times. In really BIG letters. One hundred dollars.

But still, the fool stands over the bill, singing, "This is *not* worth a hundred dollars."

It's lunacy.

God gave you worth at birth.

And no one—not even your mom who gave birth to you—can change that.

There's a famous song written in the Bible. It happens to have been written by one of the more important people in the Bible, a man named David (of David and Goliath fame). He wrote this about God:

> You made all the delicate, inner parts of my body
> and knit me together in my mother's womb.
> Thank you for making me so wonderfully complex!
> Your workmanship is marvelous—how well I know it.
> You watched me as I was being formed in utter seclusion,
> as I was woven together in the dark of the womb.
> You saw me before I was born.
> Every day of my life was recorded in your book.
> Every moment was laid out
> before a single day had passed.
> How precious are your thoughts about me, O God.
>
> PSALM 139:13–17 (NLT)

I love this psalm. I love that David used the verb *knit*.

Knitting is an act that's intentional.

Thoughtful.

Artistic, even.

Takes a long time.

God did not whip you up. Or throw you together last-minute. Or even assemble or construct you.

He **knit** you.

God gave you worth at birth. Understanding you have worth means confidently accepting this deep truth about yourself. The more you can understand this, the more you can accept yourself.

But . . .

It's very hard to feel confident that you're worth something when other people tell you you're worthless. Nobody can give you worth—because that's already been bestowed on you by God—but it sure is amazing how much people can influence how you feel about yourself.

And the sad reality is this: the more you are around people who make you feel worthless, the less likely you are to realize you're truly invaluable.

Or, put another way, if you drink that poison milkshake—if you let those lies about your worth really enter into you—it can really hurt you.

This is why it's important for you and me to really read and think about the lines from that poem in Psalm 139. It's true, they were written by King David, but they also are from God Himself. Because at the end of the day, it doesn't matter what other people say about your worth. If it doesn't line up with what God says, then it's a lie. It's not accurate.

YOU WERE GIVEN WORTH AT BIRTH

You were made by God in such a way that inspires awe.

You don't believe that, do you? Well, it's true. Let it sink in.

You were carefully handcrafted—a stunning work of artistry by God Himself.

Did someone tell you differently? Well, they're lying. This is the truth.

When you know your worth, you don't chase validation, because you already know you've been validated. God put His stamp on you.

So when those people—or those voices—try to tear you down, you need to take time to think about what's true.

What's lovely.

What's right.

Because at the end of the day, the things we believe about ourselves matter. And you're always in control of what you accept. Including lies.

So when someone slides that poison milkshake your way, don't drink it.

Don't drink the poison milkshake.

Drink in this deep truth instead:

God gave you worth at birth.

And ain't nobody can take that away.

Ever.

And that's a truth that's even better than a milkshake.

REHAB TIME

COACH PEP TALK

Don't drink the poison milkshake. Drink the good one. Here's what I want you to do: read this poem (Psalm 139) and really interact with the words in the space provided.

Read the poem. Highlight or underline the things that stand out to you.	Why did you underline what you did? Why did it stand out to you?
PSALM 139:13–17 NLT *You made all the delicate, inner parts of my body* *and knit me together in my mother's womb.* *Thank you for making me so wonderfully complex!* *Your workmanship is marvelous—how well I know it.* *You watched me as I was being formed in utter seclusion,* *As I was woven together in the dark of the womb.* *You saw me before I was born.* *Every day of my life was recorded in your book.* *Every moment was laid out before a single day had passed.* *How precious are your thoughts about me, O God.*	

LESSON 14

PROTECT YOUR PEACE

What kinds of things make your stress meter ping?

You know what I'm talking about, right? When you start to redline because of the amount of stress in your life? Because I know your stress meter is pinging.

Here are some warning signs that your stress levels are high and you're almost overloaded:

- You feel restless or wound up like a coiled spring.
- You are fatigued and always tired.
- You have difficulty focusing or concentrating.
- You're irritable (with almost everyone in your life).
- You have stress headaches and tension in your neck, head, or shoulders.
- You worry frequently.
- You can't fall asleep.
- You aren't sleeping well.

So what do you do when your stress meter pings? Because as people, we go to different places that are safe or give us comfort.

Some people run to food, because good-tasting food releases endorphins that make you feel good. But we always run to food that isn't good for us, don't we? Doritos or cookies or ice cream. Nobody gets sad and binges on broccoli.

Some people run to books. I know this one girl who was always reading, which sounds very academic. But she was reading fiction books to escape the reality of her life. It wasn't a healthy coping strategy.

Some people run to cleaning. I know it sounds strange, but cleaning is a way of controlling your environment when everything else is out of control. The problem is, no matter how much you scrub your kitchen, that doesn't make the other problems go away.

Some people turn to alcohol or drugs. Go to that party. Get your numb on. Forget about the world, and just party for a while. The problem is, of course, that the problems are still there when you wake up the next morning (usually not feeling so great).

Some people turn to work. They get productive. Which sounds very healthy, except that it turns a bit into workaholism, where you do tasks to avoid thinking about your own life. You get a lot done on the outside, but the work you need to do on the inside is neglected.

Some people turn to friends and fun, which also seems like a great thing to do. But sometimes, you simply create a busy social calendar so you won't have to deal with your own issues. As one girl said to me once, "I can't be alone with myself. I just can't."

But by far, the single most common coping mechanism for young people is screen time. Usually their phones. But here's the problem. We think, "Oh, screens will help me relax and deal with my stress." But, as research shows, screens are actually TERRIBLE coping mechanisms. Screens not only don't help with big issues of isolation, anxiety, and depression, they actually make those things worse.[1]

So back to my question. What do you tend to do when your stress meter pings? What is your "haven" or "safe place"?

And the second, more important question: When you go there, where is your soul?

Where are you?

Because I would submit to you that we are a nation of people who are starving spiritually. Starving. People don't have any idea how to take care of their souls.

We might know all about how to feed our bodies. We often know how to feed our minds with books and learning. But we rarely know how to feed our souls.

You need to protect your peace.

What do I mean by that?

I mean, you need to pay attention to you.

A while ago, I realized I was really overwhelmed by life. I was unfocused. I was constantly rushed and hurried. I was almost frantic mentally. I was going, going, going, but I didn't feel right inside.

I asked a friend of mine what to do. She was a licensed therapist and counselor. She had seen a rise in anxiety in the people she was seeing. And she had a common recommendation as a starting point.

DISCONNECT OFTEN

She told me we all need to disconnect from the world and reconnect with our soul. We need to learn to disconnect often.

How often is often? The therapist suggested daily. And if you can't do that, then at least every other day. The point of disconnecting is to put yourself in a better place so that when you show up to the world, you're in a better place. You're not stressed. You're not in response mode. You're not rattled.

So here's what I do.

I go outside, into nature.

That's it.

Go for a hike.

I started trail running and hiking outside in the hills around my home. Sometimes I'd do it early in the morning. Sometimes during my lunch break. Other times, after work, after the heat of the day as the sun was setting.

And I'm not suggesting that going outside for a hike is a one-size-fits-all solution, but here's what I found:

- Hiking outside disconnected me from tech.

    Tech is a constant interruption. Outside in nature, my thoughts can wander without being grabbed by that email or that text message. I can think clearly, and my mind can do what it needs to.
- Hiking outside disconnected me from the expectations of other people.

    Look, we all need people, but we also need time to disengage from the demands and requests of other people and concentrate on ourselves. Requests on us aren't bad—at all!—but people drain us. If we only think about other people, and never take care of ourselves, we're in trouble.
- Hiking outside connected me to my physical body.

    It's a good thing to get the blood pumping. We're not just minds, we're also bodies, and hiking outside connected my body to my mind and soul. It's a good thing.
- Hiking outside connected me to God.

    Perhaps it's because I love nature or perhaps it's because I don't have the distractions of my phone and entertainment or other people, but being alone allows me to focus on God. I have my best talks with God out in nature.
- Hiking outside connected me to myself.

    Away from all distractions and demands, I can begin to slowly pay attention to my own life. What am I actually feeling? What am I worried about? What is going on inside of me? What are my struggles? What is God showing me about my own life?

Here's why I recommend this to you. Because I've seen what doing this has done in me. This practice gave me a time, every single day, to think about my own life. The bottom line is that there are times that your stress meter pings. Life will drain you.

You need to be filled.

YOU NEED TO PROTECT YOUR PEACE

You know, I was reflecting on this the other day. In the Bible, in the book of Mark, the story records that Jesus has a pattern of doing this thing where He gets up very early and withdraws from everyone. It's like a rhythm in the life of Jesus: He withdraws to be alone and then does something major.

Jesus withdraws before major decisions.
Jesus withdraws before big events.
This is His pattern, as recorded by Mark.

Another writer who wrote about Jesus's life put it like this:

But Jesus often withdrew to lonely places and prayed.

LUKE 5:16

There's this one moment, early on, that really drives home the point.

Very early in the morning, while it was still dark, Jesus got up, left the house and went off to a solitary place, where he prayed. Simon and his companions went to look for him, and when they found him, they exclaimed: "Everyone is looking for you!"

MARK 1:35–37

The disciples are like, "Hey! Everyone needs you." Basically, they're saying the same thing that life says to you. "There are stressful things to do and loads of people counting on you." And Jesus knew this. But He also knew that if He was going to be any help to other people, He needed to be connected to Himself and to His God.

JESUS NEEDED TO DISCONNECT OFTEN, AND SO DO YOU

I mean, if Jesus needed to get away from it all, and disconnect and protect His peace, then how much more do I need to? And how much more do you?

So when your stress meter pings, instead of doing something that ignores your soul or distracts you from your soul, get alone and spend some time in nature (or whatever your peaceful, disconnect-time is) with just you and God.

You need to tend to your soul. And if you don't, your soul will send out messages, shouting to you, "Hey! I'm in here! And I'm not okay."

Maybe you feel that way RIGHT NOW.

If so, take the time now.

Protect your peace.

It won't just help you. It will help everyone who depends on you.

——————— REHAB TIME ———————

COACH PEP TALK

If you don't protect your peace and disconnect, you'll burn out. So how do you do this? I have a strategy that I've been using for a while that a lot of people have found to be helpful. I call it the FOUR A'S. Read the explanation for each A below and then fill out the chart.

A=APPRECIATION

Gratitude really helps your mindset. Often, we get so busy thinking about what we DON'T have that we don't stop to properly thank God for all the things that we DO have. I mean, first off, appreciate the fact you're alive. Appreciate the fact you have people who love you (name them). And here's a trick: don't just be grateful FOR the things you have. Be grateful TO God for giving them to you. It not only reminds you that you have good things, but that you have a Good Father who graciously GIVES you good things, like food, shelter, love, friends, and purpose. Gratitude is great for your soul.

A=AFFECTION

I know that stress is a real thing, but you know what else is a real thing? Hugs. Now, I'm not talking about random hugs. Hugging strangers is weird. I'm talking about hugs from people you love. There are studies that show that people who are hugged at least once a day feel more connected to the world (and are even less likely to get sick). Hugging actually releases oxytocin, often called "the bonding hormone." This hormone promotes attachment in relationships, and after a hug, it literally stays in your brain and influences your mood. I'm telling you: a hug a day can keep the stress away.

A=ACCOMPLISHMENT

How you start your day will influence your day. You want to start your day with a win. Set up a thing you can accomplish—and check off the list—so that you can gain positive momentum in your life. Get a small win. Maybe it's writing in your journal. Or doing a short workout. Or walking the dog. Do something small so you can say, "I did this today." You want to start the day off positive, because when you get a win (even a small one), you feel good.

A=ACTIVITY

Get your body moving. This is not only good for your body, it's good for your mind and soul. Do something that gets your body moving. Go walking or hiking or hit the weight room.

APPRECIATION	What are some things I'm deeply grateful to God for in my life?
AFFECTION	Who is someone who I love and have hugged today? NAME:
ACCOMPLISHMENT	What's a small task I can do in the morning that is an "easy win"?
ACTIVITY	What's a physical activity I like that can get my body moving?

PROTECT YOUR LIFE

I'm gonna be real with you.

You need to start protecting your life.

Not everyone deserves you. Not everyone deserves to be in your life.

I am very picky about what I place in my life. And I am very picky about *who* I place in my life. The reason is I cannot afford to have certain people—certain mindsets and certain information—in my life. It's not good for me.

I learned early on, there are people who can mess up my entire day. They're about nothing but drama. They are excessively pessimistic. They're gossipers. I can't afford to catch what they've got.

You know what I'm talking about, right? It puts pause on your purpose.

When I see negative people call my phone, it's hi and bye. I keep it pushing. I'm not saying I'm mean. I pray for folks.

But what you put in your life consistently will influence your life.

You've seen this, right? Your friend, who used to be so cool, started hanging out with that crowd, and it rubbed off on them, and they changed into a different person. And not a better person, either.

Or your friend started dating someone who is not a great person, and they started changing too. They "fell into the wrong crowd."

You will become what you surround yourself with.

Be careful who you let into your life. If they're not growing you, if they're not making you better, if they're not a positive influence . . .

It's time to protect your life.

I tell people this all the time. We protect our houses. We protect our cars. Heck, we even protect our lockers at school.

But we don't protect our lives? It doesn't make any sense.

Here's how I think about it, and I got this from my mama growing up. My mom was not a woman who suffered fools lightly. She wasn't harsh to people—my mother was one of the kindest people I've ever known. But just because she was kind didn't mean she wasn't smart or wise.

My mama was very particular about who she let into her house. She would not let just anybody into our house. You had to be trustworthy before she'd even open the door. She made people earn their way into the house. In fact, it was almost as if Mama used our house as a big metaphor for human relationships. Here's how it worked.

THE SIDEWALK

This is the most public part of your life. Tons of people are here. And they walk by your house. This is everyone you go to school with, are in a class with, everyone you work with, and everyone in your neighborhood. The sidewalk isn't really your house, and you can't really control who is on your sidewalk.

You can't remove people, or wish people gone, from social situations you have no business trying to control. For example, if you've ever heard someone say, "I wish I didn't have a class with that person" or "I wish that person wasn't working the same shift as me" or "I wish that person wasn't on the team" . . . Well, you don't get to decide that. Sorry. That's not your call.

FRONT PORCH

The front porch is the most open and public part of your house. You use your front porch as a way of getting to know people. My mom would call people up from the sidewalk or invite people over to the porch to talk and chat. She'd see a new neighbor, or a coworker would stop by, or the mailman would be delivering packages, and my mama would meet them on the porch.

The front porch happens when you spend a little time getting to know someone. Maybe you sit with them at lunch. Or talk with them before your shift or before class. You chat with them a bit on social media. You're getting to know them. Asking questions. Listening.

But here's the thing. With my mama, the split second someone seemed dangerous or threatening, she got them off her porch. I remember more than one aggressive salesman being shooed away by my mother. "No thank you, I am not interested," she would say, adding a forceful, "Good day, sir. And good luck."

One time I brought a friend over, and he said something disrespectful to my mama. It was a hot day and he barked at her, "Get us some lemonade, would you?" And my mother looked at him. I tell you, I backed away from that kid because I thought my mother's eyes were going to shoot laser beams.

"Young man, why don't we try that again?" my mother said quietly (which scared me more). "And this time, let's pretend like I'm the adult, and you're a child that respects his elders."

I don't think that kid ever came back over to our house.

So how do you know who's safe? The way they talk. What they talk about. Who they make fun of. The types of jokes they make. What words they use. There are people, as I'm getting to know them, who reveal to me that they probably aren't getting into my house.

- People who make slightly racist comments
- People who make fun of other people in a mean way

- People who are really negative
- People who are critical in an unhelpful way
- People who complain a lot
- People who cuss a ton, just in regular conversation
- People who say they like the Dodgers

These are all things that make me say, "Uh, I think we're done here."

Now, one more caveat. I want to talk to the girls out there. I know, just from listening to the women in my life, that lots of times women get approached by men on their porch. Guys just walk up on their porch, trying to get a date.

Sometimes this is awesome, and the guy turns out to be pretty cool.

But sometimes, a guy you don't know will just storm up onto your porch, and you will know, almost instantly, "I'm not interested. This guy is not for me." Or even worse, you might think, "This guy might be unsafe."

Here's what to do, and most of the time this works:

Imagine you're actually on your front porch. How would you get out of that situation? Well, you'd just go inside. And close the door.

Stop the conversation. Don't engage. Don't return texts. Just go inside. Maybe you say, "No thank you. I'm not really interested."

Most of the time, this works. When salesmen would come to my house, if they wouldn't go away and kept pressuring Mama, she'd just close the door. They'd go away pretty quickly.

LIVING ROOM

The living room is inside your house. If my mama let you into the house, you were someone whom she had determined was trustworthy enough to come inside. If you weren't, she would literally open the front door and keep the chain on the door and talk to you through the chain. She was that serious about it.

But when she took that chain off, and the door swung wide, it was because you were someone my mother trusted enough to let inside her house.

Now, here is the point my mama taught me. Not everyone deserves to be in your house. Because not everyone is safe.

And here's the thing: you are responsible for every single person that enters your house. If the person does damage, or tracks dirt in, or breaks something, you are the one with the mess.

It is up to you to clean up the mess. No one else will.

So be wise about whom you open the door for.

THE KITCHEN

If my mama loved you, and you'd proven yourself to her, she would invite you into the kitchen. This is the area you invite your closest friends into. I had a few friends who my mama loved, and when they came over, she would invite them into the kitchen, sit them down at the table, and pour them a glass of cold water or lemonade or sweet tea. She might even break out some food.

If you were in my mama's kitchen, you were loved. And you had proven yourself to be trustworthy. For my mama, entry to the kitchen equaled time plus trust.

You can't build up trust to get into the kitchen except over time. But here's what my mama taught me about the kitchen: the kitchen was where the laughter happened. The kitchen was where real conversation about real things happened. The kitchen was the place of friendship and family. In fact, the kitchen was where most of "real" life was done. The kitchen was the best.

UPSTAIRS

In our house, all the bedrooms were upstairs. And my mother was very particular about whom she let upstairs. When I was little, I can't remember that many people being allowed to play in my room upstairs. This is the most vulnerable part of your house. It's where your valuables are kept. It's also where you live, and it's sometimes messy. This area isn't for everyone.

The upstairs is the most vulnerable part of your life and heart. And because of that, this is where the most damage can be done. If you let someone untrustworthy come upstairs, they can do some real damage.

Some of you know what I'm talking about. You ever have a friend who gets a boyfriend or a girlfriend, and they spend all their time with them, and even let them upstairs (yes, I'm also talking about sex here)—and the person turns out to be a terrible person?

Real damage happens, doesn't it?

Upstairs is for only a few people. In my own life, the people I allow to come upstairs are my parents, my wife, my son. That might be it. Like three to four people.

So who is in the house of your life? Should they be in your house in the first place?

Because here's the issue. If you let people into your house who have no business being there, who are untrustworthy or toxic, they will make a mess. They will break things. And then they will leave, and it will be up to you to clean things up.

I talk to people all the time who have people in their lives who are treating them very poorly. And I say, as kindly as I can, "Are people treating you in certain ways that you don't like? Why is that? Why are they even in your life? How did they get so close to you? Why did you open the door?"

It's time to protect your life.

REHAB TIME

COACH PEP TALK

It's time to figure out who's in the house of your life and think about whether or not that person should be in that room. It's possible you need to move people out or around. Take some time to examine who's in your house and what effect they are having on your life.

ROOM	WHO'S IN THIS ROOM?	IS THIS PERSON GOOD FOR YOU? YES/NO/UNKNOWN
FRONT PORCH		
LIVING ROOM		
KITCHEN		
UPSTAIRS		

IV.
STRAIGHT UP
ABOUT YOUR ENVIRONMENT

NUTRIENT-RICH SOIL

My grandpa looked down at the acorn in the palm of my hand. I was maybe four or five years old. I had found the acorn on the playground and picked it up in my little hand. I showed it to my grandfather.

"You know what's in there?" he said, looking at me with wonder.

"No!" I said. "What?" I couldn't imagine what could be inside this tiny brown nut.

"A great and mighty tree, taller than the sky!" he said, laughing. I didn't believe him.

"You're teasing me," I said.

"No, no, I most assuredly am not," said my grandfather, taking my hand. He explained to me that inside this little acorn was an oak tree that could produce a thousand acorns. And those could produce an entire forest. On one condition.

"We have to plant it in good soil," he said.

"Well, let's do it!" I said, excitedly. "Let's do it now!"

So, on a fall day in 1989 in Little Rock, Arkansas, I planted an acorn on the edge of my grandfather's property line. It had good soil. And it grew. When I came over to his house, I would check on the little sapling. I would water the tree, especially in the summer, when it was dry and hot.

And that's when I learned something important.

Environment is everything.

It doesn't matter how much potential an acorn has inside it—an entire majestic oak tree, even—if that acorn is planted in the Sahara Desert. It needs good soil. It needs rich nutrients from the earth. It needs water from the sky. It needs direct sunlight for energy.

Environment is everything for plants.

Environment is everything for animals.

And environment is everything for people.

Your environment can bring out the very best in you, helping you achieve your highest potential.

Or.

It can choke your joy, fill you with stress, and damage your future.

Of course, you know this. Let's pretend we have a time machine, and let's go back to the first day of school, let's say in seventh grade. Here are the two scenarios:

CLASS ONE

TEACHER 1 stands by the door and greets students as they walk in. There's a passion about the subject that's evident from the first day of class that never stops. The teacher outlines clear expectations as to what students must do in the class and when assignments are due. You see evidence that the teacher is willing to change things on the fly if something isn't making sense to the students. There's a lot of time for classroom discussion about the subject. The teacher challenges you to do your best work, saying that anything less would be unfair to the potential that's in you. The teacher doesn't take him or herself too seriously but takes your achievement and learning very seriously.

CLASS TWO

TEACHER 2 sits behind a big desk as the students file in. The white walls are mostly blank. The bell rings, and Teacher 2 begins passing out a classroom syllabus and a list of classroom rules. The teacher often reminds students who is in charge. (Hint: it's not you.) There's a sense that the lesson plan for this class has been the same for years. The teacher puts a strong emphasis on the room being quiet and students following the rules. You don't sense any perceivable passion for the subject in the teacher, who frequently speaks in a monotone voice. There's no real discussion in the class—education is clearly a one-way street for this teacher. When the test comes, you only vaguely know what might be on it.

Okay. So. Which classroom are you more likely to learn in? Which teacher will create the better learning environment? Which classroom are you more likely to grow in?

Just like an acorn, you can have all the potential in the world . . . **but if you're not in the right environment, you won't grow.**

In fact, many researchers are saying that your environment matters a great deal for things like trying to lose weight or trying to quit smoking. Think about smoking for a second. Smoking will literally kill you. Smoking remains the leading preventable cause of mortality in high-income countries like the US.[1] So quitting smoking is a big deal.

And wouldn't you know it, smokers who hung out with friends who smoked were far less likely to quit.[2] It's tough to quit when you have a whole bunch of friends who smoke, offer you cigarettes, speak highly of cigarettes, and discourage you from quitting the thing they're doing.

Just makes sense, right? There's no support.

Environment is everything.

After my time in the NFL came to a sudden close, I realized that my environment was going to have to change tremendously. This was difficult for me, because it wasn't like I was hanging around with meth dealers or members of a Russian Mafia. I had a lot of friends in my life who I liked. Who were cool.

They weren't bad.

They just weren't . . . uh . . . good.

I wasn't being fed any inspiration from my friend group.

I couldn't look around and see anyone moving toward goals.

I couldn't look around and see anyone who was inspiring me with where they were trying to go.

I couldn't look around and see anyone growing.

I couldn't look around and see anyone I wanted to be like.

This was concerning to me. After all my time in football, I knew something about teams and squads. I knew if I was the best player on the entire team, I wasn't going to be pushed or inspired to grow.

I knew I had to change my environment.

If you're not in the right environment, you won't grow.

I began to seek out people who were farther ahead in the journey I wanted to take. I wanted to surround myself with people who would help create a positive environment where I could grow. What does this look like? Here's what I know.

If you feel inspired to be your best you, that's a good environment.

If you feel known and valued simply for who you are, that's a good environment.

If you feel challenged and yet supported, that's a good environment.

But . . .

If you feel left out all the time (like people could take you or leave you), then that's a toxic environment.

If you feel out of place, like nobody understands or wants to understand you, that's a toxic environment.

If you're stressed out all the time, that's a toxic environment.

I know what you might be saying. "That's easy for you to say,

Trent. There are things about my life I simply can't change. I can't just move away from my parents or my house or my school. It's not that easy."

I get that, but you can still change your mindset. You can still go after mentors. You can change your friend circle. If everyone around you wants to stay where they are, you can keep going after it.

It's been years since I planted that acorn. Twenty years? More?

That tree is now grown. It's taller than my grandfather's house. And what's more, the sidewalk along the front of his neighbor's house is buckled up, jutting up and broken. It's so damaged, you couldn't even ride your bike over it.

That sidewalk was poured by the city years ago. Big trucks came in and dumped concrete into wooden forms. They thought that sidewalk would last a hundred years.

But what they didn't know was that nearby, I had planted a tiny acorn in the ground in the front yard. Nothing special. Just an acorn. But over the next twenty years, that tiny acorn grew. Into a giant oak tree.

That little tiny acorn burst out of its acorn shell and grew into a small sapling, and that sapling grew into a young tree, and then into a bigger tree, and then into a mighty oak tree. And that mighty oak tree over the period of twenty years grew roots that eventually got underneath this giant slab of concrete. And slowly and surely it cracked that piece of concrete right in half.

If you get in the right environment, nothing will stop your growth.

Nothing. Not any obstacle. Not even concrete.

But none of that happens without the right environment.

So make sure your environment is fertile.

Get around other people.

Go hard on trying to seek out people who are for you.

Who will help you.

Who love you.

Who will push you.
Who *like* you.
This is in your control.
So get after it.

REHAB TIME

COACH PEP TALK

It's time to evaluate the impact of the people around you. Think about the ten people you spend the most time with. Put their names on the list below. Then rank how much time you spend with them and how much of a positive influence they have on you (-10 is the lowest score and +10 is the highest). Multiply the two numbers together to see the total impact this person has on your life. Are there any changes you might need to make to your environment? Note: this exercise only works if you are honest.

PERSON'S NAME	AMOUNT OF TIME YOU SPEND WITH THEM (Scale of 1–10)	HOW MUCH OF A POSITIVE INFLUENCE ARE THEY ON YOUR LIFE (Scale of -10 to +10)	TOTAL IMPACT (Multiply the two numbers)

EVERY HERO NEEDS A GUIDE

People always say, "Experience is the best teacher."

And that is true. If you touch a hot grill, you will learn firsthand (ha!) not to do that.

But do you know what is better?

To learn from someone else who touched a hot grill not to do that. Why go through something if you don't have to? In fact, I would put it more strongly.

Someone else's experience is actually the best teacher.

I learned this early on. I had two older brothers. I quickly learned that it was better to sit back and examine what they were doing to see what worked (and what didn't). And man, did I sure learn what NOT to do.

You want something? Don't play Mom against Dad. They'll find out.

You're told to do something? Do NOT complain to Dad. He'll double your work.

You're in trouble? Do NOT talk back to mom. She will end you.

But I also, on a positive side, learned all sorts of great things about life from my brothers.

Not everyone is gifted in the same way, but everyone has a gift.

When you're wrong, say you're sorry, and mean it. That's the only way forward.

Family time is sacred. Make time, no matter what.

A mentor is described as "an experienced or trusted advisor." Normally, and ideally, this means someone who is in your life. Who knows you. Who helps you. But it doesn't always mean that. Here are a few types of mentors I have had in my own life.

VIRTUAL MENTORS

You might have a mentor you've never met in person. For example, in my own life, the author John Maxwell taught me about leadership. He was the first person to teach me about personal development. His books taught me what it means to lead yourself, and what it means to truly lead others. He showed me that leadership is not about gaining power for yourself (this is what weak and selfish people do)—it's about leveraging your whole life to help other people. I remember the first time I read one of Maxwell's books, I highlighted everything that hit me hard, and I looked back and saw that I'd practically highlighted the entire page. And when I was done, I was like, "That was amazing. I wonder if he's written anything else." I found out he had fifteen other books. I bet I have read them all and highlighted the heck out of them. I would absolutely call John Maxwell a personal mentor of mine. He's been an experienced and trusted guide. And even though I have never sat down and had a face-to-face conversation with John Maxwell, he's been a great mentor to me. I love virtual mentors. I love reading books, listening to podcasts, and watching TED Talks. If you want to grow, find people who inspire you and educate you and challenge you, and drink in their content.

SHINING EXAMPLES

If you're trying to get better at something, it's usually wise to try to find a mentor who has had incredible success at that thing and figure out what they're doing (and then do it). When I was trying to make it into the NFL as a receiver with the Indianapolis Colts, I had a chance to work out with a receiver named Reggie Wayne, whose number of receptions as of January 2020 ranks him tenth all-time in NFL history.[1] He's a legend. And during practice, I would study every single thing he did. If Reggie Wayne did it, I did it. I wanted to learn every tip and trick he had. He was a shining example—someone who was excelling and leading in an area that I wanted to be better at. (I also learned a ton from Santana Moss when I was with the Redskins. Shout out to him.)

Post-football, there have been areas in my life I've wanted to improve, and in the process, I've chosen people who know a lot about the subjects and have had real success. So when I wanted to improve my fitness, I sought out fitness gurus. When I wanted to start a business as a professional speaker, I found people who had done it successfully and asked them about a million questions.

FLAWED MENTORS

Nobody is perfect. No mentor is perfect, but a lot of your mentors will have one thing they teach you perfectly. One of my favorite mentors is Tupac Shakur. I was raised on hip-hop, and Tupac taught me a lot of things. He never let the harshness of his life crush his spirit. Despite his surroundings, he found a way to climb up. He taught me that real men can be artistic and write poetry. Also, he never backed down, and he was never afraid to say what he thought. His rhymes were frequently filled with deep truths about life. Those are things that I deeply respect about Tupac. Now, do I agree with everything Tupac did and said? No way. Were there aspects of Tupac's life that I would NOT want to emulate? For sure. But I can pick and choose. I can accept that he was deeply flawed but also deeply helpful.

It's like Thomas Jefferson. Is he an important Founding Father?

Yes. Are his words and ideals worth studying? Absolutely. Did he own slaves? Yes. Take the good. Filter out the bad. Nobody is perfect. You can still learn from them. You must still learn from them.

EVERYDAY-PEOPLE-AROUND-YOU MENTORS

I always tell people, "Life is my greatest mentor." Here's what I mean by that. As an introvert, I often get a chance to sit back and observe life and how it's playing out inside the people around me.

I try to be a sponge. I try to learn as much about how life works from other people.

Success always leaves clues. And destruction also leaves clues.

Sitting back and watching others around me has served me well. I try to pay attention to life. If someone around me has success, I can study their life and ask them questions to see how they got to be where they are. If someone's life crashes and burns, I can examine and learn from them what not to do. Follow others through the open doors of success that they find. Back away from the destructive messes that other folks cause. Learn from their successes. And learn from their failures.

DEEPLY PERSONAL MENTORS

There's one more category that's both incredibly important and incredibly rare. These are mentors who enter into your life with whom you have a special bond. For me (as you can probably tell from other parts of this book), the people who played this role were my parents and grandparents. To this day, I think the mentoring, guidance, and love I received from my parents and grandparents are the biggest gifts that God has ever given to me. But I know not everyone out there has that. I know not everyone is born into a great family.

That doesn't mean you're alone.

And that doesn't mean God doesn't have a mentor for you.

I find it fascinating that nearly every hero in every epic saga faces an impossible obstacle. And that hero has a guide and mentor to help them overcome that obstacle. It's just the way that nearly every beloved story works. Whether it's Daniel in *The Karate Kid* with Mr. Miyagi, or Frodo with Gandalf, or Harry Potter with Dumbledore, or Luke Skywalker with Obi-Wan AND Yoda (he was so off, he needed two mentors).

So along your journey, keep your eyes open for people who might be able to help you, and then ask for help. Because here's what I know: most good people (who are worthy of mentoring someone) really, deeply want to help you. I've never met a decent human being who—when I asked them for help—said no.

Every hero will face an insurmountable obstacle.

It's true.

And every hero needs a guide.

But the good news is that every guide is looking for a hero to help. So ask for help.

REHAB TIME

COACH PEP TALK

I read once that every person needs at least twelve caring adults—people older than them—in their community and circle. That's a lot of people, actually. This exercise is designed to help you see who your guides are, and who you should add to your list of guides.

QUESTION 1

Make a list of every adult you have in your life who truly cares about you and pours into your life. How many people did you come up with?

....
....
....
....
....
....
....

QUESTION 2

Is there someone in your life (who is older than you) who you admire or respect? What is it about them or their life that you look up to? What would it look like to ask them for help or spend more time with them so they could help you in your life?

....
....
....
....
....
....
....

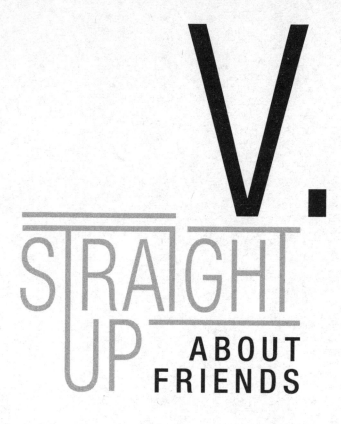

V.
STRAIGHT UP
ABOUT FRIENDS

NOT EVERYONE IS YOUR FRIEND

Listen. This is as real as I can put this. I need you to get this.

Everybody ain't your friend.

Everybody you call a friend might not be a friend.

People pretend well. And sometimes it's the ones riding with you who aren't really riding for you. Just because they're smiling to your face doesn't mean they won't go behind your back.

And just because someone's been in your life a long time doesn't mean they're a real friend. Don't confuse the length of the friendship with the strength of the friendship.

Just because they're in your life now doesn't mean they'll stay in your life when trouble comes. Real situations expose fake people. So, when it gets real, you're going to find out who's real.

And just because someone says they're your best friend doesn't mean they want the best for you. Just because they're by your side, that doesn't mean they're on your side.

Your friends are incredibly important. Who you hang around with affects where you're going. And in this stage of life, your friends actually affect your destiny. Which is why it's so critical to choose the right friends.

I want to go through the types of friendships I've seen to help you analyze some patterns. Because at the end of the day, your friends are the bow, and you're the arrow. You'll only fly as far as they shoot you. And it's important you have friends who will help your life, not hurt your life. So let's get into it.

SITUATIONAL FRIENDS

This is the most basic form of friendship. You're friends with a person because some situation in your life has thrust you together.

> **You share the same location.** When you're younger, you're mostly friends with people because they are physically close to you. Like you both went to summer camp and were put in the same cabin, and now you're besties. Or they happened to grow up in the house next door to you, and so you played together all the time.
>
> **You share a similarity.** These are friendships that happen because you have something in common. Maybe you like the same music, or at recess, you both liked the swings more than the teeter-totters. I remember in kindergarten, we were always lined up by height. I started talking to the kids in line who were roughly the same height as I was. And that's how I made some friends. This is not how I do it now. I don't go around looking for people roughly 1.83 meters high. But this is how it happened when I was a kid.
>
> **You share an activity.** Sometimes you become friends with people because they're doing the same thing as you. You hang out because you're in the same soccer club, or on the same gymnastics team, or in the same Boy Scout troop. Because you both like doing the same thing, you're in the same place, and share a similarity, you become friends.

The problem with all three of these friendships is that they're actually pretty shallow. For example, if you change your location (move somewhere else) or stop doing that activity (switch to another sport or switch after-school clubs), and then your friendship with that person crumbles, it usually means it wasn't a very deep friendship. This is okay, of course. I just want to point out that this is the most basic form of friendship, and it's not incredibly deep.

FUN FRIENDS

This is the second level of friendship. These are friends who are always down for fun. They are awesome companions for ice skating, or going to the movies, or just hanging out at home. They're a blast to be with. Now, do not get this twisted: fun and friendship go hand in hand. And sometimes, this type of friendship can seem awesome.

But fun friends are actually pretty shallow friends too.

First off, some things that are fun aren't good for you. And fun friends will push and encourage you to do those things, because they're fun, even if they're destructive. That isn't good friendship. Also, fun isn't the most important aspect of life. This type of friendship doesn't work when life gets complicated. What happens when life isn't fun? If your friends are only down for fun, what about when that relative in your family dies and you need someone to talk to? Or when you have a problem at school? Fun friends won't stick around, leaving you feeling even worse. You thought you had a real friend, but they only wanted to hang as long as the relationship didn't require anything from them.

DORY FRIENDS

I named this after one of the main characters in the classic Pixar film *Finding Nemo*. Do you remember Dory? She was a loyal friend. Man, was she loyal. She was a ride-or-die regal blue tang. She stuck by Marlin at great personal risk to herself. She was willing to sacrifice. She proved her loyalty.

And that's beautiful. Really, it is.

But—and I got to be honest here—Dory was useless. She couldn't remember anything apart from the initial address. Marlin had an important, vital task, and she couldn't help him during very important parts of it. In fact, at one point in the story, Dory accidentally leads them into a very dangerous field of jellyfish. She didn't mean to. But she did.

There are friends who aren't helping you get to where you need to go. They're not bad. In fact, they're very loyal. But they're not helping you grow and develop. I'm not saying you should cut off Dory friends, but you have to be really careful with them. You can't let them lead your life.

BEST FRIENDS

This final group is the rarest and by far the most valuable. These friends understand that the phrase "best friend" means that they will be a friend who always pushes you to be your best and do your best.

These are friends who serve as compasses. They will always point to true north, no matter what the situation. These are friends based on core values, who go beyond just having fun or just being loyal. These are friends who help you become better than you already are. They stand with you to help you become who God wants you to become. They believe in you. And they will never stand with you if what you're doing is a violation of your own principles and values. They will challenge you, because they truly want the best for you.

Here's the honest truth: Some of you need to take a good, hard, honest look at the friends around you.

If your friends don't want to see you win.

If they don't want to see the best you.

If they don't inspire you.

If they don't motivate you.

If they don't stick around when tough times come.

Then I hate to tell you this, but you don't have a circle of friends. You have a cage.

It might be time to do some surgery and cut some friends out of your life. Sometimes the best way to add to your life is to subtract from it.

Everybody ain't your friend.

It's time that you start realizing that.

And act accordingly.

REHAB TIME

COACH PEP TALK

Figuring out who's around you and what kind of friend they are is the first step. The chart below will help you think about who is around you right now (or who has been around you in the past) and what kind of friend they might be.

TYPE OF FRIEND	DESCRIPTION	NAMES
Situational Friends	You're just friends because you're in the same place (like school) or do the same thing (like a sport or club)	
Fun Friends	You do fun stuff together, but you're not sure they'd help you if you needed it	
Dory Friends	They're loyal, but not truly helping you grow or develop	
Best Friends	They help you get better, point you to what's right, and help you get closer to God and who He made you to be	

LOYALTY IS RARE

If all you had to offer was friendship, who would still be around?

If you didn't have anything else except yourself, who would still call you a friend?

Who would still show up?

I learned a painful lesson right out of college. I realized that the people I thought were my friends weren't actually my friends. They didn't like me—they liked the things they got from me. And that's not real friendship.

Look, I was by no means a famous athlete, but I did have some success in college and in the NFL. People began to hang around me. And I didn't realize it at the time, but they did this because they wanted something from me. They looked at me and thought:

You're big.

You're in the NFL.

You're young.

You're fit and muscular.

And if I'm around you, I will feel good about myself too.

This is how fame works. Fame says two things. First, to the "famous" person, it says, "You have something that a whole lot of people want. Sell yourself to them. Let them consume you, evaluate you, and flood you with approval. Then you'll be valuable."

(In this case, I was valuable only because I was an athlete in the NFL.)

And then to the people around the famous person, it says, "If you tie yourself to that person, hang around them, and ride their coattails, that will make YOU important too."

(In this case, I was valuable to other people not as a friend or a person, but as a means to gaining popularity.)

Everything fame says is a lie.

Fame is fleeting. I know. I was a hot commodity for a minute. Then, like a shooting star, that bright future in professional sports went out. And suddenly, people started disappearing from my life.

I realized I was fighting for people who wouldn't throw a punch for me.

I realized I had people in my circle who weren't in my corner.

These people wanted something from me. They didn't value me. They valued what I gave them.

For some, you're just an opportunity. This is how these fake friends will do you: they'll present to you what you want just so they can take what they need. When they can no longer benefit from you, their loyalty leaves.

Do they really have love for you?

Or do they just fake it?

Do they really have love for you?

Or do they love to use you?

Here are some warning signs I saw in my own life that I want you to be aware of. Think of these as red flags.

PROCEED WITH CAUTION IF . . .

THEY'RE JEALOUS WHEN YOU SUCCEED

Pay attention to friends who are silent when you win. True friends want the best for each other. They want each other to succeed. If they're not happy when you succeed, it's not friendship: it's jealousy.

It's a scarcity mindset, believing that if something good happens to you, that's one less good thing that could happen to them. This is absurd logic.

My buddy's wife had a childhood friend who refused to attend her wedding. She returned the wedding invitation with the note, "Seeing you happy is just too difficult for me." I have no idea what that even means. What kind of person believes that if you're happy, that means less happiness is left in the world for them? What a shame. But I'm telling you, it's a real thing.

THEY START PUTTING YOU DOWN IN LITTLE WAYS

As real as I can put it, sarcasm isn't funny. Look, I love to have fun with my friends. And making jokes with each other is friendship. But sometimes it crosses a line. Sometimes those jokes cut. In fact, that's what the word *sarcasm* actually means. The Greek root for sarcasm, *sarkazein*, means to "tear flesh." Sometimes sarcasm is simply hostility in disguise. Pay attention to how you feel. If the jokes sort of hurt, or hit a soft spot, or seem unkind, you need to have an honest conversation. They might not know the effect their jokes are having on you. So tell them. If they change the way they joke, they're your friend, because friends don't put down their friends. And if they don't . . . well, there's your answer.

Like I say, "Everybody in your boat might not be rowing, but they might be drilling holes."

THEY GET MAD IF YOU SAY NO TO A REQUEST

One of the biggest red flags of false friendship is if a person only comes around when they want something from you. I remember this time when I was right out of college, and one of my friends—who I thought was a true part of my crew—asked me to do something for them. I think it might have been a request to get tickets to a game or something. And I said, "No, man, I can't do that." And they flipped the script on me and got super mad. It wasn't gentle disappointment.

They got hot. And it dawned on me that what they most wanted from me was the cool stuff I was giving them, and as soon as that dried up, so did their friendship. That was a tough lesson to learn.

YOU'RE ASKING THIS QUESTION ABOUT SOMEONE IN PARTICULAR

If you're asking the question, "Am I sure this person is really my friend?" that's a pretty good indication they're not. Look, you should never have to question something that's real. You just know. So, if you have doubt . . . that doubt is usually there for a good reason.

TRUE FRIENDS ARE IN IT

I recently watched a documentary on rock climbing.[1] This is a grueling and dangerous sport. One thing you'll nearly always see: professional rock climbers climb in pairs. Rock climbing is never safe, but having a buddy there at least makes it somewhat less dangerous. You're literally tied to each other and hooked into the rock. That way, if you slip or fall, there's someone there who has your line and can anchor themselves and pull you up. And there's a sacred and unspoken rule in climbing: never ever cut the rope. It means, "You never cut the rope just to save yourself."

It's a sobering thing.

It means, "Either we both get down from this mountain, or neither of us does."

That's a real friend. That's a good metaphor for life. I know in my own life, when I've hit rock bottom, when I've been in trouble, I've had friends who refused to cut the rope.

When it gets real, you're going to see who's real.

This is based on trust. Can you trust this person? Can you depend on this person?

I always tell people to pay attention. Look for people who just love you for you.

Are they happy for you?

Do your friends truly value you?

If so, run with it. You've got a good squad. And if not—let me say this as clearly as I can—MAKE SOME CHANGES.

If all you had to offer was friendship, who would you still be able to call your friend?

REHAB TIME

COACH PEP TALK

I know it's a sobering reality to think that maybe the people you're hanging around with aren't actually FOR you. Sometimes it's easier to be friends with the wrong people than to be alone. I get that. But in the end, we have to know who our real friends are. That's what this activity is designed to do. At the very least, look for the warning signs, and if you see them, you know, "This person is around me, but they're not really FOR me." That might save you some heartache.

ACTIVITY

Think about your friend group. Fill out this circle with everyone who might be "in your corner."

As you read this chapter, did anyone in this circle come to mind? As you look at the names in your circle, do you have friends who:

Get jealous when you succeed?
Get mad at you when you say no to them?
Put you down, even a little bit?
Encourage you to do stuff you know is wrong?

YOUR CIRCLE MIGHT NEED TO SHRINK

As real as I can say it: some of you need to make some changes in your circle of friends.

When I look at my closest friends, I realize there's something all of them have in common. They are trustworthy. Our relationship is based on trust.

This was not always the case.

As I recounted before, I realized I had people in my life who weren't really my friends. They liked me because of what they GOT from me. They weren't really loyal to me.

And sometime in my twenties, I realized that my definition of friendship had to change. My squad goals had to shift. Because I promise you this, your friends will determine your destiny.

WHAT IS A TRUE FRIEND?

The first thing I had to do was get a good definition of friendship. Because my dad was a pastor, I started looking at the book of Proverbs, and the Bible in general, to find some general truths about friendship. There's actually a lot in there.

Here are some of the words of wisdom, which I have translated in ways that make sense to me. Call this the TSV, the Trent Shelton Version.

- If you're a person with unreliable friends, you'll soon come to ruin. But there is a friend that is loyal—more loyal than a biological brother, even (based on Proverbs 18:24).
- Do not make friends with a hot-tempered person. Seriously, don't hang out with them. They'll rub off on you, and pretty soon, you'll be acting a fool, just like them (based on Proverbs 22:24–25).
- Walk with the people who are wise—who are trying to figure out from God how to be good at life—and you will become wise. Hang out with fools, and life's going to be really hard (based on Proverbs 13:20).
- A true friend will challenge you and tell you when you're dead wrong and get in your face to stop you from doing something that's completely wrong. Trust that person. It hurts, but it's a good wound. You know what your enemy will do? Stand and smile as you walk into destruction, cheering you on the whole way (based on Proverbs 27:5–6).
- Good friends don't leave when life gets tough. They'll stay and help you. It's in tough times that you find out who's really for you (based on Proverbs 17:17).
- Want to win at life? Always choose your friends carefully. Because the wrong friends will surely try to get you to go down the wrong path in life (based on Proverbs 12:26).

Here's my definition of a true friend. A true friend says, "My friendship with you isn't just based on fun or loyalty. I want to help you stay connected to God so that you can become who God made you to be."

It's not about the size of your circle, it's about the loyalty that's in it. Nothing can stop a squad that's dedicated to fighting for the same mission.

So what does that friendship look like?

A REAL FRIEND WILL STAND UP

I remember when I was in elementary school, there was this kid who wanted to fight me. (I didn't want to fight.) So after school, there was a big group of people waiting for me at the fence at the back of the school, waiting for us to fight. I guess it's entertaining to watch two fifth graders cage fight.

But then something strange happened.

A couple of my friends stepped forward. They formed a line in between the two of us. They said this beef was stupid and that they weren't going to let us fight. They reminded the big guy who wanted to fight me that we actually used to be friends. The message was pretty clear: "Fighting is dumb. But . . . if you want to fight, I guess you'll have to fight all of us at once."

Once everyone saw there wasn't going to be a fight, the whole thing just fizzled out. The tension went away. And after that, we were able to sort of be cool with each other. I learned something that day, back in elementary school: friends step up.

STANDING UP FOR FOLKS ONLINE

When I was growing up, we didn't have social media. But nowadays, I see a ton of horrible stuff on social media. People straight up bully each other. And it's not cool. Part of being a good friend is standing up for them online. What does this look like?

The first thing you can do is tell the bully to stop it. If you know the person who is doing the cyberbullying, tell them to knock it off. Explain that it's not cool to be a jerk to others. Whatever you do, chime in. If you remain silent, you are basically telling them that it's okay to do it. Don't stand on the sidelines.

The second thing you can do is to tell the truth about your friend. If someone says they're a loser, come at that comment and correct it.

You called him a loser. You couldn't be more wrong. This guy right here is awesome and keeps it 100.

Disagree with what he said, that's fine, but the personal attacks aren't cool, man.

The fact is, some people try to hurt other people online. But you can stop a lot of cyberbullying just by standing up to it.

A REAL FRIEND COMES WITH SOLUTIONS

I used to believe that a true friend was someone who always agreed with you, no matter what. If you're on the playground, arguing with people that LeBron is better than Kobe AND MJ, they jump in and take your side—even though you're very, very wrong. But that's not friendship.

A friend doesn't always agree with you. Especially if you're wrong.

A friend will sometimes get in your grill. But here's the difference. When your friend comes at you with criticism or correction, they will also come with solutions. It's easy to point out when someone else is doing something wrong. But a true friend won't just point out what you're doing wrong, they'll also show you what you can take to make it right. And then they will either do it with you or help you do it. A true friend will say, "Listen, this is what I see, and it's a problem, but here's how you get out of this."

I saw this in college. My buddy was not great at math, and he had to take a precalculus class freshman year, and he didn't get it, so he just sort of gave up. He literally stopped coming to class. I don't know what he expected would happen—that somehow the athletic office wouldn't notice that F? But our friend who was great at math called him out on it. "You're going to lose your scholarship over a math course, bro," he said. But it wasn't just fire. He said, "Here's what I'm going to do to help you," and for the next month, they met at the library and my friend tutored him.

A person who is truly for you will always help you out, because they want to see you succeed. Your success matters to them. That's friendship.

So I'm going to ask you a direct question.

And it's a tough one.

Who do you need to add to your team? This is someone who you know is a good person, who is for you, and who you should invest more time in. You really should make it a point to hang out more, to build that friendship.

Here's another question.

Who do you need to cut from your team? This is someone who you know isn't a true friend. In fact, they might not even care if you're friends with them anymore because they only tolerate you being around. This isn't friendship.

Friends determine your destiny.

Be careful who you hang out with.

Not everyone deserves you.

And sometimes the best way to grow is to invest in a good friendship.

And sometimes the best way to grow is to cut someone out of your life.

REHAB TIME

COACH PEP TALK

Your friends influence your life. You are who your friends are, and in a very real way, your friends can mean the difference between losing and succeeding. So it's time to evaluate the people in your life—and the impact they're having on your life. Complete the following questions, being as honest as you can.

ADD TO YOUR TEAM

Who is someone you should initiate a friendship with or spend more time with? In other words, who's someone you should INVEST in?

....

What would that look like? Write down a couple of ways you could build that friendship.

....

....

....

CUT FROM YOUR TEAM

Who is someone you should SEVER ties with, for your benefit and theirs?

....

What would that look like? What are some things you'll have to change, or stop doing, to distance yourself from that person?

....

....

....

FRIENDS TELL EACH OTHER THE TRUTH

On the first day of school, our school sent an official note home with every kid in the sixth grade. This was an official letter from the school district. It was printed on school letterhead. It was signed by the principal. And it had to be signed by our parents and returned to our homeroom teacher by the end of the week.

What was the content of that letter? What issue was so important and pressing that it required hand-delivered letters to every parent?

I will tell you what the issue was.

The issue was deodorant.

That's right. This official letter from school district literally talked about the importance of sixth graders showering daily and using deodorant.

And do you know why the school did this?

Because of Robbie.[1]

Robbie was my friend and had been since third grade. But starting in sixth grade, Robbie's body started changing. And Robbie's armpits started smelling bad. Real bad. Robbie's general scent was okay in the morning, but after recess in the hot New Orleans sun,

Robbie smelled like someone had rubbed dead skunks under his armpits.

And for some reason, Robbie couldn't smell it.

People in Canada could probably smell Robbie. But he couldn't. Which was ironic, because the nose closest to Robbie's armpits was HIS OWN.

But Robbie was my friend.

And everyone was talking about him. Whispering behind his back.

And that wasn't cool.

So I decided to be brave and tell Robbie.

Because friends tell friends the truth.

That's one of the hallmarks of being a good friend. You are brave enough to tell them the truth when other people are not.

I did not have many options in this situation.

1. I could pretend like Robbie didn't smell, and maybe snort Febreze or glue my nostrils shut.
2. I could gossip with the other kids behind Robbie's back (and downwind).
3. I could be brave and let Robbie know that he smelled.

The first two options would not help Robbie. Option three was the *only one* that would.

And so I decided to pull Robbie aside in private and tell him. I didn't want to do this. I was afraid Robbie might get mad at me or be embarrassed and point out all my flaws as a defense. But I did.

Because friends tell friends the truth.

Since then, I have had many difficult conversations with friends. They were never easy. And ten times out of ten, I did NOT want to have those conversations. I would much rather have simply avoided the conversation.

- I had a friend who made fun of other people too much. It was like he was trying to put other people down to feel good about himself.
- I had a friend who talked too much in groups. He always seemed to dominate the conversation and didn't let other people talk.
- I had a friend who wasn't honest with me. And it wasn't the first time something like that had happened.
- I had a friend who talked to his mom in a way that was straight up disrespectful. It made me really uncomfortable. And it wasn't okay.
- I had a friend who just ate more than he should have, and it wasn't healthy. He just wasn't taking care of his body.
- I had a friend who was dating a dude who was NO GOOD. And she knew it.

Those are all conversations I've had to have.

Rough, huh?

But here's what I learned. I learned that when you're having tough conversations, you have to say it in a way helps people receive it.

You have to communicate in a way people can hear you.

People need the truth. But . . .

People also need the truth wrapped in kindness.

If you say tough things without kindness, people can't hear you.

If you say kind things without the truth, people won't change.

So here's my little formula that I developed. I'm not saying it works every time, but I've tried it out quite a few times and it seems to work pretty well. I call it the ARC method.

A = APPRECIATION

Always start by appreciating the other person. Before you bring up any concerns or issues you have, let the person know you value them.

Here's the key: you have to be honest, and you have to be specific. It does no good to say, "You're awesome." That's super bland. And it doesn't stick. It feels inauthentic, even if you don't mean it that way. Pick out a few particular things that are awesome about the person or something they did that stands out to you.

> Robbie—first off, the other day at recess, you were throwing BOMBS on the playground. I think you're the best quarterback in our whole class. I'll have you throw to me anytime.

R = REASSURANCE

This is where you reassure the person about how valuable they are to you, and how awesome you think they are. This is also where I usually say something like, "True friends tell each other the truth, and if the situation were reversed, I know you'd help me." Sometimes I also say, "I could be wrong about this, and if I am, I promise I don't mean to be."

> When I first came to this school, you were the first person to reach out to me. In this whole school, you're one of my best friends, and I want you to know that. I seriously think you should stick with football, because if you keep at it, you could be starting QB in high school.

C = CONCERN

This is where you bring up the issue. You can't beat around the bush. You have to be as direct and honest as possible. Rip the Band-Aid off. But it's okay, because if you've done the first two steps right, the person will be in a better place to receive it, AND you'll be in a better place to say the hard truth because you've been reminded of your friendship with the person.

Recently, I have noticed that after recess, you have body odor. Like, you really smell. And I think other kids are starting to notice, and I don't want that for you. This is easy to fix, man. Just wear deodorant. Put some on in the morning, and *bam*, the issue will be solved. I just want the best for you. Does that make sense?

So the next time you have a problem with a friend, use the ARC method. It will help you be the kind of person who tells their friends the honest TRUTH in a way they can receive.

And then things can change for the better.

And you won't have to smell Robbie's armpits.

See? Everyone wins.

REHAB TIME

COACH PEP TALK

I'm going to have you practice the ARC method of communication. But I need you to understand something: the ARC method only really works with people you actually know and love. Don't do this with strangers or people you don't really know that well—it won't work.

QUESTION 1

Have you ever had to have a tough conversation like the ones I listed in this chapter? What was that like? Why was it tough?

....

....

....

....

....

....

....

QUESTION 2

In the space below, make a list of all the friends who are like Robbie to you—you care about them, and they care about you. These should be people you know would also tell YOU the truth.

....

....

....

....

....

....

....

QUESTION 3

Are there any tough, important conversations you KNOW you need to have with any of the friends on that list? Use the worksheet below to practice having a conversation with them about what's bothering you.

ARC WORKSHEET

ARC	
APPRECIATION	Make a list of two or three SPECIFIC things you honestly love about the person.
REASSURANCE	What does this person mean to you? Why is your life better because of them?
CONCERN	What is the issue, in one sentence? Be as direct as possible. Is there a way to say it in a way that's kinder?

YOU CAN'T CHANGE PEOPLE

Have you ever watched a new parent try to feed a baby? It's incredible, for a number of reasons.

First of all, if the baby decides that they don't want to eat the food, there's pretty much *nothing* the adult can do.

This mystified me when my son was a baby. There I was, a fully grown adult man, with vastly more money, power, strength, and wisdom than this tiny baby, and *he* was the one calling the shots. I was practically powerless, just sitting there, tiny spoon in my hand.

It seems that even at the earliest ages, we're reminded that we can't control one another. We don't have that power.

Watching adults try to feed babies always reminds me of an important, but sometimes painful, truth.

We can't change other people.

There are times I wish I had this power. Because sometimes, let's be honest, we're right. Like with my infant son; I know he needs to eat those smashed carrots to grow big and strong. He doesn't know better. I do. And I wish I could just make him do what I want.

But I can't.

And this is sometimes a painful reality.

WE CAN'T CHANGE OTHER PEOPLE

The painful truth is we can't save people. Because sometimes the people you love do stuff you wish they would not do. Sometimes they behave in ways that are destructive to their own potential, and you just wish they would wake up and knock it off. Get on a better path.

Sometimes the people you love behave in ways that are destructive to those around them. And you wish you could just change them. But you cannot.

It reminds me of my friend Grant. When he was about seven years old, Grant learned in school that cigarettes were bad for you. That the tar in them coated the delicate sacs in your lungs called alveoli that absorb oxygen, doing real damage to your lungs. But there was a problem: both Grant's grandmother and grandfather smoked.

So Grant started a campaign. He made informational posters with facts about the harmful effects of smoking and put them up all over his grandparents' house.

He took anti-smoking pamphlets from the school nurse and stuffed them into his grandparents' mailbox.

At family dinners, Grant would volunteer to pray for the meal, and at the end of the prayer, he'd always close with "And God, please help Grandma and Grandpa stop smoking."

Every time he saw them, Grant would ask his grandparents to stop smoking.

Grant kept this nagging up for months.

And months.

He didn't stop.

Neither did they. Grant learned a terrible truth.

You cannot change people.

You can hope for them to change.

You can pray for them to change.

You can plead for them to change.

But until they want to change, they're not going to change. When someone doesn't even see an issue with their actions, they're not going to change their actions. Some people are just too set in their ways.

But that doesn't mean the situation is hopeless.

YOU CAN'T CHANGE PEOPLE, BUT YOU CAN INFLUENCE THEM

Grant sat his grandparents down and explained why he was nagging them.

He showed them how lung damage from smoking is very reversible, and how the lungs can heal dramatically from years of abuse and smoke after just a few months of not smoking.

He made a projection of how many years they could add to their lives if they stopped smoking today—and what would happen to their lifespan if they didn't.

And he made a timeline of events in his future that he wanted his grandparents to see and be there for—things like learning to drive, graduating from high school, getting married.

And wouldn't you know it, Grant's grandparents gave up smoking. It went from something Grant wanted for them to something THEY wanted for them. But that didn't mean the battle was over.

Changing habits is tough, especially when you've been doing it for a long time. So Grant started trying to help his grandparents in their decision to quit.

He went through the house and got rid of all the ashtrays.

He helped his grandparents steam clean the curtains and carpets to remove the smell of smoke.

And he wrote encouraging notes to his grandparents every week, hiding them in the freezer, in the medicine cabinet, and in the garage. And in the process, Grant learned another lesson.

YOU CAN'T CHANGE PEOPLE, BUT YOU CAN SUPPORT THEM

Being a good friend means trying to be a good influence and helping your friends make good decisions. And it also means supporting them when they make a good decision. You can't change people.

But you can influence them.

And support them.

And one of the best ways you can do this is being the change you want them to make. Be the person who is doing what they think they cannot do. As you progress and move forward, show them what it looks like to be happy and fulfilled. Because everybody wants to be happy and fulfilled. Give them the model AND create the environment where doing the right thing is actually the norm. For example:

- Let's not be slackers out there on the court.
- We don't need to vape. We don't need that to be cool. Let's pass on that.
- We can be a group of friends that has a blast and laughs until we're weak . . . without using drugs.

Help the people you love want to make the change by embodying it in your own life. This happened to me. After I hit rock bottom, I knew I had to make some major changes. I cut things out. I added things in. I started talking about all the time. But my friends were hesitant. Who is this new Trent? What is he doing?

But then they saw me close-up. They saw that my life was a lot more fulfilled. I wasn't wallowing. I wasn't numbing out. I was happier—much happier. I was the proof. My life was the proof. I was practicing what I was preaching, and it was working.

Not all my friends came along on the ride. Some continued doing what they were doing (and honestly, my friendship with them started to fade. Just being real with you).

But there were others who came along with me. And saw for themselves. It was cool.

You have more influence than you know. Your life really matters, especially in the hearts of the people you're closest to.

Use that influence for good.

Because it really does matter.

REHAB TIME

COACH PEP TALK

Being a good friend means helping your friends make good choices, both influencing them and supporting them to make (and continue to make) good choices.

STEP 1

Who is the most supportive person in your life? What kinds of things do they do to make you feel encouraged?

....

....

....

....

....

....

STEP 2

Choose five of your closest friends. Individually send each of them this text:

TEXT MESSAGE

Hey. So, I was just reading Trent Shelton's book *Straight Up*. In one of the chapters on friendship, it said that good friends SUPPORT each other in making good choices. I was thinking, is there a way that I could be more supportive of you?

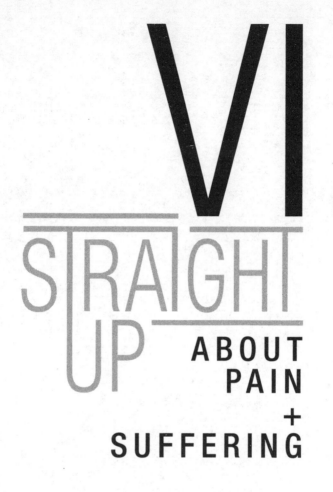

VI.

STRAIGHT UP

ABOUT PAIN + SUFFERING

YOUR DEEPEST PAIN CAN BE YOUR BEST FRIEND

Here's the straight truth. Rock bottom changed my life. Rock bottom is the reason I am who I am. In fact, to be blunt, the deep pain of rock bottom might very well be the best thing that's ever happened to me. You read that right. And I know that maybe you're thinking to yourself . . .

Trent, how can pain be good? How can pain help me?

First off, no growth happens without pain. If you think about your own body, you only get stronger when the muscles are pushed and broken down. There's always pain and soreness after you work out hard. But it's not just with muscles. It's in all areas of life.

There is no one who is an expert in anything that didn't have to go through some pain. They had to go through something.

This has proven itself to be so true in my own life that I've even stopped using the phrase, "That thing that happened was bad."

Was it? How do I know? What if something really important happened to me because of that bad thing? What if one door that closed led to the next door, which I needed? When life is tough, that doesn't mean God is punishing you. He could very well be protecting you. Guiding you.

Too many times, we want to skip the process of pain. But we can't.

Your hardest times can create your greatest faith.

Your worst times can create your greatest life.

By going through what you are going through, it qualifies you to help other people get through it. Because now you know what it's like.

Let me tell you how by telling a story.

A few years ago, my friend Rob found a bump on his arm. The doctors thought it was nothing, but when they sent a sample to the lab, they discovered it was a tumor from a rare form of cancer. This cancer was not only aggressive, but deadly.

Surgeons cut the tumor out, and then doctors pounded Rob's body with chemotherapy and direct radiation therapy on his arm. The stakes were high: if they didn't kill every single cancer cell of this tumor, it would spread through his body and kill him.

The chemo treatments were a nightmare. The chemical poisons they dripped into Rob's body made him sick, made his mind foggy, made his hair fall out. It was a miserable experience.

But it was made far worse by this one nurse.

I don't know how this woman ever got to be a professional medical provider, but she was terrible. She hurt Rob when she put the needles in. She was rough. She was curt and generally unpleasant. And at one point, she left his Mediport (a small valve that connected to a large vein in Rob's chest to deliver medicine) wide open. Rob started bleeding. He lost four pints of blood (the human body only has about twelve) in thirty minutes and passed out in his bed. If his wife hadn't discovered this, he would have died.

This nurse was terrible.

So they changed nurses.

And the next woman, who we'll call Glo (short for Gloria),[1] was amazing. She was not only sunny and bubbly, but eminently professional.

The best part about Glo was how good she was at administering the procedures. She walked Rob through every part of it. She'd explain what she was doing. She'd warn him about the parts that were uncomfortable or would hurt. And she was about as gentle as humanly possible.

At one point, Rob asked Glo a question.

"My previous nurse was terrible at this," he said. "Why are you so good at it?"

"It's easy," Glo said as she hooked Rob up to the monitors. "I had a cancer very similar to yours, and I had to go through these very same procedures."

Gloria was a great nurse because she had already been through all these terrible procedures herself.

And this is how your pain can be a good thing.

THE LESSONS YOU LEARN IN YOUR PAIN CAN HELP OTHERS

In fact, this might be the very way that God uses your pain—this season of awful in your life—and redeems it.

Your pain isn't wasted if you work with God and use it to help other people.

Some of you reading this know what it's like to be a child of divorce. What it's like to not live with both parents. To have to share holidays and birthdays with two parents. Some of you know what that does to a person. What it's like to blame yourself and wonder if you could have kept your parents together by being a better kid. Some of you have walked that path. And you can help other people going through that exact same situation.

Some of you know what it's like to lose friends because you weren't willing to do what they thought was cool. What it feels like to be kicked to the curb because you were trying to do what's right. What it feels like to be alone. And you can help other people who just lost friends because they refused to bow to peer pressure. You can help them feel less alone.

Some of you know what it's like to be cut from the team. What it's like to be teased because of your skin color. Or your accent. Or the way you look. You know what it's like to not be the smartest kid in your class. What it's like to constantly be compared to your older sibling.

And you can help other folks who are going through that right now.

Some of you know what it's like to grow up with not a lot of money. You didn't have the newest shoes or the latest styles because your family didn't have the money. You know what it means to have God provide for you. He always made sure you had what you needed. You always had enough. You can help someone who's feeling scared about that right now.

Some of you know what it's like to lose someone you love deeply. What it's like to be at a funeral you don't want to be at. To stare at a coffin and realize that the person you love isn't coming back. What it feels like to have your heart break. What grief feels like, and how it feels an awful lot like fear. You've been there. You know that. And you can help someone going through that for the very first time.

You see, we think it's our BEST moments that make us who we are. Our highlight reel.

But it's not.

IT'S IN OUR WORST MOMENTS THAT GOD SHOWS UP THE MOST

In the Bible, there was a king named David who knew a little something about hitting rock bottom. He knew what it was like to lose everything. And he wrote this beautiful poem, where he said:

> The LORD is close to the brokenhearted
> and saves those who are crushed in spirit.
>
> PSALM 34:18

In 2 Corinthians 12:9, Paul says that God's power "is made perfect in weakness." Paul recounts that when he was in his weakest moments, God showed up. When we are weak and rely on God, that's when we become strong.

If we let God use our weakness to help other people, that makes THEM strong, and it turns an awful situation into one that now has meaning.

I used to think that my best moment in life would be catching a touchdown in an NFL playoff game. Being carried off the field, victorious. I thought people would like me a lot—and that I would help a lot of people—if I were a Super Bowl champion with multiple rings on my fingers.

But that's not how life works. We love heroes, but they're not relatable.

You know what has been the moment in my life that's helped the most amount of people?

Getting cut from the NFL.

Losing my dream.

Dealing with deep disappointment.

Starting at zero.

People can relate to that. And because God helped me through that rough time, I can now help other people going through the exact same thing. This is the reason why I have all the influence I have—because I know the terrain of loss and suffering. I know the path through.

Because I have been there myself.

And there's no way to shortcut that or fake it.

Your deepest pain can be your best friend.

Because it's where God can meet you.

Where you can begin to get healing.

And it could be the very thing you use to help other people who are going through similar circumstances.

My grandmother used to say to me, "Trent, God never wastes anything."

She's right.

If you let God, He can turn your WORST moment into the thing that helps a lot of people.

And your WORST moment can actually be flipped around and become your BEST moment.

That's the truth.

———————————— REHAB TIME ————————————

COACH PEP TALK

If you're anything like I was, you don't believe that something really good and beautiful can come out of your worst moments. That's fine. But do this for me. In this exercise, you're going to talk to two people you respect who are at least twenty years older than you. You're going to ask both of them this question individually.

TEXT MESSAGE:

So I'm reading this book *Straight Up* by Trent Shelton, and he said something in one of the chapters, and I wanted to know if you agree with it. He said that sometimes the lessons you learn in your worst moment in life can be used to help other people. What do you think about this? Do you think this is true?

LESSON 24

DEALING WITH HATERS

L isten.

Haters are people who admire what you do; they just have a different way of showing it.

If you don't want haters in your life, don't do anything, be anything, or say anything. But if you're going to try to work hard, if you're going to go after something you love, or if you're going to try to make a difference in this world, then you're going to have haters. There are people who are trying to bring you down (because you're up).

But haters don't hate you, even if it seems that way. Because if they're paying attention to you, it means they don't hate you. And I'm going to prove to you why this is true.

Think about this. If you were in a buffet line, and they had a whole section of seafood, and you absolutely hated seafood, would you spend time at that section of the buffet? No. You'd pay NO attention to it. And if you hated a TV show and it came on, would you spend time paying attention to it? No.

The things you hate you pay no attention to.

Which means if someone is giving you attention, they don't hate you. If someone is following you on social media sites, they obviously don't hate you. If someone knows more about your life than most people, they're not a hater. In fact, I don't even call these folks haters. I call them "confused supporters." When I do that, people often laugh, but it's true.

Haters actually admire you.

It's just admiration mixed with real immaturity. They want what you have, and they don't know how to show it. The reason they want to bring you down is because you're above them. And they feel jealousy. Jealousy happens when your life reminds other people of what they don't have. In the words of that ancient Canadian poet Drake, "Jealousy is just love and hate at the same time."

I want to change your mindset about haters.

When I played football, the defensive players I lined up against were almost always talking trash. Talk about haters. Football players might be the worst at this. And the reason is pretty simple: players are trying to create mental distractions so they have a competitive advantage.

Those cornerbacks didn't really believe what they were saying.

They were saying those things to get me off my game.

To distract me.

Or, put another way—they couldn't beat me head-to-head, so they wanted to create a condition where they could get in my head. They couldn't beat me, so they wanted to try to convince me to beat myself.

But that means they admired me. You don't try to get an advantage over a player you KNOW you can beat.

Though here's the thing: Life is full of trash talkers. Not just in football, but everywhere.

DON'T LET THEIR PETTINESS STEAL YOUR HAPPINESS

Here's what you need to know: there are some people in life who are going to trash talk you. For some reason—maybe because they feel bad about their own life—they get their high from making other people feel low.

Often this is because they don't like where they are in life, but instead of improving themselves, they try to tear you down. Instead of climbing up higher to be where you are, they think they should just try to pull you down. Or they're jealous of you—your hard work reminds them they haven't done that, and they lash out. They're miserable, so they want to make everyone else miserable.

They don't have control in their own life, so they try to control other people's lives to make themselves feel powerful. If they can frustrate you at any given moment, that gives them power. And these kinds of negative people are dangerous, because they understand something that's very true. They know that if they can control your emotions, they can control your life.

But those haters don't deserve a single drop of your energy. They should not be able to stop your progress. In fact, they can't hurt your life or stop you without your permission. Nobody can actually get to you without your permission. Someone talking about you can't stop your success.

You have to learn to be emotionally strong enough NOT to take the bait. You have to be mentally tough. Remember, trash talkers want you to react in anger. So don't.

Here's the weird thing I learned while playing football: when that trash talk got into my head and got me emotional, I always played worse. Always. Never better. That trash talk took my focus off my routes, off the play, off what I should be doing. One of my coaches once called trash talking "the game within the game."

I like that.

My coaches knew something: responding gives hate power. The only response is to put your head down and keep pursuing your excellence. Run that route. Catch the ball. Do your best.

You see, those trash-talking defensive backs were playing a game. It was a game of "Try to Get Trent Really Upset."

If I get upset, I lose the game.

If I don't get upset, I win the game.

And I want to win.

So. What should we do?

KILL THEM WITH KINDNESS

I have a shirt that I wear that says, "They even hated Jesus." Jesus was the most perfect person to ever walk the earth, and the hatred leveled at Him was so strong that they crucified Him. So if you're expecting to walk through life unscathed, I don't know what to tell you. If Jesus had haters, so will you. And I'm not saying it's not going to affect you. Of course it will—you're human, after all.

But there's something else you need to know. Where does hate come from? You will never meet a hater who's filled with joy. You'll never meet a hater who's doing better than you in life. You'll never meet a hater who's happy. Period.

Here is what has helped me be patient and kind: their hate comes from their hurt. Haters are hurt. They're miserable. They're keyboard gangstas typing up criticism from afar. They think that giving pain is the way to heal their pain. But here's the truth: if you're hating on someone else, it means you're not working on yourself.

If I understand this, I realize that the hate is NOT about me. It's about them. So I don't have to take it personally. And it shows me the way forward.

Kindness can defuse their hate.

The Bible talks about this as well.

Do not repay anyone evil for evil . . . On the contrary: "If your enemy is hungry, feed him; if he is thirsty, give him something to drink. In doing this, you will heap burning coals on his head." Do not be overcome by evil, but overcome evil with good.

ROMANS 12:17, 20–21

I love that. Paul is saying, "If you're nice to people when they're trying to be mean to you, it's like heaping hot coals on their head."

In other words: you win the game. And they lose. And people don't like playing games they always lose.

Just allow the hate to bounce right off you.

This isn't easy.

A while ago, I posted a positive video on Facebook. And this one guy sent me a message.

> I hate you Trent. You should die. The world would be better without you.

I mean, it was nuts. Who writes that? To a stranger? But instead of taking it personally, I responded with kindness. I wrote him back:

> I don't hate you. I love you, and I'm praying for you.

The guy didn't stop. He wrote back again.

> You don't understand. I hate you. I hate your messages. Everything you say is trash. I can't stand you.

I realized that this had nothing to do with me. Though I wasn't going to spend a whole lot of time trying to get this guy to like me. What was I going to do? Try to convince him with facts that I was a pretty good person, and my presence in the world was positive? That's a fool's errand. So I wrote back:

> I'm sorry to hear that, man. I got nothing but love for you, and hope things get better for you.

We played ping-pong back and forth with messages. Each time, he responded with vile anger. And each time, I tried to respond with as much kindness as I could. And then finally, something incredible happened. The guy broke.

> You know what Trent, I'm going through so much and I didn't know what to do. I knew I had to do something outlandish to get your attention because you have so many followers. The things that you say are so true, but I don't want to face it, and it makes me angry inside. I'm sorry, man.

And from there, we were able to chat. I sent him some videos and other material that dealt with the issues he was dealing with. And to this day, he's a supporter.

That exchange helped me realize that a lot of times, it's hurt people who hurt people. And so if you respond with kindness, it will either help them (best case) or they won't get the reaction they want and leave. But either way, the hate stops.

I wish I could tell you that life is easy, and haters and trash talkers are super rare, and you probably won't ever run into them.

But that's just not true.

But if you realize why there are haters, and respond with kindness, you can make it through. And maybe even help some hurt people along the way.

——— REHAB TIME ———

COACH PEP TALK

Dealing with haters is never easy. Answer these questions to figure out who the negative people are in your life—and how you can neutralize their ability to affect you.

QUESTION 1

Have you ever had to deal with a hater or someone who verbally bullied you? How did you handle it? Did it work?

....
....
....

QUESTION 2

Is there someone in your life now who comes at you with negative talk or tries to tear you down to make themselves look better? What do they say or do?

....
....
....

QUESTION 3

What would it look like to kill them with kindness? What words would you say?

....
....
....

PERFECTION DOESN'T EXIST

Let me be straight with you.

Don't let the world make you think that there's something wrong with you because you're going through hard times.

I want to be clear.

Everybody goes through struggles.

Everybody has their struggles.

Everybody.

You don't have to suffer in silence. You don't have to go through stuff alone.

You don't have to hide.

So many people are trying to pretend they're okay, because if you're not strong, that means you're weak.

One of the greatest strengths is being able to admit you're not okay.

It's okay to say, "I'm tired."

It's okay to say, "This season of my life is really tough."

It's okay to say, "I don't know how much more I can take."

It's okay to say, "I'm scared."

About a month ago, I had this back-to-back-to-back encounter that opened my eyes.

First, I was at lunch at a nice burger joint, and my buddy Eric was deeply discouraged. For some reason I will never understand, Eric's boss was blind to his incredible talents. My friend was locked in a job where he was deeply underutilized. He was opening up to me about it and getting pretty emotional.

And then he did this thing. He just stopped talking. He looked down and to the left.

"But whatever," he said, quietly. "It's okay."

I lit into him.

"What are you talking about?" I said, putting down my burger. "Your boss doesn't see you. You're offering up your gifts, and he doesn't use them. That's not okay, man. That hurts. That's deeply discouraging. And until you admit that it's NOT OKAY, you're going to be trapped in your own emotions."

And from there, we were able to have a real conversation about what to do next. It wasn't until he acknowledged what was actually going on—that he was really hurt and wounded from this situation— that we could get to the root of it.

One of the greatest strengths is being able to admit you're not okay.

Pretending—playing ostrich and burying your head in the sand—doesn't work.

About twenty-four hours later, I was at a camp outside New York City with a whole bunch of teenagers. When I arrived, the camp director's son Justin was there, who I'd met the year before. Justin was a sophomore basketball player, and he'd grown and put on muscle. I started talking to him about the season. It didn't go so well. He started telling me about his coach, who favored the upperclassmen. Justin worked his butt off and bit his tongue, hoping that performing on the court in practice would be enough to convince the coach to put him in. But despite his best efforts, the coach benched him.

And then Justin stopped talking. He looked down and to the left. "But whatever," he said, quietly. "It's okay."

The same line as my buddy Eric.

"No, man, stop that mess," I said. "Stop pretending it's okay and you're okay. It's deeply disappointing. You feel trapped. You work hard, and it's not being rewarded."

And then we talked about what to do. But first, Justin had to stop pretending.

One of the greatest strengths is being able to admit you're not okay.

A few hours later at dinner, I was chatting with another student. Her name was Cristiana. She was an incredibly outgoing, bubbly senior. The kind of student who lights up every room she's in.

"What are you doing next year?" I asked her.

She told me her plan was to be a pediatric surgeon, but she was staying close to home to go to community college. I knew she had the grades to go anywhere, so that was a little puzzling to me.

"Why?" I asked.

She talked about how her parents were going through an incredibly messy divorce. Her dad had an affair with a woman half his age. Because of the legal battle fees, Cristiana had to get a job and work twenty-five hours a week, on top of school and soccer practice, just to pay the bills. And even worse, her dad had vanished out of her life.

"He moved out the day before soccer tryouts and two days before the SATs, in August," she told me. "Do you know how hard it was to keep myself together for those things?"

She told me she felt rejected by her dad. Once, joking, she said, "Are you going to get married to this new woman, Dad?" Her dad said he didn't know.

Cristiana nervously laughed, "Well I hope I don't end up with a surprise baby brother or sister."

Her dad looked at her.

"Maybe I'll have another baby. A girl. And I'll name her Cristiana," he said. "Maybe this one will turn out right."

As she told me this, Cristiana's eyes filled with tears.

"Why would he say that?" she said, covering her face.

I shook my head. I've heard a lot of messed-up things, but this was easily one of the cruelest. What kind of father says that to his daughter? I simply cannot imagine ever uttering this.

"But whatever," Cristiana said quietly, looking down and to the left. "It's okay."

There it was again.

That same line.

Three times in a row.

What is going on with that?

I called over some other adults, and later that night we all sat around listening to Cristiana and helping her process the loss and grief and pain she was going through. But we couldn't do any of that until she stopped pretending she was okay.

You will never fix what you're not willing to face.

I don't know why everyone seems to hide their struggles. Maybe it has to do with Instagram, and how everyone wants to present their best life. Nobody online is out there posting their struggles.

Now, I'm not saying you should just post all your struggles online for everyone to read ("I just had the worst diarrhea. Man!").

But here's what I know.

Perfection is not the goal. In fact, perfection is not even possible.

All those people who appear to be living their best life online deal with struggles after the camera is put away.

All those people who show perfection are almost always battling things you have no idea about.

You're not alone.

I know it's hard when the pain chooses you. But going through what you're going through doesn't make you weak.

It doesn't make you less.

It makes you human.

So don't hide your struggles. Because it's hiding your humanity.

—————— REHAB TIME ——————

COACH PEP TALK

One of the most important parts of relationships is to share honestly about the tough parts of life. Here are some questions to help you figure out how well you do this.

QUESTION 1

On a scale of 1–10 (with 1 being "not at all" and 10 being "very"), how vulnerable and honest are you with your friends and family about the tough things that you face in life?

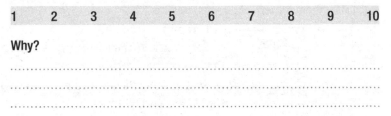

| 1 | 2 | 3 | 4 | 5 | 6 | 7 | 8 | 9 | 10 |

Why?

....

....

....

QUESTION 2

Who are the people you trust the most to share tough things with?

....

....

....

QUESTION 3

What is the toughest thing that you're going through right now? Have you shared this with anyone?

....

....

....

HOW TO KEEP GOING

Here's the straight truth.

There's no way for anyone on this planet to go through life without going through suffering.

I wish there was.

But there is not.

Though knowing that suffering is a part of life and that it's coming can actually help. Because part of the problem of suffering is that so many people are surprised when it happens.

A silly example: the other day, my friend invited me to go trail running on a course I'd never been on. I asked him, "Are there any hills?"

My buddy paused and said "No."

The next day, we started out on this trail, and I am telling you, it was murder. So difficult. At the end of the run, I turned to my buddy.

"I thought you said there were no hills, man," I said, feeling deeply betrayed. "Why you trying to trick me?"

"I didn't say that!" he exclaimed.

"I asked you yesterday if there were hills," I said.

"Oh!" he said. "I thought you said, 'Are there any wheels?' I thought you meant mountain bikes or something."

I'm still a little mad about that one.

"Are there any wheels?" Who would ask it like that?

The point is because I thought the course was flat, I was dismayed and even felt a little betrayed by my friend. "You could have warned me," I thought to myself. "I would have brought more water."

The next time we ran it, I was prepared. And you know what—it really wasn't so bad that time.

In a small way, that's what life is like. So here are some ways to prepare yourself so that when the storms of life come—and they will come—you'll be a little more ready.

It won't be easier, really. But at least you'll know what to do.

NOT IF, BUT WHEN

As I said earlier, it's not an issue of *if* suffering and bad things will happen to you, but *when*. I wish this were not so, but one of the surest truths of life is that suffering will happen to you. Jesus even says at one point to His followers, "In this world you will have trouble" (John 16:33).

In fact, if you love anyone or anything a great deal, there's a good chance you will suffer quite a bit. As the famous author C. S. Lewis once wrote:

> To love at all is to be vulnerable. Love anything and your heart will be wrung and possibly broken. If you want to make sure of keeping it intact you must give it to no one, not even an animal. Wrap it carefully round with hobbies and little luxuries; avoid all entanglements. Lock it up safe in the casket or coffin of your selfishness. But in that casket, safe, dark, motionless, airless, it will change. It will not be broken; it will become unbreakable, impenetrable, irredeemable. To love is to be vulnerable.[1]

NOT WHY, BUT WHAT

My friends who have been around a great deal of suffering tell me that the most common question people ask after experiencing a great loss is "Why?" As in, "Why did this happen?" or even "Why did God let this happen?" This is the question we want to ask first, and it's actually the question least likely to be answered. You're probably never going to know why.

And even if you got the answer, it wouldn't help.

Instead, ask God the question "What?"

God, what are you up to here?
God, what are you doing in my life?
What—if anything—is my role in this? (There are times we suffer because of our own choices. Be careful not to slip into false guilt, though, because sometimes suffering has literally nothing to do with us.)

Another thought. If God actually explained why He allows things to happen as they do, it would be too much for our finite brains. My daughter, when she was younger, often would cry when her mother or I didn't let her do something she wanted to do. She didn't understand why we didn't let her, for example, play with the sharp knives we emptied from the dishwasher. She was too little. But we would pick her up and hug her and let her know we loved her, even if we wouldn't let her play with the knives. She might not understand the why, but she could understand that we loved her. And that's what she needed the most. I can't understand all of what God is up to, but I know He loves me. I know He loves you. Jesus on the cross proves it.

NOT AROUND, BUT THROUGH

We almost always want to do whatever it takes to avoid pain. We try to numb it, or distract ourselves, or get away from it. It's natural. It's what we do. But this is not how to deal with suffering. In fact, this is like if you have a gaping cut on your leg and you walk around pretending you don't have a serious wound. You actually make it worse. There's no way around the pain. We can't pretend our way out of it. We have to go right through the painful valley. But there is good news. The good news is that this is where God is. He promises to walk with us through the valley of the shadow of death. He walks with us.

NOT EVIL, BUT GOOD

In the midst of suffering, we have two tendencies that will paralyze us. The first is the tendency to believe that everything is ruined. When suffering happens, we think, "Things will never be the same, and everything is wrecked." That's almost never true. How many times in the Bible does God take a situation that seems helpless or hopeless and make a way out of it? God does this all the time. One of God's great superpowers is to write stories with surprise endings, where bad things come undone.

The second tendency is to believe that because this bad thing happened, it means God is bad. Or maybe not bad, but definitely mean. But God didn't create the world with evil in it. That's the result of mankind turning away. But even though there is suffering, God doesn't turn away. In fact, if the Bible is to be believed, God rushes in to help us.

As the theologian John Stott once wrote, "I could never myself believe in God if it were not for the Cross. In the real world of pain, how could one worship a God who was immune to it?"[2] So we must resist the temptation to believe that because the world is bad, God is bad.

Jesus proves otherwise.

—————— REHAB TIME ——————

COACH PEP TALK

One of the toughest parts about suffering is believing something good can come out of that season. This is where it's important to remember and pay attention to your life. Think about your past struggles and how good things eventually came out of those hard times. This can give you hope that if it turned around before, God can do the same thing again.

What I went through	When I went through it	Something good that came from it in my life

VII.

STRAIGHT UP

ABOUT RELATION-SHIPS

HOW TO DEAL WITH HEARTBREAK

Straight up—the pain of heartbreak is unlike any other type of pain.

It's like rejection mixed with grief mixed with a punch in your gut. You want to be rational, but there might not be any rational answers. You want to be rational, but your emotions are in the driver's seat. And every song that comes on is like salt on the wound. Ugh.

I certainly didn't start doing RehabTime to be a relationship coach, but I get tons of comments and emails each day from people who are dealing with the heartbreak of a breakup.

I wanted to talk about this, because it's so personal and affects so many people.

According to a *Fast Company* article, around the world, there are about three million first dates every single day.

Three million!

That's a lot of awkward. But that's also a lot of opportunity. As the article says, "That's three million chances for sparks to fly. Three million chances to discover the person you're going to spend the rest of your life with!"[1]

Also, three million chances the relationship will fizzle and lead to the opposite of that: the breakup.

The most common reasons people break up, according to the article, are:

- Distance (16 percent for women, 21 percent for men)
- Cheating (22 percent for women, 18 percent for men)
- Lost interest (26 percent for women, 28 percent for men)
- Parents/friends didn't approve (3.5 percent for both)[2]

Another fascinating fact: most breakups occur in March and the first two weeks of December. The fewest breakups occur on Christmas Day,[3] which is good, because that's just cruel.

Also, only 7 percent of all breakups are mutual. So the chances are good that you will either have to break up with someone or have someone break up with you.

UNDERSTAND WHAT'S HAPPENING TO YOU

Breaking up is hard to do. This isn't my opinion. There's actually scientific proof.

In a study by Helen Fisher at Rutgers University, fifteen people who had just experienced romantic rejection were shown a picture of their ex while Fisher scanned their brains in an fMRI machine. Their brain activity was similar to those of withdrawing addicts.

"We found activity in regions of the brain associated with cocaine and nicotine addiction," Fisher said.[4]

COCAINE!

Cocaine, people.

You feel out of whack because your body actually is out of whack. This is helpful to know because it means that, like a withdrawal from an addictive drug, this process is going to be the most difficult at first. But it does get a little bit better every day.

YOU HAVE TO GET SUPPORT

Your brain is a jumbled mess of conflicting emotions after a breakup. And you're going to want to withdraw socially from everybody. This is when you need your friends to help you out.

Now sometimes friends try to help by saying things like, "You're better off without him!" or "I never liked her anyway." This sounds supportive, but in reality, it isn't really helpful. It's minimizing the fact you are experiencing real loss. It's like if you blew out your ACL and someone said, "Walking is overrated. It will be so fun to be in a wheelchair for the next six months." See? Not very helpful.

It's better to feel the wave of painful emotion, acknowledge it, and move on. And your friends can help you by listening to you, helping you process, and getting you out of the house and going on with daily life.

KILL THE RELATIONSHIP, NOT YOUR EX

In college, I knew a guy who went through a messy breakup. He'd joke that he and his girlfriend broke up for religious reasons. "I was Protestant," he said, "and she was the devil." When a relationship ends, the tendency is to shift all the blame for the failure of the relationship entirely onto the other person. This is not only unfair, it's actually untrue. One of the reasons we date is to try to find out if the other person is a good match for us. In the words of the great American poets Rob Base and DJ EZ Rock, "It takes two to make a thing go right."

If the other person is not a good match for you, that doesn't make them a bad person. It means they don't fit with you. In fact, if you think about it, your ex is probably someone else's perfect match.

I know that failed relationships can feel very, very painful because they feel like rejection. But they're not really rejection, so much as an honest recognition that the two of you don't go together very well. And that's often not anybody's fault. It just is.

So the relationship went bad. It doesn't mean the other person is. And changing your mindset on this can help you keep away from bitterness (it's all their fault) and even move forward with hope (I can't wait to find someone who fits with me).

TAKE YOURSELF OUT OF THE GAME AND REHAB

After a breakup, the very last thing you need is to rush into another relationship. You need to stop putting yourself out there for a while until you have time to figure things out and heal. This is tough, but the impact after a breakup is real. You need time to just be by yourself. And I don't mean for a week. People ask me all the time, "How long does it take to heal from a breakup?" Look, everyone is different, but a good rule of thumb is "Don't date for roughly half as long as the relationship lasted." That means if you dated someone for a year, take six months off. Minimum.

But something else I know about rehab: it usually takes longer than you want it to.

During this time, reflect with God on the lessons you learned from this. Those lessons might include: What did you learn from this season? What did you learn from this person? What would you go back and change if you could? What should you definitely do going forward? What did you learn about yourself because of this experience?

Learning from life is part of the process of closure. But this process might also be a little bit painful, because you might realize that some of the issues have to do with you.

So now, I want to go through the three most common reasons why I've seen relationships fail. I'm not saying this to judge you, just to give you some help.

YOU DIDN'T HAVE A WINGMAN

How many times have you seen this: a friend makes a stupid decision about who to date, plows through all the red flags, and the situation winds up horrible for everyone. It's a tale as old as time. Look—just because they're cute doesn't mean they are good for you. When it comes to dating, we all sometimes drink the dumb-dumb juice and do stupid things. This is why you need a wingman (or a wingwoman). This is like having a designated driver for your relationships. You give your trusted friends the keys. You entrust them to help you make wise decisions and keep you out of harm's way. You have to trust them to give you honest feedback. And then you have to LISTEN to that feedback.

YOU EXPECTED TOO MUCH

Look, just because the person is going out with you doesn't mean they're automatically your soul mate. Almost every married person I know has a failed relationship in their past. You have to be realistic about this process: there's a good chance it won't be a good fit. That's okay.

YOU VIOLATED YOUR OWN VALUES

One of the primary causes of heartbreak—and something I've seen over and over again in emails and comments—is that the desire to be in a relationship is stronger than the desire to be in a good, healthy, respectful relationship. You can't negotiate on the things that are nonnegotiable just because you really don't want to be alone. If you do, you'll end up feeling miserable and resentful of both the other person and yourself.

The bottom line is that chances are you're going to have to go through a painful breakup at some point in your life.

This might feel like the end of the world, but it doesn't have to be.

—————— REHAB TIME ——————

COACH PEP TALK

Okay, I know it's no fun to stop and think about all the pain you experienced from your last heartbreak, but if you don't dig in, you don't break through. Complete this exercise to see what you can learn from your past failed relationships.

QUESTION 1

Have you ever been through a breakup? What did you learn about yourself (and life and love) from that breakup?

....
....
....

QUESTION 2

If you've been through a breakup before, rate yourself on how likely you are to do the three following things.

Get support from friends vs. Isolate

1	2	3	4	5	6	7	8	9	10

I tend to reach out to my friends. I tend to isolate and be alone.

Kill the relationship, not your ex

1	2	3	4	5	6	7	8	9	10

I vilify my ex in my mind. I accept that my ex wasn't bad, they were just a bad match for me.

Take yourself out of the game and rehab

1	2	3	4	5	6	7	8	9	10

I take myself out of the dating game and work on myself. I jump into other relationships so I can feel better about myself.

RED FLAGS IN RELATIONSHIPS

Straight up—one of the quickest ways to misery is to be in an unhealthy or immature relationship with an unhealthy or immature person.

Misery, I tell you.

I get so many comments and emails and texts and DMs from young people who say they're trapped in bad relationships and don't know what to do.

So I ask, why did you start dating this person?

He was cute.

She was pretty.

I mean, I get it. There's such a thing as physical attraction. But come on. The person's looks should be at the very least the SECOND most important thing you look for when you start to date someone. I mean, right?

Here's what I learned. You don't date a person's looks. You date their character.

We get so easily distracted by the external that we forget that the external isn't really who we date. We date the person's internal, their character.

Think about this: Do you know someone who is physically attractive, but their personality is so ugly it actually makes them less attractive to you? That's facts, isn't it? Some of the most attractive people I know are actually horrible people.

So before we go any further, I need to outline what to look for in any healthy and mature relationship. There are three things that are critical.[1]

SAFETY

You should always feel safe in any relationship, but especially so in a romantic one. Safe to be yourself. Safe to express your thoughts, feelings, and opinions without shame, disapproval, or judgment. And absolutely safe from physical, emotional, or verbal attacks and abuse.

RESPECT

Respect is when someone treats you like an equal who has incredibly high worth and value. You've seen relationships where one person wants to have power or control? Yeah, that's not respect. If the other person doesn't care what you think, doesn't ask what you feel, doesn't care where you came from, and doesn't bother to find out where you want to grow, then they're not interested in you as a person. They're not respecting you.

THEY HELP YOU GROW (AND DON'T TRY TO CHANGE YOU)

I have a theory that relationships (both friendly and romantic) should be going somewhere. The goal of all relationships isn't just to have fun, but also to help you move toward becoming the person God made you to be. This does NOT mean, however, that the person is trying to change who you are. They simply want the best for you. You can tell the difference. In his book *Changes that Heal*, Dr. Henry

Cloud calls this "grace," saying: "Perhaps you have experienced this kind of love and grace with someone. You can be exactly who you are. You do not need to hide your thoughts or feelings; you do not need to perform; you do not need to do anything to be loved. Someone knows the real you and loves you anyway."[2]

So now that we know what to look for, let me outline a few red flags that indicate you're dealing with someone who at best is really immature and needs to grow up, and at worst is selfish and manipulative and needs to change before they hurt someone. These are things that should cause you to pump your brakes and take a good hard look at whether this relationship is helping you.

RED FLAG 1: THE PROBLEM IS ALWAYS YOU, NEVER THEM

There's no way to avoid conflict in relationships, but how it's handled is key. If the other person is constantly pointing out all the things that you did wrong, but never willing to admit their part in the issue, that's a big red flag. If you're always saying sorry and they're never saying it, that's a big problem. It could be that they are unwilling to even look at their own problems, let alone admit them, let alone WORK on them. This is always a bad sign.

RED FLAG 2: THEY ISOLATE YOU FROM YOUR FRIENDS

This is a classic control move. Usually this is done because the other person doesn't want the people who know you best to know what a snake they are. So if they get you away from your friends, then you're isolated from good advice, such as "You should dump that guy and run away." A solid relationship always includes integration into your friend circle and respect for the people who know and love you well. In the words of famed British poets the Spice Girls, "If you wanna be my lover, you gotta get with my friends."

RED FLAG 3: THEY INVALIDATE YOUR FEELINGS

Nothing breaks human connection faster than when you honestly and vulnerably share something in your life (your pain or your emotions) and the other person invalidates your feelings. Maybe they say you shouldn't feel the way you feel, or that you're dumb to feel that way. Sometimes this is called gaslighting. It's a reference to an old movie where an abusive husband turns off the gas to the lights in the house, making them flicker, and then when his wife notices, he pretends like she's seeing things and tries to convince her that she's insane.[3] Gaslighting can occur when you bring up an issue in the relationship and the other person tries to convince you that you're making it all up, that what they're doing is just fine. This breaks trust, and it's manipulative.

RED FLAG 4: THEY DEMAND TRUST BUT DON'T WANT TO EARN IT

People think that trust is a thing that's given. It's not. It's a thing that's slowly earned over time by doing the right thing again and again and again. There's no shortcut to trust. Ever. And in my experience, people who demand to be trusted without having to earn it are not trustworthy. Don't fall for this. I will give you my trust when you've earned it, and if you value me, you will do what it takes to earn my trust. That's how it works.

RED FLAG 5: IT'S ALL ABOUT WHAT THEY NEED

Relationships are not one-way streets. But some people think they are. Look, I'm going to be honest with you, there are a LOT of people out there who are self-centered and who only think about themselves. This means they're immature. And immature people think relationships are ways for them to get what they want . . . not ways to love another person sacrificially. Ask yourself this question: Does this person ever go out of his/her way to help or serve me? Are there any examples you can cite?

RED FLAG 6: THEY PLAY GAMES

One of the most important aspects of all relationships is honest, direct communication. But some people are incapable of this. So when your significant other talks about you to your friend or someone else, and then that information gets back to you: that's an immature game. Tell them to knock it off. Other immature games are giving you the silent treatment, being sarcastic, or any passive-aggressive behavior. If they can't be brave enough to communicate what they're actually feeling to your face, maybe they're not brave enough to be in a real relationship.

FINAL THOUGHT

In 1890, the average age that women got married was 22. For guys, it was 26.1.[4] By 2018, that number had shot up to 27.8 for women and 29.8 for men.[5] This means there are a lot of people waiting longer to get married. I don't know exactly why this is. But here's what all the research is showing us: relationships are very difficult when you're young. This is why almost all high school relationships fail, as well as tons of relationships people have in their twenties. We have a culture that's very selfish right now, and selfishness and healthy relationships are like oil and water.

Here's something else I know.

It's tough to find someone who fits with you if you don't know who you are.

There's that famous line in the movie *Jerry Maguire* where Tom Cruise says, "You complete me."

As real as I can put it, I love me some Tom Cruise, but this line is garbage. It's a dangerous thing to ask another person to be the missing puzzle piece to your entire personhood. What if they get killed by a bus? Do you walk around the rest of your life half-completed?

No other person can complete us. Only God can do that. What other people can do is bring deep meaning into our lives as we learn how to love them sacrificially, as we learn how to love them even more than we love ourselves, as we learn how to show them our truest selves without fear and shame, and as we learn how to accept the love and grace we desperately need from them.

But these are things only mature people can do. These are things that we can only do (honestly) with the help of God.

So maybe if all your relationships are failing, it's not because you haven't found the right person, but because you haven't focused on becoming the right person.

Work on that.

Work on yourself.

And then it will be easier to spot someone who fits perfectly with you because you'll finally know who you are.

———————— REHAB TIME ————————

COACH PEP TALK

The baseline for all relationships, romantic or not, is that there should be safety and respect, and the person should help you grow. As you answer these questions and review the red flags, keep that in mind. And if the relationship does NOT meet that baseline, you have to be honest enough and brave enough to end it. It's better to be alone than with someone who is a bad fit for you.

QUESTION 1

Are you in a relationship with someone right now?
YES / NO

IF YES . . . go through this checklist. Do any of these red flags apply to your current relationship?

> The problem is always you, never them.
> They isolate you from your friends.
> They invalidate your feelings.
> They demand trust, but don't want to earn it.
> It's all about what they need.
> They play games.

If the answer is yes to any of these, what are you going to do about this?

. . . .

. . . .

. . . .

IF NO . . . do you see any of those red flags in any of your friends' relationships? How can you talk to them about it?

. . . .

. . . .

. . . .

LESSON 29

STRAIGHT TALK ABOUT SEX

I want to talk about sex.

But I want to talk about it in terms of freedom.

You would think in a culture that has so many ties to the word *freedom* that we would understand what it is.

But we don't.

So first, let's look at the modern definition, which is this:

FREEDOM MEANS DOING WHATEVER YOU WANT

One of the most influential thinkers in the modern world is a man named Sigmund Freud, who is sometimes called "the father of modern psychology." To take it down to basics, Freud said that we all have desires, and that pretending like we don't is bad. He then concluded that true freedom is the ability to follow or desires without anyone telling us no.

Now, this sounds good. And it sounds like freedom. But I'm going to be honest with you, it's just not true.

Because—and I learned this the hard way—you can use your freedom in a way that actually results in LESS freedom overall.

Think about this scenario. You are a kid, and your mom tells you that you can't play outside until you pick up your room. Now, can your mom MAKE your pick up your room? No. You have the freedom to flop on your bed and refuse to move a single muscle to pick up a single toy. That's your freedom.

BUT.

If you use your freedom in THAT way, you actually LOSE freedom, because now you can't go outside and play.

Another illustration. I had a friend in high school who was very, very good at football. He was for sure going to get a Division I scholarship and might have had a decent shot at making the NFL. But he didn't like school. So he decided to not do any homework. He used his freedom to not do any classwork.

As a result, he didn't make grades and got kicked off the football team. Then he used his freedom to stop coming to school. As a result, he didn't graduate high school. As a result, he didn't make it to college or the NFL.

He used his freedom in a way that LIMITED his freedom. He shut down his options for the future.

The misuse of his freedom led to less freedom.

I had another friend, also on our football team, who was equally gifted and also clearly heading to Division I. He used his freedom to sleep with his girlfriend, and she got pregnant. As a result of that, he had to work multiple jobs to support the baby. As a result of that, he didn't get good enough grades to get into those Division I schools. He used his freedom, but it led to less options and less freedom in his life.

And the young woman he got pregnant? She was in no way ready for a child. She had to put her goals and dreams on hold and raise a child she was not ready for. She used her freedom, but it led to less options and less freedom in her life.

Is that really freedom?

Shouldn't freedom lead to more options and a better life?

It's like this.

Imagine there's a fish in a giant lake. The lake is brimming with life and is vast enough to offer adventure and exploration for all the fish's days. But right near the shore, there's a wooden dock. And the fish begins to think, "I really want to go up there on that wooden dock." But his parents and friends and teachers all tell him, "Don't go up on the dock."

The fish grows indignant.

"Who are THEY to tell ME what to do with MY BODY?" the fish says. And then he leaps out of the water and onto the dock. He is there, flapping around. He yells to the universe, "I am free!!!"

And then a pelican swoops down and eats him.[1]

Sometimes, freedom isn't really freedom.

Let's talk about how this relates to sex.

The dominant idea in our culture is that sex is always good, and that any repression of any sexual desire is always bad. Do whatever feels good. Sex is about self-expression and pleasure. It's an evolutionary urge that must be followed.

But.

Uh.

This just is not true. Sex is not just a biological act. There's something more going on. If it was just physical, then would so many people be emotionally wounded by it? It's a part of relationships, but it can also be used to hurt people.

And many people I know—including myself—have deep regret over a sexual encounter that they really wish had not happened.

You can use your sexual freedom in a way that hurts others.

And.

You can use your sexual freedom in a way that hurts you.

What we need is a different, wiser definition of freedom.

Like the one is taught by the Bible.

FREEDOM MEANS SAYING NO TO ANYTHING THAT DOESN'T POSTIVELY BENEFIT YOURSELF AND OTHERS

Sometimes freedom means saying NO, even though you want to do something, for the sake of something that's BETTER. Something that produces a better life. Something that makes you better or makes the world a better place. Something that results in deeper joy or deeper personal fulfillment. For example:

- You say no to eating McDonald's because it's better for your body in the long run to eat real food.
- You say no to dropping out of high school because it's better to maximize your potential.
- You say no to coming home right after school because it's better to be a part of that school play, which will be awesome.
- You say no to free time because you want to practice gymnastics.
- You say no to all other people because you want to marry that ONE person.[2]

Now, let's bring this back to sex.

The Bible teaches that sex isn't only about pleasure, it's also about deep, human connection. That sex is physical, but it's also spiritual. One of my pastors once said that sex was "sacred energy exchanged." That stuck with me. Sex is a way for two people to become united as one.

So if part of the overall design of sex is to unite you to someone else, then maybe it's best to be smart about who you unite yourself with.

Or, let me put it another way.

If sex is about pleasure AND showing commitment AND deep human connection, then what happens if the person you're with only wants the pleasure part?

What if they only are interested in having sex with you because THEY get something out of it?

Do you really want to give yourself to somebody who doesn't deserve you? Who doesn't even really want all of you?

Look, I get that sex feels good. It's pleasure. It's designed that way, biologically. But I think there's a toll on the human soul when sex is separated from connection and commitment.

It's better to use your FREEDOM to NOT use sex that way so that you FIND SOMETHING BETTER.

Sex is designed by God for deep connection and commitment. It's a way for two people to show that they will be with each other and united to each other no matter what.

Anything less, and you're cheating yourself.

──────────────── REHAB TIME ────────────────

COACH PEP TALK

This is a delicate topic, and I'm not telling you how to run your life. I just don't want you to use your freedom in a way that hurts you or your future. Here are some questions about sex that only you can answer for yourself. Take some time and be thoughtful about your answers.

QUESTION 1

Have you seen sexuality used in a way that hurts people? What was the situation?

....
....
....

QUESTION 2

Is sex more than just pleasure? Do you agree with the statement from this chapter that sex is pleasure AND commitment AND connection? Why or why not?

....
....
....

QUESTION 3

You don't want to give yourself to somebody who doesn't deserve you. What might it look like for someone to deserve you? What kind of person would they be? How would you know if they deserved you?

....

....

....

VIII.
STRAIGHT UP
ABOUT HARD WORK

LESSON 30

IT'S NOT FAILING IF YOU'RE TRYING

When I was in kindergarten, I enjoyed going over to my grandfather's house in Little Rock, Arkansas. My grandfather loved to garden. I would help him prepare the ground and till it up. I would help him make the little rows. And the best part was planting the seeds. I would take the tiny seed, make a hole with my finger in the soft, warm earth, put the seed in, and cover it up.

I was so excited.

But.

I didn't understand how gardening worked. In my little kindergarten mind, I thought that when I woke up the next day, all the plants in the garden would be fully grown. Red, ripe tomatoes would be hanging on the vines, green and red peppers would be popping up, watermelons would be sitting there fully formed. Just BAM, instant garden.

I ran out to the garden the next morning.

It looked *exactly* the same as it did the day before.

I was crestfallen.

"Grandpa! When is it going to grow?" I asked.

My grandfather got down on one knee. "You have to be patient, Trent," he said. "For gardeners, the name of the game is patience."

"I don't want to be patient!" I said. "I want things to grow."

"Oh, things are growing, Trent."

"But I don't see anything."

And then my grandfather broke it down and dropped some knowledge on my five-year-old self. And he said something that I still remember.

"Even if you can't see growth, you have to understand that growth is happening.

"It's just under the surface, where you can't see it."

Man, grandpas are the best.

The problem with living in the modern world is that most of us no longer understand anything about gardening. Most of us don't live on farms or grow our own food. We've lost some wisdom about life because of that. We think that food just comes from the supermarket.

But it doesn't.

It grows.

Slowly.

Painfully slowly.

Over a period of months.

That's how plants grow.

And the thing is, that's how we grow too. But we don't like that. We want mechanical growth—something quick and almost automatic.

Mechanical growth is like what happens when they build a new Target or a giant shopping mall or condominiums. Big machines come in, and they remove all this dirt and push it around. Giant piles of dirt and gravel. Then they bring in some bricks and wood and concrete, and in a few months there's a brand-new building. Unlike planting saplings in that area, which take years and years and years to grow into something resembling a wooded area.

Mechanical growth is super impressive.

And fast.

And we want that for our own lives. We want to have our lives built like that. But that's not how it works.

PATIENCE IS A TALENT

God does not do mechanical growth. He does biological growth. Nearly every single metaphor that God and Jesus use in the Bible for human growth has something to do with plants—with organic botanical growth.

Organic growth is slow and happens over time, and in some ways, it is almost imperceptible.

God grows us like plants. Slowly.

I know we want quick results. I know you want the work that you put in today to show up as results tomorrow.

But it just doesn't happen like that.

The work you put in today might not show up until months down the road. Or even years down the road.

When I knew I would be going to the NFL combine, I realized I needed to impress scouts with my speed. I wanted to run a 4.3 forty-yard dash.

But I wasn't that fast. I was running roughly a 4.5 forty-yard dash. So I started working with a speed and conditioning coach.

For an entire month, I worked for HOURS a day to get faster. I did so many drills, so many exercises to shave tenths of seconds off my time. I worked every day for a month. And at the end of that month, I still was running a 4.5.

Man.

All that work. All that effort. And nothing to show for it. But my coach reminded me that I was doing the right things. I had to trust the process. So I worked for another solid month. I ran a 4.49. Two months of work for practically nothing.

Then one day, bam, I ran a 4.39. Just like that. All the work suddenly paid off.

But I had to be patient. I had to trust that something was happening in me, even if I couldn't see it. And that's when I learned that it's easy to give up when you don't see results. But being patient is a talent.

And it's a talent that most people don't have. The person who is patient and consistent will reap the results in time. Working and waiting is a hard process, and most people won't do it. But if you operate with faith that something is happening, then you can separate yourself from your peers because you've been patient.

There's a verse in Philippians where Paul talks about God's slow work in us:

> He who began a good work in you will carry it on to completion until the day of Christ Jesus.
>
> PHILIPPIANS 1:6

There's another place in 1 Corinthians where Paul continues this idea. He writes:

> I planted the seed, Apollos watered it, but God has been making it grow. So neither the one who plants nor the one who waters is anything, but only God, who makes things grow.
>
> 1 CORINTHIANS 3:6–7

God is responsible for the growth. God makes the field blossom. Now, the problem with organic growth is that—to our modern eyes—it often does not seem that impressive.

That Target is going to done by March. It wasn't there, and then—BAM—it's there in all its red-and-white Target-ness. But with organic growth, it's much less dramatic. There are seasons, in fact, when it looks like nothing is growing. Those wintry seasons are very difficult. But it doesn't mean that God is not growing the tree, because pretty soon spring happens and then you see the explosion of color. Just an explosion of growth and buds and flowering.

Botanical growth requires incredible patience. It requires us to take the long view of life.

GROWTH IS NOT SOMETHING THAT HAPPENS OVERNIGHT

I stayed with my grandparents for an entire week, and when I left, still nothing had grown.

Maybe you feel that way now. Maybe you feel like nothing is growing. That God isn't really doing anything in your life. That nothing is moving. Nothing is taking shape.

Here's what I always come back to in those moments, when it's tempting to give up on the idea that anything is growing in my life at all, or that things will ever be any different. I ask myself:

Am I trying to grow?
Am I trying to take steps?
Do I have the things I need to grow?
Am I putting in the work?
Am I trying to make things better? Doing what I can? Owning what I can own?
Am I going to the gym?
Am I staying connected to my friends?
Am I putting aside time to connect with God and my family?
Am I trying?

And if the answer is no, then I change that. I can control that. But if the answer is yes, then I just remember my grandfather.

My grandfather once told me the story of the Chinese bamboo tree. As the old fable goes, there was a man who set out to grow a bamboo tree. Like any plant, it needed good soil and water and nutrients. But unlike other plants, the bamboo would not grow above the soil during the entire first year.

In fact, it did not grow above the soil the first FIVE YEARS after the man planted it. The neighbors mocked the man. "Are you going to keep watering the ground for nothing?" they joked.

But the man knew something his neighbors did not. He knew all the growth would happen in the fifth year. So he kept on watering that seed.

Then, in year five, it happened. The bamboo tree grew. And not just a little. It shot up above the houses and the powerlines. It grew eighty feet in forty days!

That's the power of botanical growth.

It may be slow.

But nothing can stop it.

And that's what God is trying to do in all of our lives.

God wants to grow us.

It might not be as fast as you'd like.

Things may be going slower than you'd wish.

But you're not failing if you're trying.

Make a choice to be committed. And patient. Just because you can't see the growth doesn't mean it's not happening.

— REHAB TIME —

COACH PEP TALK

Seeds can't grow without soil, water, and sun. There are things each of us needs in order to grow too. As long as you have them, rest assured God is up to something. These questions have helped me figure out what I need in order to grow (especially spiritually).

QUESTION 1

Jesus once said, "Remain in me, and I will remain in you. For a branch cannot produce fruit if it is severed from the vine, and you cannot be fruitful unless you remain in me" (John 15:4 NLT). What are the times when you've felt most connected to God? What was going on in your life? Who was there? Was there anything unique going on?

....
....
....

QUESTION 2

What are the times in your life when you've grown the most? What was going on in your life? Who was there? Was there anything unique going on?

....
....
....

QUESTION 3

Do you need to do anything in order to grow? Is there something you might need to add? Something you might need to cut out to make space and time for something more important? What steps could you take?

....
....
....

LESSON 31

YOU CAN'T FIX LAZY

Around 600 BC, in ancient Greece, there was a man named Aesop, who told stories to illustrate important ideas about life. You have probably heard his stories. Classics like:

The Hare and the Tortoise (Slow and steady wins the race.)
The Fox and the Grapes (You often hate what you can't have.)
The Lion and the Mouse (Kindness is never wasted.)

But one of the most famous of Aesop's fables is *The Ants and the Grasshopper*. The story basically goes like this:

It's summer, and the ants are all working to harvest food for the winter, but the grasshopper makes fun of them. He says, "Why are you working so hard?" He only wants to play music and have fun. The ants keep doing what they're doing. Later, it's winter, and the grasshopper comes to the ants. He's run out of food.

"What were you doing all summer?" the ants ask him. "Where's your stored food?"

"I was too busy playing music to harvest food," the grasshopper says.

Then, in a pretty dark turn, the ants turn their backs on the grasshopper in disgust, and he's left to starve and die out in the cold.

What a great lesson for kids!

But besides the cold-hearted, compassionless response of the ants, I really like this story. Because it reminds me of something I've seen time and time again in life.

YOU CAN'T FIX LAZY

Lazy is defined as someone who is "disinclined to activity or exertion."[1] Now, this doesn't mean I'm advocating for everyone to work all the time. We all have moments when we need a break from the churn of work to recharge. That's what vacations, weekends, and evenings are for. And they're super important.

However, what I'm referring to in this case is someone who is in a perpetual state of spring break.

You know the type.

- They ask to copy your work right before class because they didn't do their homework.
- They're asked to do a chore, and they put as little effort in as possible.
- They have a part in the group project and don't do it (and you have to stay up late to get their stuff done).
- The coach tells the team to run ten laps, and they purposely run only eight and then claim they ran ten.
- There's a chapter assigned in English class, and they don't read it. Ever.

Here's the truth. As sad as it sounds, there are people who don't want to work.

All through my football career, from junior high through college, I've had teammates who drove me (and everyone else on the team) up the wall. I mean, football isn't the most important thing in the entire world, but I was playing it because

1. I wanted to contribute as much as I could to the team, and
2. I wanted the team to do as well as possible.

This meant working hard. Right? I mean, if you want to personally contribute as much as you can, you have to be at your personal best. Which means pushing yourself and doing as much as you can. And if you want the team to succeed, that means you want to create a culture where everyone is after the same thing.

But there were some guys who wanted to do as little as possible, just enough to get through practice. They hoped the coaches didn't notice them slacking off. These kinds of people flourish in a culture where there is no accountability, no expectation, and no method of keeping score.

And there's nothing anyone can do about it.

I once complained to a friend about a lazy teammate of mine who really wasn't taking the team seriously, and my buddy said something that stuck with me. He said:

IF YOU AIN'T WILLING TO GO GET IT, DON'T COMPLAIN ABOUT WHAT YOU GET

You can fix a lot of things. You can fix "not very good." I watched football players who weren't naturally gifted train themselves into pretty amazing athletes. People who could have never made the team turned themselves into starters.

But they put in the work.

You can fix "bad luck." I have watched teammates get hurt on a freak play. And it didn't keep them down. They took time off and got healed.

But they put in the work.

In fact, I've even seen hard work beat talent. What's that saying? "Hard work beats talent when talent don't work hard." I have seen some incredible athletes who refused to work hard, and they got beat by less talented people who hustled their butts off.

THERE'S ONLY ONE WAY TO SUCCESS: HARD WORK

This isn't just true in sports. This is true in literally almost every arena of life.

I love what Oprah Winfrey once said about what she thought was the secret to success: "The big secret in life is that there is no big secret. Whatever your goal, you can get there if you're willing to work."[2]

Which means the opposite is true.

If you aren't willing to work, you won't get there.

But here's the crazy part to me.

If you don't work hard, it's still going to be hard.

Think about Aesop's grasshopper. He didn't want to do the hard thing (in this case, harvesting food). He wanted to play. But he didn't escape the hard thing. He just delayed it until winter. And then it was *really* hard.

The issue is not "Can I avoid the hard thing?"

No. No, you cannot.

As the ants show us, hard work pays off later, but it requires some discomfort NOW.

As the grasshopper shows us, laziness pays off now, but it GUARANTEES some discomfort later.

If you ain't willing to go get it, don't complain about what you get.

And I gotta tell you. There's always room in the world for a hard worker. Hard work will always blaze you a trail. But laziness will always hurt you in the long term, and your laziness will cause your life to suffer. Maybe not today. But rest assured, it will eventually.

Don't be lazy about things that are important to you. Don't be lazy about the things that matter to you.

Because hard work can cover over a multiple of issues.

But you can't fix lazy.

—————— REHAB TIME ——————

COACH PEP TALK

We're all a little lazy at something. Take some time to do some reflection about where in your life you've gotten a little lazy about something that's actually important. If you can't think of anything, there's an easy solution: talk to your parents about this. They have X-ray vision for this. Believe me, if you come to them and explain what you're trying to do, they will be *thrilled* to help.

Important thing I'm actually pretty lazy about	One small step I can take to get better at it and stop being lazy **(Make sure it's something you can measure)**	Date/Time I will complete this small step

GET COMFORTABLE WITH BEING UNCOMFORTABLE

Outside your comfort zone is where growth happens.
It's where change happens.

Period.

Muhammed Ali once famously said, "I don't count my sit-ups; I only start counting when it starts hurting because they're the only ones that count."[1]

No growth ever happens in the comfort zone. In fact . . .

GROWTH HAPPENS THE MOST WHEN YOU'RE UNCOMFORTABLE

This isn't my opinion. Scientists have studied the subject of human performance for years, wondering what helps people truly grow and optimize their gifts and talents.

There's something called the Yerkes-Dodson Law that was developed all the way back in 1908 and has been examined in various ways over the last century.[2] Here's what they found (and I'm paraphrasing the geek stuff):

Too little pressure/pushing/challenge?

You become bored and unmotivated.

Too much pressure/pushing/challenge?

You break down and burn out.

Just enough pressure/pushing/challenge?

Incredible growth.

So what's "just enough" pressure and pushing and challenge? Well, it's up to you to find that balance. But it's got to be something that pushes you beyond what you reasonably expect you can do or have done in the past. A challenge. Something new. Something that carries with it the real possibility of failure. An adventure.

It's like that moment in the 2001 film based on J. R. R. Tolkien's epic tale *The Fellowship of the Ring*, when Frodo and Samwise leave the Shire to meet Gandalf on the dangerous mission to destroy the ring. They're walking through a field in the Shire, and Samwise suddenly stops.

"This is it," he says to Frodo. "If I take one more step, this will be the farthest away from home I've ever been."[3]

That's what I'm talking about.

Take one more step.

Away from you comfort zone.

Away from where you've been.

Away from what you've always done.

Into a new place.

A grand adventure.

For the sake of Middle Earth!

(Sorry. I really like *The Lord of the Rings*.)

Now, I know what you're thinking. Some of you are saying to yourself . . .

I DON'T WANT TO BE UNCOMFORTABLE

I get this. But I gotta be straight up with you. If you never push yourself outside your comfort zone, then I tell you, you will not grow. And if you don't ever grow, then ironically, you will BE VERY

UNCOMFORTABLE. Not changing and staying right where you are will actually make you incredibly uncomfortable, because you were meant to GROW and be something greater than you currently are.

I love what Jesus says when He's asked what the point of his life was. He says in John 10:10 (NKJV), "I have come that they may have life, and that they may have it more abundantly."

Full life.

Overflowing life.

In fact, Jesus was CONSTANTLY using agricultural comparisons to describe what our lives should look like. In Matthew 13:32, He talks about how our lives are like trees, and His goal is that those trees would grow up, become strong and huge, providing shade for all the birds of the air. And in verse 23, Jesus is basically saying, "That's what I want for you. My dream for your life is for you to grow and be fruitful."

To produce much fruit.

To grow.

To make a real and lasting impact on this world.

That can't happen if you don't grow. And you can't grow unless you push yourself to grow. Push yourself to be uncomfortable.

THE BENEFITS OF BEING UNCOMFORTABLE

Here's the thing. The Uncomfortable Zone is actually pretty cool. If you're spending some time in the Uncomfortable Zone, I can bet that more than likely:

You'll be conquering your fears.
You'll be excited about your own life.
You'll be conquering your struggles.
You'll be conquering your laziness.

This is where you become better. And if you have dreams for

your life to be fruitful—to grow and become all that you can be—you're going to have to be in this Uncomfortable Zone.

I learned this pretty early on. My chances of being in the NFL were incredibly low. In 2019, only about 7.1 percent of high school senior players even went on to play NCAA men's football, and only about 1.6 percent of NCAA senior players were drafted by an NFL team.[4] So, out of all high school players, only about nine in 10,000 get drafted, or .09 percent. That's a really low percentage.

I had to push myself to beat those odds, which meant learning how to be comfortable with being uncomfortable.

I had to get up early and go to workouts by myself.

I had to stay late after practice.

I had to train in 100-degree heat.

I had to do two-a-days when I didn't want to.

Was that comfortable?

No.

It was definitely uncomfortable.

But I had to do it. Because I had a dream, and also because I was gifted by God with athletic ability, and I wanted to see if I could push myself to my ultimate best as an athlete. I didn't want to leave anything on the table. I wanted to see if I could make it in the NFL.

I had to become comfortable with being uncomfortable.

WHAT HAPPENS IF YOU DECIDE TO BE COMFORTABLE?

If you decide to live a comfortable life, you're probably going to end up filled with regret.

You think you'll be happier, not pushing yourself to be uncomfortable. But you'll never fully realize your potential.

There's a famous scene in the movie *Braveheart*, which is about William Wallace, who led Scotland's fight for independence from British rule. Right before a big battle, a Scottish soldier sees the great British army and yells out, "Fight? Against that? No, we will run; and we will live." Wallace knows that the man is not saying something wise but giving in to his cowardice and fear. Wallace's response is one of the great lines in movie history. He says to the man:

> Aye, fight and you may die. Run, and you'll live. At least a while. And dying in your beds many years from now would you be willing to trade all the days from this day to that for one chance, just one chance, to come back here and tell our enemies that they may take our lives, but they'll never take our freedom?[5]

Chills.

What Wallace is saying is this: "You can be comfortable. Yes. But you will regret it all the days of your life because you missed out on something important."

OUTSIDE THE COMFORT ZONE IS NOT CROWDED

When I get up early in the morning to do my trail runs in the hills around my house at six a.m., it is not busy. There is not a line. There are plenty of parking spaces. There is no one else out there. I know I'm outside my own comfort zone. I know I'm outside the comfort zone. Because most people won't do it.

Inside the comfort zone is average.

It's mediocre.

It's settling.

It's mild.

It's getting by.

It's content with just surviving.

It's NOT thriving.

It's NOT thrilling.

It's NOT realizing your fullest potential.

Look, friends.

I'm not trying to make you be uncomfortable for the sake of discomfort. I'm not saying there's value in being in pain for the sake of pain. I'm not telling you to sleep on beds of nails or to never wear shoes.

I'm trying to get you to avoid the greatest discomfort of all.

Because there's no greater discomfort than knowing that you (to paraphrase the musical *Hamilton*) threw away your shot.

That you left your true potential untapped and unexamined.

That you left something on the table.

There's no greater discomfort than regret. Nothing is worse. I don't want that for you. I want you to avoid that at all costs.

So if you want to go beyond average,

make the world respect your greatness,

become the greatest you possible,

make an impact on this world,

you have to get comfortable with being uncomfortable.

Let's get to it.

--------- REHAB TIME ---------

COACH PEP TALK

I want to be clear on this: being uncomfortable for no reason other than being uncomfortable is dumb. I'm not asking you to do that. What I am asking you to do is push yourself in areas that matter to you so that you eliminate regret. Like I tell my son all the time, "I don't want you to settle for a C when some effort could get you a B. If you can't get an A, that's fine, but don't settle for a C." Make sense? These questions will help you.

QUESTION 1

Answer these questions as honestly as you can. They might help reveal places where you have settled for being comfortable.

Is there any area that is important to me (that I'm good at and want to grow in) where I have been lazy?

....

Is there any area I've become bored in that I really want to be fully engaged in?

....

Is there any an area I've purposely NOT challenged myself in that I really should be challenging myself in?

....

QUESTION 2

Based on my answers, what is a small step I can take to push myself out of my comfort zone to grow?

....

What do I hope might happen because I've pushed myself? What kind of growth or change would be awesome in my life?

....

BUSYNESS IS SOMETIMES LAZINESS

There's a tale I heard about a man who went on a sightseeing safari in the Serengeti. He wanted to see all the stunning animals of the African plains. And he paid quite a bit of money to some local guides to make sure he saw everything.

He kept pushing his guides to go faster, so they drove fast. And hiked fast. And set up camp fast. They saw elephants and rhinos and cheetahs and lions and warthogs and baboons and hyenas and wildebeest. It was like stepping into a live remake of *The Lion King*. Hakuna Matata!

On the fourth day, after practically sprinting through the safari, the man awoke in his tent. But he did not hear the clatter of the guides packing up the camp and getting ready for the day's adventure. He did not hear the bustle of the Land Rovers getting loaded up with gear. In fact, there was only silence.

The man emerged from his tent and saw his guides sitting around the campfire, drinking their morning coffee. They were not even in their field clothes!

"What are you doing?" the man said, surprised. "We have to get going! There are things to see."

"Oh, we cannot go today," the guides said.

"Why not?" asked the man. "Are the vehicles broken?"

"Oh, no, they work fine," the guides said.

"Well then, what is it?" asked the man.

"You see, we traveled so fast the past few days," the guides said, "that we all have to wait here so that our souls can catch up."[1]

You ever feel like that?

You ever feel like you're going so fast, moving at such an incredible pace, that you've lost touch with even yourself?

You've gone so fast for so long that your soul hasn't caught up?

It's exhausting.

And if you're like most young people, you can relate.

There's a reason so many high schoolers and young adults are tired.

Like that man on safari, they're going at a pace that's ridiculous.

You have to achieve. College applications expect a long list of extracurriculars. And you have to fill that résumé.

Your coach expects 100 percent commitment.

Your English teacher expects 100 percent commitment.

And so do your chemistry, math, and history teachers, by the way.

You have two events after school multiple days a week for that club or that sport or that leadership council or that youth group or that band or that theater production.

Maybe you have a part-time job.

Plus homework.

And family responsibilities (your room isn't going to clean itself).

And you have to find time to sleep in there. Specialists tell us you need about nine hours, but if you're like most of your peers, you're lucky if you snag seven.[2]

You're overscheduled.

Overcommitted.

Going from one thing to the next.

To paraphrase Jesus . . .

WHAT'S THE POINT IN GAINING THE WHOLE WORLD IF YOU LOSE YOURSELF?

Do I need to tell you this isn't good?

No.

You can't stay on all the time. Take a lightbulb. A light's job is to illuminate the darkness, which is an important task. But if that light never turns off, it will burn out.

There's no gain that's worth burning out like that. There's nothing that important.

Do I need to tell you that slowing down isn't easy?

Also no.

But there is something you can do. Because I have learned this lesson from my own life. Sometimes we're busy for the sake of being busy. And sometimes, being busy all the time is actually a sign that you're being sloppy with your time and your priorities. Activity is not the same thing as productivity. In fact . . .

SOMETIMES, BUSYNESS IS A SIGN OF LAZINESS

We're doing a lot of stuff, but perhaps we're not being very thoughtful about what we SHOULD be doing with our time.

The bottom line is that you and I are only given twenty-four hours per day.

That's all.

And how we choose to spend that time is really important. We need to be more thoughtful about it. In fact, if you feel like right now, in your life, you don't have enough time, that means you don't have your priorities in order.[3]

You're riding a bike without a chain.

Or swimming against a strong ocean current.

It doesn't matter how hard you try. You won't get anywhere.

SOMETIMES PEOPLE DO THE LEAST BY DOING THE MOST

Let me give you a real-world example. We have a family friend named Tim, and he told me about a recent crisis he had. At the time of that crisis, Tim was a high school senior. Here's what he was involved in:

- He played on the school basketball team.
- He was secretary of his school's student leadership council.
- He was president of a robotics club.
- He played on the worship team for his youth group.
- He was taking four AP classes (math, physics, history, and English).
- He worked at a local grocery store (on weekends and one school night).
- He was a ref on Saturday mornings for a youth soccer league.

Tim told me that he hit a breaking point one Sunday when, after church, his dad invited him to go to lunch with the family, and he realized he couldn't go because he had to be at work at one o'clock.

Tim was so frustrated that he actually started to cry. And Tim was NOT a guy who cried. His dad realized something was wrong, and they sat and talked about what was going on. Like the man on safari, Tim had gone so fast for so long that he needed time to let his soul catch up.

Together with his parents, Tim outlined all the things that he was doing and then ranked them on a scale of one to ten based on how important they were to him.

Tim quickly realized there were things he was doing because he felt like he *should* be doing them, or because there was some other pressure, not because they were important to him. He felt a sense of relief, not loss, when his parents gave him permission to let go of them. So here's what Tim did.

- He dropped AP history. Tim was a science and math guy and was going to go to college for engineering. The pressure of that class was too much. Regular history would be good enough.
- He quit his job. He realized he needed spare time with his family on the weekends more than he needed money. Plus, he had the ref job for extra cash.
- He turned over the robotics club presidency to a friend. Tim still participated, but he gave the weight of leading everything to someone else who was competent.
- He decided to only ref soccer games that started after nine a.m. on Saturdays so he could have a little time to sleep in.

All in all, this thoughtful analysis of his schedule allowed Tim to get back eighteen hours of time in his schedule per week.

You read that right.

Eighteen hours.

And Tim learned an important lesson with his mom and dad that day.

Sometimes busyness is a sign of laziness.

Just because you're busy doesn't mean you're being smart about your time management. Adding things to your life and working 24/7 doesn't mean you're succeeding. What it really means is that you're setting yourself up to crash.

Everything good takes rest. I mean, even God had to rest, right?

How are you spending your time?

Is what you're doing helping you become the person you want to be?

Is what you're doing helping you work toward your goals?

Is what you're doing important to you?

Because at the end of the day, you only have twenty-four hours. Don't waste it by working all the time.

REHAB TIME

COACH PEP TALK

Like Tim, sometimes we aren't thoughtful about the ways we're spending our time. Sometimes we do things because we think other people want us to do them, or because we think we *should* do them, not because we want to. This activity is a chance to examine how you spend your time.

NOTE: Don't you dare try to cut out important stuff just because you don't want to do it, like household chores or homework.

NOTE: You probably spend too much time on entertainment and video games. I want you to think about what's helpful to your life and what's not.

TIME AUDIT

Multiply the last three boxes together for a total score. (If there are activities with a really high number, that's an indicator).				
What I spend my time doing	How many hours per week I spend on this	How much this activity helps me grow (scale of 1–10)	How important this activity is to me (scale of 1–10)	How much I would miss this if I stopped doing it (scale of 1–10)

SWEAT THE SMALL STUFF

Straight up—the little things matter.

People say all the time, "Don't sweat the small stuff."

And if that means "Don't waste a lot of your time worrying about things that ultimately don't matter," then I agree.

But if it means "Little things don't matter as much as big things," then I wholeheartedly disagree.

A lot of times, it's the little things that make the biggest difference.

I learned this lesson acutely several years ago. You'll recall that right after college, I began training for the NFL tryouts. Because I was going out for the position of wide receiver, I knew I needed to impress the coaches and scouts with my speed. I had to catch their attention. Which meant I had to drop my 40-yard time down from 4.5 seconds to 4.3 seconds. So I trained. And I trained. And after months and months of speed training and agility activities and stretching, I could not get my time to drop.

Then, I made a change.

A small change.

And the very first time I made this change, I ran a 4.3.

Want to know what I did?

I moved my right foot back about two centimeters (roughly three-quarters of an inch). And I moved that foot away from my body about two inches.

That's it.

Two centimeters.

And two inches.

I had a slightly bigger base to push off from, and all that work on my leg strength allowed me to explode off the block, and that took my time down to a 4.3.

Tiny change.

Big difference.

(Actually, it's a tiny, tiny difference, but you get what I'm saying.)

SMALL CHANGES CAN MAKE A BIG DIFFERENCE

I want you to think about your own life. I know you want to make some changes to be better in some area of your life. So I want to ask you, what is one small thing you can do that will create momentum throughout your life?

One small thing you can absolutely do.

When I was a trainer, people would say, "I want to get in shape," or "I want to lose some weight." And they'd go from not working out at all to working out seven times a week.

I would tell them, "Don't." Don't do that. Choose something you can do in your life. Choose something you can absolutely commit to. Work out ONE day a week. Meet with me ONCE a week. Don't break that commitment. Then, once you do that for a while, and have that under control, move to TWICE a week.

Don't run ten miles a day.

Aim for three.

Then, get that under control.

Starting small gives you confidence. AND it allows you to fully commit to a lifestyle change one step at a time.

DOING SMALL THINGS FLEXES YOUR DISCIPLINE MUSCLE

Habits always start small. They're about making a decision and then following through on it, day after day. This is how things happen. And it's the little tweak you can consistently commit to that makes the big change.

I was thinking about this, and I made a list of five little things that often snowball into major life changes.

DAILY FAMILY DINNERS

According to a study by Stanford Children's Health, family dinner together might be one of the most important and foundational habits to children's well-being. Researchers found that family meals dramatically increase family bonding, decrease stress, and might even be tied to better grades and less drug use.[1] Yes, it's a hassle to make meals every evening. But the benefits are off the charts. I love family meals, and I don't care how busy my life gets (or our kids' lives get), we will always make family dinner a priority because that time communicates very important ideas. That we share as a family. That we are here for each other as a family. And those lessons are priceless. So something as small as eating dinner together can lead to something much bigger.

EXERCISING DAILY

Your body is the means by which you move about in this world and accomplish everything you do. If your body fails, uh . . . you're in trouble. So it makes sense to take care of it. And all the research says that exercising a couple of times a week really matters for your physical health. But did you know that it might also make you smarter? Researchers don't know why exactly (perhaps it's increased blood flow to your brain), but exercising makes your mind and focus sharper. And if you're trying to lose weight, there's evidence that exercise helps you make healthier food choices, too.[2] So moving your body and breaking a sweat is a small thing that leads to a big thing, like a healthier life.

SAVING MONEY WEEKLY

I recently read a story about five friends from Philadelphia, all in their early twenties, who realized they needed to make a change. They each saved fifty dollars per week for the next two years. After two years went by, the group had enough money to buy their first investment property.[3] This habit forced the group of friends to think daily about their financial realities and what their goals were. Putting aside this money every single week was a small thing that led to a big thing.

CLEANING THE KITCHEN EVERY DAY

I had a friend who was constantly fighting to try to keep her house clean. The area she hated the most was the kitchen, which always seemed to be filled with dirty dishes, papers, and clutter. So she made a change. Every day, she would clean her kitchen sink.[4] She'd remove all the dishes and get out the stainless steel cleaner and make that sucker shine. Seems like a curious goal, but what she found is that the spotless sink put more focus on the kitchen and helped her clean outward. It was easier for her to clean up the little things five times a week than let it build up into a giant chore once a week. For her, cleaning the sink was the small thing that led to the big thing.

MAKING YOUR BED EVERY MORNING

First off, your bed is the biggest piece of furniture in your house, and seeing it there all messy has a psychological effect on you. Making the bed gives you a little bit of joy and makes the whole room seem . . . neater. But I'm not the only one who thinks this. Navy Seal William H. McRaven, commander of the forces that led the raid to kill Osama bin Laden, gave the 2014 commencement speech at the University of Texas. He gave a startling bit of advice. "If you want to change the world, start off by making your bed. If you make your bed every morning, you will have accomplished the first task of the day. It will give you a small sense of pride, and it will encourage you to do another task, and another, and another. And by the end of the day that one task completed will have turned into many tasks completed."[5] Who knew? Making your bed is a small thing that leads to big things.

So I want you to think on this. What is one small thing that you can commit to that will get you closer to your goal? What's something you can do to move the needle?

Figure it out.

Write it down.

And do it.

Because the little things often wind up making the biggest difference.

——————————— REHAB TIME ———————————

COACH PEP TALK

You need to take a small step. But what is it? I want you to spend some time thinking about what your big goal is, and what is one small step you can ABSOLUTELY do without fail for the next thirty days. Remember, if it's too difficult to absolutely commit to for thirty days, then make it simpler. The point is movement in a direction toward your goal, not perfection.

OVERALL GOAL	
ONE SMALL STEP (that I can absolutely commit to for the next thirty days)	
HOW OFTEN I WILL DO IT?	
WHO WILL I TELL ABOUT IT? (so I can be accountable)	

IX.

STRAIGHT UP

ABOUT CHANGE

LESSON 35

HOW TO CHANGE
(PART 1: COMMITMENT)

When I was playing college football, the rallying cry across all the major Division I programs was pretty much the same.

Win championships.

From Alabama to Florida to Ohio State to USC, every program's coaches would say the same thing: the goal is to win championships. Plural. Not just one. Multiple.

Our coaches at Baylor called this a "championship mindset." I always appreciated this, because I am a fairly competitive person, and why even play if you're not interested in winning?

The thing is, championships don't just happen. They don't just accidentally occur. They take a great deal of focus and determination, and sometimes that can be overwhelming. So for the next five chapters, I want to look at the five steps to developing a championship mindset. These five things will help you move. Let's start with the first step (arguably the most important).

COMMITMENT

Definition: *Staying loyal to what you said you were going to do long after the mood has left you.*

Okay, I might have gotten ahead of myself. Before you commit to something, you need to think about WHAT you're going to commit to. The first thing you have to do in any venture is decide what you're going to do. What's the pressure point in your life? What's the one area that's weak, that's not good, that isn't where you want it to be?

I hear so many people say things like, "I wish that my grade in chemistry wasn't so low."

This is simply wishful thinking. I wish all sorts of things. I wish I were in Hawaii right now.

Wishing isn't commitment. It's just daydreaming. And it's never changed anything.

But if you just dig a little farther, you can move from wishful thinking to an actual goal. All you have to do is think about what you want to be different in the future, and then put a time stamp on it. So the formula is:

Time Frame + Desired Outcome = Goal

Back to that student with the bad grade in the chemistry class. What if they said:

By the end of the semester, I want to improve my chemistry grade from a C to at least a B.

Ooh.

You see.

That's a goal. It's moved from wishful thinking to a plan. Now, you need to sit and brainstorm for a little bit. What concrete steps do you need to take to help you achieve this goal?

What steps do I need to take to make this happen?
I'll meet with the teacher before school on Wednesday mornings.
I'll join the study group that meets in the library on Monday and Thursday.
I'll get extra tutoring.

Okay, so now that we know what we need to do, we have to

decide to do it. All this planning, this clear goal setting, is all very important, but it's literally meaningless if you don't actually commit to doing those things.

I'd say about 50 percent of people I know never move beyond the wishful thinking stage. And of the 50 percent who do come up with a clear goal and action steps, probably 75 percent of those people stall out and don't keep their commitment.

Why?

Because we say we want something, but then, because we're human, that mood goes away.

I want to work out. I feel a surge of commitment. I'm very excited about this. I will get up early, and it will be amazing.

But then the alarm goes off at five a.m.

And suddenly, that doesn't sound so good. It's chilly out there. And my bed is oh-so-soft and oh-so-warm.

Commitment is what gets you out of bed.

The great philosopher Thomas Aquinas said that the ability to do what you should even when you don't want to (what he called temperance) was one of the four most important virtues a person could have (he called it a "cardinal" or "foundational" virtue).[1] For him, it was the decision to not do what you want to do in order to avoid sinful excess. But we can also adapt that idea toward a similar idea: it's also important to do what you DON'T want to do to avoid an excess in the form of bad habits.

Here's the truth.

Commitment is foundational.

Commitment is an investment in yourself.

Whenever my son Tristan is working out, I always say to him, "Are we working for now? Or are we working for later?" He's learned that the answer is always later. I tell him that you're doing something now in order to get results down the road.

I love the title of Drew Dyck's book on self-control: *Your Future Self Will Thank You.* That's exactly right. You're making this commitment to your own self in the future.[2]

Michael Phelps is one of the greatest Olympians of all time. He began swimming at the age of seven. By the age of ten he was setting records for his age group, and at fifteen he qualified for the US Olympic team.[3,4]

Phelps knew he was good at swimming. But that wasn't enough. His goal was to be the greatest swimmer in the history of the Olympics—to win more gold medals than anyone had ever done before.

That's a lot of gold medals.

So he committed to train. Every day, he'd be in the pool training, doing whatever his coaches told him to.

Phelps told reporters that early in his career, he trained in the water *every* day of the week for five years. During the eight-year peak of his training (the four years leading up to the Athens games and the four years leading up to the Beijing games), Phelps's longtime coach Bob Bowman reported that Phelps trained six days a week and spent, on average, five hours per day in the pool.[5,6] Reportedly, Phelps swam a minimum of eight miles a day.[7]

I'll do the math for you. If we assume Phelps swam at least eight miles a day during his Athens and Beijing Olympic training years, he swam more than nineteen thousand miles. If the entire state of Texas were a giant swimming pool, that would be like swimming twenty-four and a half times across the length of Texas.

For more than twenty years, Phelps spent nearly every day in a pool.

That's an investment in his future self. Mark Spitz had set the standard with nine gold medals. Phelps retired with twenty-three gold medals. That's two and a half times the number of gold medals than the previous most decorated Olympic swimmer.

I know I use a lot of sports examples, but this is not just about athletic achievement.

I have a friend named Heather whose life was very difficult when she was in high school. She had a rough family life, compounded by some tragedies in her family, compounded by some of her own bad decisions. She was very smart and academically capable, but she had never graduated from college.

She didn't like this about herself. Heather was working for a major health care company, doing some administrative work, and it was clear she had a lot more leadership potential. It was clear she had the real capability to do so much more.

But all those jobs required a college degree.

So Heather made a commitment to her future self: "I'm going to graduate from college."

There were all sorts of things in Heather's way.

Heather was a single mom.

Heather was financially strapped.

Heather didn't have any support from her family.

But she made a commitment. She started taking night classes. Stayed up late, got up early, used her lunch breaks to read and study. She started chipping away. And in about three years, Heather got her degree. Her company knew what her plan was, and after graduating, she was promoted immediately.

One year later, another promotion.

Today, Heather finally is using her skills and gifts in a job she can do (and do well).

Why did Heather do this?

This wasn't just about money (although this new job pays substantially more than she used to make). It was also about Heather not cheating her future self. It was about Heather's future self being able to realize more of her own potential.

She wanted her future self to be a person who had graduated from college. Was this easy? No. But in the end, she knew she'd regret it if she didn't at least try. Her commitment, in the end, was to be faithful to herself and her own gifts.

Look, if you're reading this book, I might not know you, but I know this about you: you have a lot more potential in you than you think.

And I don't want you to waste it. Let it go undeveloped.

I want you to be the BEST you possible.

I want you to move beyond simple wishful thinking. I want you to imagine your best you and then figure out what steps you need to take.

And then commit to those steps because you're committed to becoming your best you.

The world needs you to be the best you possible.

But more than that, you need you to be the best you possible.

Let's get it.

——— REHAB TIME ———

COACH PEP TALK

I want you to complete this exercise so you can move from wishful thinking to actual goals with real action steps.

STEP 1

Here are several areas of life. Of these, which you feel is most important for you to focus on right now? Circle one.

SCHOOL / MONEY / FRIENDS / FAMILY / DATING / PHYSICAL HEALTH / CONNECTION WITH GOD / WORK / SERVING OTHER PEOPLE WITH MY GIFTS

STEP 2

What is the reality of this area in your life right now? Be honest. It does no good to sugarcoat things.

....

....

....

STEP 3

Be specific about what you want to be different in your life.
Complete this fill in the blank:

By _____ I want _____ to happen in my life.
　(insert a specific time frame)　　　　　(insert specific life goal)

STEP 4

Brainstorm all the things that you could do to help you achieve the sentence you filled in above.

....

....

....

STEP 5

Pick 1–3 things you are convinced will help you achieve that goal. Write them down below. Be sure to include how often you will do them.

1. ....

2. ....

3. ....

HOW TO CHANGE (PART 2: DISCIPLINE)

In our previous lesson, we talked about moving from wishful thinking to a place of commitment. I want to explore that a little bit more. Commitment and discipline are tied together. And neither are about "trying harder." In my experience, it's a lot deeper than that.

But first, we need a definition.

DISCIPLINE

Definition: *Saying no to things that don't get you a yes.*

Life is all about yes and no.

Life is a series of decisions about what you say yes to and what you say no to. And those decisions really matter. And they add up.

You have a big yes inside you. It's what you want. It's what you're going after. And your life and your energy will go into whatever your big yes is. I imagine it in my head as a big, inflatable beach ball in a pool. Have you ever held down a beach ball in a pool? What always happens? You can hold it under the water, but only for a little while. It always pops to the surface.

The same is true with your big yes. You will go after what you most want. You just will.

This doesn't mean your big yes is a good thing. For example, I know people whose big yes is money, and they do whatever they can to get more of it. They use people, bend the rules, break the rules, and burn relational bridges. Money is that important to them. Money is their big yes—and they go after it with every ounce of passion and life they have. They're miserable, awful people. But they get what they want.

That's how that big yes inside of you works. It drives you. For good or for bad.

The Bible has a word for this idea of your big yes. It's the word *heart*. The word for heart in Hebrew is *lebab* or *leb*, and in Greek it's *kardia*. These words are used in the Bible more than one thousand times. I bet when you think of the word *heart*, your mind goes toward the actual organ that beats inside a person's rib cage—but in these ancient languages it also means much, much more.

Old Testament scholars Dr. Tremper Longman and Dr. Bruce K. Waltke both wrote commentaries on the book of Proverbs. One of the most important words used in that ancient book is the word *heart*—used 46 times in Proverbs and 858 times in the Old Testament. But both Longman and Waltke had a problem: there's no good English equivalent for this Hebrew word. It's not merely your emotions, Longman says, but more like your "core personality."[1] Waltke says, "The direction or bent of the heart determines its decisions and thus the person's actions"—which means that heart is so much more than merely emotions.[2] It's more like "who you are and what you're about." Or a better English equivalent might be "your core motives."

It's the big yes.

The heart is your big yes. It's what motivates you. It's what you'll spend your energy going after. It's what your mind fixates on. It's what your emotions love. It's what you direct your will toward. It's what you most want.

For example, some people are willing to lose power in order to get people to like them. Other people don't mind losing relationships as long as they win and maintain power. Those are two entirely different hearts.

Another example using Longman and Waltke's ideas about the heart: If you're stingy and aren't generous, it's likely because your big yes is to money (or more accurately, what money can give you—either comfort or status or something else). If you are deeply offended and hurt when someone insults you, then likely your big yes is protecting your reputation and standing in society. You want people to think of you as successful.

The Bible is constantly asking us to examine our heart. What is your big yes? What are you really after? What have you set as your deepest goal? What really gives you meaning? What do you most want in this life? Where is your heart, really?

You will say yes to the thing you most want in life. So it's worth spending some time thinking about that. What's your big yes? And is it worth devoting your entire life's energy toward?

Now, here's why this is so important. Discipline is always tied to your big yes.

Let me tell you first off: you're never going to do anything in life if it's just one more thing on your to-do list. That's going to deflate you.

When I say no to television or no to sleeping in, I'm not saying no to those things as much as I'm saying yes to the idea of trying to create some positive content for RehabTime.

So I gotta ask you a question: What is it that you want? What is most deeply in your heart?

It's all about choices. Every day you have a choice to move forward or stay the same.

That's all on you. Nobody can control your choices.

You make a choice. In order to get something out of life, you have to put the work in.

Let me tell you about a time when I realized I had to change my big yes. And how changing that big yes changed my discipline and changed my life.

When my son Tristan was born, I realized I had to change some things. I had to start saying no to some things so I could become the best possible father to this little boy. My big yes in my heart was my son. So, I had to say no to quite a few other things.

This is what fatherhood means. You might remember from a previous chapter my mentor and good friend who loves to play golf. But it's an expensive and time-consuming sport. So when his first child was born, he decided to sell the clubs and stop playing golf until the kids were out of the house. It was just what he had to do to become the father and the husband he knew he wanted to be.

Your big yes will make it easy to say a big no.

Have you ever met someone who is bound and determined to do something? Perhaps it was something good, or perhaps it was wildly destructive. It's pretty impressive what humans can accomplish when they're highly motivated to do something. We can go to the moon and back. Also invent New Coke.

The question is not, "Can a human being accomplish something amazing if he or she focuses their life's energy on it?" The question is rather, "What am I devoting my life's energy to? And is that getting me what I most want?"

What's your big yes?

Because your life's energy will go after that.

So maybe it's time to start saying no to some things that aren't getting you toward your big yes.

─── REHAB TIME ───

COACH PEP TALK

If it's true you'll spend your energy on what you most want, it would be good to spend some time thinking about that. Answer these questions below and do the hard work of excavating what your big yes might be.

QUESTION 1

What is your big yes right now?

....

QUESTION 2

What are some things you need to say no to in order to move toward your big yes?

....

....

....

LESSON 37

HOW TO CHANGE
(PART 3: CONSISTENCY)

Straight up—once you've decided to do a thing (commitment) and that thing is tied to the big yes inside of you (discipline), you need to do the hard work of being consistent.

The world will always make a place for someone who is consistent. It's one of the most important aspects of success. Here's my definition.

CONSISTENCY

Definition: *Every single day, I will show up.*

There aren't many things more important in football than consistency. In fact, as I think about it, the whole point of practice—and I'm talking hours and hours and HOURS of practice—is to grow in this one small area: to become more consistent.

As a wide receiver, I knew that if I didn't practice, I would be inconsistent. If I only caught thirteen out of twenty balls thrown to me, that wouldn't be good enough. That's only a 65 percent chance I'd catch the ball. The quarterback would not trust me enough to throw me the ball.

But if I worked hard in practice and caught nineteen out of twenty balls thrown to me, that's a 95 percent chance I'd catch the ball. The QB would know I'm reliable. He'd have greater confidence in me. And more passes would come my way.

CONSISTENCY = TRUST

And honestly, consistency (and trust) are crucial, not just for a receiver, but for every position. The quarterback has to consistently make the right throw. The running back has to consistently make the right cut. The linebackers have to consistently make the tackle. The safety has to consistently make the right read. Football taught me that consistency matters because it builds trust.

Here's the thing I also learned. Talent alone doesn't automatically mean you're consistent, and consistency matters more than talent. You don't have to be the best. There were always receivers who were faster or flashier than me. They might have had more natural talent than me. But they only showed brilliance in flashes. They were on-again, off-again. They were not reliable. And in football—and in life—reliable matters a great deal. In crunch time, people want to know who to trust. And reliability matters.

There's a story from the Beijing Olympics in which a team of NBA superstars, including LeBron James, Chris Paul, and Dwayne Wade, were all meeting for their first practice session. It was early morning, and the players were lazily slumping in their chairs.

Then Kobe Bryant walked into the meeting. He was sweaty, because he'd been doing his own workout while all the other players were still in bed.

Even though it was summer.

Even though the team was about to work out.

Even though he was jet-lagged.

Kobe didn't miss a day. Bryant was credited by coaches and players for transforming the work ethic and culture of Team USA and dramatically impacting the personal habits of the stars on that team.[1]

Kobe's message was clear: talent doesn't win. Consistency does. Even the best in the world have to consistently put in the work.

CONSISTENCY = MOVEMENT

It's not about perfection. It's about movement. Every day.

In his book *Great by Choice*, Jim Collins calls this kind of consistency the principle of the "20 Mile March." The story he recounts is taken from true history. In October 1911, Roald Amundsen and Robert Falcon Scott set off on a dangerous race. Each man led a team with the goal of becoming the first to reach the South Pole. This was an incredibly dangerous journey—they would need to travel more than 1,400 miles, in a place where winds howled and temperatures often reached under 20 below Fahrenheit.

Amundsen and Scott both had the same goal. But one was successful, and the other one died along with the rest of his team.

Same journey. Same goal. What was the difference? Well, there were many, but one of the things that Collins calls out is that Amundsen had his team trek around twenty miles a day. On the days with good weather, Amundsen's men could easily travel a lot more than twenty miles. But Amundsen would not let them. He wanted them to conserve their energy. But then, in terrible weather, during brutal winter storms with gale-force winds, they still had to trek as close to twenty miles as they could. No matter what the conditions, the team would set off for twenty miles. Consistency. Always.

Scott's team was more haphazard. Sometimes, if the weather was clear, they'd make a huge push and go very far. But then they'd be exhausted and have to wait out a storm. They were inconsistent. They had big days when the conditions were good, but no progress at all when conditions were bad. They frequently exhausted themselves. Other days they didn't move at all. There was no consistency.

Can you guess which team was successful? Amundsen's team came back home, victorious. Scott's team didn't reach the South Pole until over a month later, and then they all died on their way back when a deadly winter storm overtook them.[2]

Consistency matters. In his book, Collins extrapolates why Amundsen's twenty-mile-march approach worked for him, and how it can help you and me.

IT GIVES YOU A CLEAR WAY TO KNOW YOU'RE MOVING.

Most of the really difficult things we do take a long time. It's very easy to get discouraged. But if we break a giant task down into daily, measurable goals, then we know what victory for the day looks like. The goal is to move twenty miles a day. This isn't confusing. It's clear. And when you accomplish that twenty-mile trek, you're done. You've done your job. And that success is very motivating to you.

IT ELIMINATES ALL EXCUSES, ALLOWING YOU TO PUSH THROUGH BAD DAYS.

Most people complain and whine when things don't go their way. Let's be honest: whether it's trekking through Antarctica or trying to pass that difficult economics class, we're all looking for excuses to not do the hard things. The twenty-mile-per-day program eliminates your excuses, because you go into the day knowing what to expect. Be it making sure you pay attention no matter how you are feeling, or knowing you have a quiz that day you need to pass.

IT MOVES YOU CLOSER TO YOUR GOAL EVERY SINGLE DAY.

My son used to get overwhelmed at the size of the tasks in front of him. He didn't feel big enough or strong enough. But I would tell him, "If you took tiny steps, like baby steps, right now, and started walking, where could you get to in an hour?" He'd point to a cone across the field. "Okay, what about if you took baby steps for an hour for an entire week. What about a month? Where would you be? Now where would you be after a year? You'd be halfway to Minnesota or something." Movement adds up.

Having a clear "20 Mile March" focuses your mind and helps you stay consistent.

Some examples of 20 Mile Marches from Rehabbers:

- Every Sunday night, we're going to have the whole family over for dinner.
- Even though this is a busy season, we're going to have a date night every Thursday night.
- Six days a week, I'm going to log at least three miles running/ walking.
- Every single Tuesday night, I'm going to meet with other Christian friends to talk about our lives, pray for each other, and hold each other accountable for the things we need to do.
- Every day, I'm going to get up early and spend some time reading the Bible or a devotional book.
- Every night before I go to bed, I'm going to read five pages of a book.
- Every single week, I'm going to save fifty dollars and put it into a savings account.
- Six times a week, I'm going to sit my butt down in a chair and write for one hour.

You want to make progress? Figure out what your 20 Mile March looks like.

REHAB TIME

COACH PEP TALK

You need to be consistent to be successful. In the previous lessons, I had you think about what you wanted your goal to be. Now, put some time and thought into figuring out what consistent steps you can take toward it. For example, I want to improve my fitness (a high value for me), so I run trails every morning (six times a week, with a Sabbath). Answer these questions to find your own 20 Mile March.

QUESTION 1

Go back to Lesson 34. What's your goal? Write it below.

....

QUESTION 2

In your quest for consistency, what is your personal 20 Mile March? What is something you should do very regularly to accomplish your goal?

....

....

....

HOW TO CHANGE
(PART 4: FAITH)

Straight up—life is tough, and you will be battered. Without the confidence that God is with you and for you, it's very easy to get overwhelmed, off track, and deeply discouraged.

Faith is a tricky word—and I know that there are a lot of theologians who are much smarter than me who have their own definitions—but this is the definition that has helped me the most.

FAITH

Definition: *Acting in a way that shows you believe God's got you.*

I'm writing this at a strange and confusing time in American history.

Mass shootings across the country, from San Bernardino to Las Vegas to Charleston to Gilroy to Dayton to El Paso, have shocked, angered, and saddened a nation weary of this kind of tragedy.

And in the midst of this, people respond the only way they can—by using familiar words and phrases to convey how sorry they are that this is happening. People don't know what to say, so they say, "My thoughts and prayers are with you."

But some people think that's a dumb thing to say.

"Thoughts and prayers!" some people write, "What help is that to us now? That's meaningless! What we need is action!"[1]

Hold on.

Just. Hold on.

I want to talk a little about prayer. And faith. And life. Because there's a lot of confusion.

First off, "thoughts and prayers" have been the way that people of faith (not just Christians like me, but anyone who is religious) have made sense of life—especially the terrible and awful parts of life—for millennia. And in my faith tradition, the Psalms (the largest book of the Bible) show us that when something tragic happens, prayer is a way for people to put their entire life before God, showing Him their whole range of emotions and asking Him for help in dealing with their fear, outrage, and grief.

But it goes deeper than that. It's not just about dealing with emotions. Prayer is based on the belief that there is a God who is in control and seeks to help broken people (like me, like you) when no one else will. The story of God in the Bible is, among other things, the story of a God who helps people who have no other hope. Prayer is asking God for help (when the odds are impossible), for wisdom (when you don't know what to do), for strength (when life has beaten you up), and for courage (when you know what to do, but it's scary).

But it goes even deeper than that. Prayer is also a way of trying to connect with God, of getting things in order. We have to think, process, get God's wisdom, receive our marching orders, and grow in firm conviction BEFORE we act. Otherwise, we'll just be a flurry of activity going nowhere, like people on a bike with no chain.

The point is this—and this is important. Prayer isn't useless. But it's also not meant to be the end of the story. First we pray, then we act. That's the order of things. All through the gospel of Mark, the author recounts this pattern with Jesus. Jesus would go away in solitude and silence to be with His Father in prayer . . . and then come out swinging. Big movements and decisions always happen AFTER these times of prayer. First prayer, then action.

For Jesus, there was always action.

It was never simply just private prayer.

There is power in prayer.

But there also must be action after the prayer.

What we do after the prayer shows whether we truly believe that God is with us.

You can't pray a victorious prayer and go out and live a defeated life.

If you truly believe in what you're praying for, and believe that God is with you, then you'll move. Prayer is the way our faith is activated, and then we will walk out in it.

Faith is believing God can beat the odds even when the odds seem impossible.

Do you believe God's got your back?

I'm not a Bible scholar, but I am the son of a preacher. The Bible contains a whole slew of stories about people who were rescued by God in some way or another. In fact, one of the primary things I learned from listening to the Bible Sunday after Sunday was this profound truth: When it looks hopeless, it really isn't. God has your back.

When Moses—and the rest of the Hebrew people—had their backs up against the Red Sea, with the armies of Egypt racing after them to force them back into slavery, or worse, they were afraid. But God had their back. God parted the Red Sea, and they crossed through to safety and freedom.

When Daniel was trying to be faithful to God in a place that was very hostile and was thrown into a den of lions as a result, he was afraid. But God had his back. God closed the lions' mouths, and Daniel wasn't harmed.

When Jonah was a stubborn brat, refusing to listen to God, and even trying to run away from God, he found himself sinking in an ocean storm. He was afraid and cried out to God to help him. God had his back. He saved him in the most unlikely way.

When Ruth, a widow and immigrant in a foreign land, was desperate for food and protection, she cried out for help. God had her back. He made sure she not only had food but found a husband who would love and protect her. God gave her a family.

Or pick any one of the twenty-six stories we can read in the New Testament where someone came up to Jesus with physical issues they could not fix: blind men, lepers, a woman who had been bleeding for twelve years, a man who was paralyzed.[2] They were afraid—they had no way to get better. But God had their backs. Jesus went to each of them and healed them.

I want to close with one more example.

One of my favorite verses in the Bible is Jeremiah 29:11. But it's not just me. Loads of people love this verse. Out of curiosity, I searched #jeremiah2911 on Instagram. There are more than 34,000 posts. Here's what Jeremiah 29:11 says:

> "For I know the plans I have for you," declares the LORD, "plans to prosper you and not to harm you, plans to give you hope and a future."

On first glance, it looks like God is saying, "I'm going to make your life really good and easy!" But this verse is written to a particular people for a particular reason.

The Jewish people disobeyed God in every possible way, and instead of being a nation filled with examples of how to live life with God, they did evil upon evil. As a direct result, bad things happened: the Babylonian empire conquered them. And—as is the case so often in life—when the people of Israel woke up and saw where the road of their actions had taken them, they realized how bad off they were.

God sent comfort: He told them that eventually things would be better. But not immediately. They'd still live in exile. But God says something along the lines of, "Even though things aren't what you expected, I'm with you. Live well, and remember that I will work everything out, even if it's not as fast as you'd like."

Basically, God was saying, "Even though you messed up royally, I still have your back. I will always have your back."

Don't live in fear when God has your back.

Don't live as though you're an orphan when God has your back.

Don't live in defeat when God has your back.

Don't live in hopelessness when God has your back.

Faith is in your feet. If you truly have it, you'll live it out.

REHAB TIME

COACH PEP TALK

Prayer is a deeply personal thing and is tied to your religious beliefs. The following activities are meant to help you connect with your faith in God and are written from my faith tradition. But I understand that some folks aren't Christian, and some folks aren't particularly religious at all. That's totally cool (I got nothing but love for you). But if that's you, go ahead and read these activities and feel free to skip them if you don't think they're helpful.

ACTIVITY 1

Read the following verse, taken from Matthew 7:7–11, where Jesus is teaching about prayer and faith:

> Ask and it will be given to you; seek and you will find; knock and the door will be opened to you. For everyone who asks receives; the one who seeks finds; and to the one who knocks, the door will be opened. Which of you, if your son asks for bread, will give him a stone? Or if he asks for a fish, will give him a snake? If you, then, though you are evil, know how to give good gifts to your children, how much more will your Father in heaven give good gifts to those who ask him!

Reflect on this verse for a while. Highlight what stands out to you. What is Jesus saying in this verse about His Father? What is He saying God's attitude is toward us? What does this verse teach us about prayer?

....

....

....

ACTIVITY 2

Life is not static, and we need different things from God at different points in our life. In the list below, which of the following reflects what you most need from God right now? Circle one or two.

I need God to see me and understand my situation.

I need God to love me and provide what I need.

I need to know God is with me.

I need God to guide me and give me wisdom.

I need God to give me strength and courage to do what's difficult and right.

ACTIVITY 3

Write out a short prayer to God regarding your area(s) of need, keeping in mind the teachings of Jesus in Matthew 7:7–11.

....

....

....

HOW TO CHANGE
(PART 5: HEART)

A few years ago, I was running a half marathon. These are tough to do, mainly because your body is using so much energy. Distance runners often talk about "hitting the wall." This is the moment where your muscles lose energy because you're out of glucose in your blood. Your body basically screams at you, "I'm done. Sit down."

This is why marathoners and long-distance cyclists eat during their race and guzzle Gatorade to try to get enough energy in their body.

But the wall is also psychological. Sometimes it's not about nutrients. Your body just hurts. Things go from being hard to being really, really hard.

During my training for the half marathon, I'd never hit a wall. This is probably because in training, I'd never actually run a whole half marathon. I'd never run that far before.

But during the race, around the ninth mile, I hit the wall. It was not fun.

And I thought about dropping out, walking over to the medical tent, and sleeping for a few hours.

I really, really wanted to quit.

I was done.

Out of energy.

I was not going to make it to the finish line.

But then I thought about the finish line. "Wait," I said to myself. "My son will be at the finish line."

That little thought was major for me.

I suddenly didn't want to give up. Not for myself, but for my son. I wanted to show Tristan that you can push through pain. I wanted to show my son that sometimes life is tough, but you can keep going, even though you think you cannot.

I wanted to give my son that example.

And the whole thing shifted for me. It wasn't about me anymore. It was about Tristan.

That moment allowed me to push through. And I finished the race.

My time was terrible—I think a seventy-six-year-old might have passed me at one point—but I finished. And that's what mattered.

That's what heart is about. It's having a reason big enough to pull you through tough times.

When the reason is big enough, no struggle is great enough.

That's what heart is about.

HEART

Definition: *Finding the strength to give more, even when everything else says you have nothing left.*

When my grandmother died, our whole family and extended family had to drive from Texas to Little Rock, Arkansas (about a four-hour trip).

As we were driving, we ran into a storm. And I want to be clear about this. I am not talking rain showers. I am talking the kind of storms that cause that area to be called Tornado Alley.

In all my life, I've never experienced a worse storm. The wind was so intense, my two-thousand-pound car would periodically be shaken and moved on the road by the gusts of wind. Rain was coming in sideways. Visibility on the road was probably two feet in front of the car.

People were pulling off the highway. People were stopping under bridges. Truckers—professional drivers—pulled off the road as if to say, "Forget this. I'm going to take a nap."

My dad called me. "I'm going to stop," he said. "This storm is too intense."

I pulled over under a bridge, pulled out my phone, and looked at the weather app. I saw the storm radar.

"Dad," I said. "I know it's bad, but the edge of the storm is only about ten miles away."

My dad wasn't convinced.

So I left the protection of the bridge and started back out on the road while he stayed behind in his car.

As soon as I left, the rain and the wind came down even harder, which I literally did not think was possible. I have never experienced so much rain falling. Imagine fifteen people on top of your car, pouring fifteen buckets of water over your windshield all at once, and that's close to what it was like.

"Maybe I made a bad decision," I thought to myself. But I kept going, driving at probably twenty miles per hour.

The weather radar was correct. After about ten minutes, the rain slowed to a drizzle, and then a pitter-patter, and eventually it cleared up.

My dad and some of the other members of my family sat under that bridge for two more hours. Two hours! The storm didn't move, and neither did they. Eventually, they listened to me, followed my advice, and slowly made their way out from under the bridge and out of the storm.

I think what might have caused them to move is when I said, "Dad. No storm is going to keep me from Grandma's funeral."

Sometimes you have to keep going because the destination is too important.

I think about that story a lot. I hope I'm never in a storm like that again. But it's a reminder that sometimes you can't stop. Your destination is too important.

One final story about heart. And it's the final piece to this. Heart means giving, even when you don't you have anything left to give. And it's not just because it will get you closer to your destination. It's because sometimes, it's the only thing that can keep you going.

A few years ago, I met a guy named Luke.[1] Luke came from a military family, and he enlisted right out of high school. He served in the Marines during the Iraq War. When I found out he had served in active duty during an actual war, I asked him what that was like.

He told me about the blistering heat in Iraq and Afghanistan.

He told me about the fear every time his group would go out on a patrol because there were insurgents who often planted bombs along the roads.

He told me what it was like to come back safe from a patrol, collapse into his bunk, and wake up to learn that another group had been hit by an explosive mine.

He told me about the mental exhaustion that comes from facing possible death every day.

I sat in silence. It was a sobering reminder that no matter what I'm facing in my life, it will likely never be as intense as what Luke went through.

"It was hell," Luke said, "And I wouldn't wish it on anyone."

He paused.

"But I did learn something important," he said. "Maybe even something that made it all worth it."

"What's that?" I asked.

"I learned the secret to making it through tough times. Through suffering."

Luke took a sip of his coffee.

I leaned forward.

"When you're at the end of yourself, when you're utterly exhausted, when you have nothing left, when you want to literally lay down and die, when there's no way forward that you can see and you can't think you can take another step . . . there is a way to keep going."

Luke paused.

"You look around and see who else is hurting."

He continued, "And then you try to help them get through. That's the secret. That will keep you going. That's what gets you through suffering."

I don't think I'll ever forget that conversation with Luke.

Look around.

See who else is hurting.

Help them keep going.

That's what will keep you going.

I know some of you have hit the wall. Your courage is waning. The storm is too great. Please keep going. Not only for your sake, but for the sake of all the people who are around you.

Give for the sake of others. Even when you don't feel like you have anything to give. That's what love is.

And it's the greatest motivator mankind's ever known.

—————————— REHAB TIME ——————————

COACH PEP TALK

Pushing through tough times is never easy. I want you to use the following questions to think about your own life and how you've pushed through tough times in the past.

QUESTION 1

Think about a time when you gave up because it was too tough. Looking back on it, is there anything you wish you had done differently?

....

....

....

QUESTION 2

Is there any area in your own life right now where you're tempted to quit because the storm is too intense? What is that situation?

....

....

....

QUESTION 3

Do either of these heart motivators apply to your situation? Which one could help you keep going even though you're weary?

- The destination is too important.
- There are still people who need help.

....

....

....

FACE THE DOG

Fear has killed more dreams than failure ever did.

Because so many people never try because they're afraid to fail. Or afraid to be judged. Or afraid they'll be embarrassed.

But fear keeps people in tiny prisons. And it's time to get out. Here's how.

Let me tell you a slightly true story.[1] There once was a boy named Jon, and every day, he and his elementary school classmates would walk through their neighborhood to their school.

The problem was, about halfway along their route, down Poplar Street, there was a house with a dog that would chase Jon and his friends as they passed by.

Looking back on it, Jon is sure the dog—whose name he and his friends vaguely remember as Rufus—wasn't a very big dog. But when you're eight years old, even a smallish terrier seems fierce and giant. And any dog that runs after you while barking seems like a hound of hell.

The problem for Jon and his friends was that there was no alternative route they could take to get to school that would bypass Poplar Street. It was a necessary evil.

The boys tried everything.

They tried tiptoeing past the house. Rufus was too smart for that.

They tried passing by on the other side of the street. Rufus streaked right across that road.

And so, out of options, the boys did they only thing they could think of.

They ran.

When they heard the deep, fearsome tones of Rufus barking, the boys would hightail it down the sidewalk as fast as their second-grade legs could carry them, their school backpacks swinging wildly on their backs.

Rufus never chased them more than a house or two, and then, perhaps because of his training (or maybe because of boredom), he'd stop and slowly walk back to his own house.

Jon and his friends would slow up, panting and out of breath, their hearts racing in their chests not only from the spurt of physical exertion, but also from the sheer terror.

One of the boys was named Mark, and Mark had a mild form of asthma. Mark didn't like running, and he especially hated running in the cold autumn air, which constricted his lungs and made breathing more difficult.

And so, one day in late October, on the sidewalk on Poplar Street in front of Rufus's house, Mark did the unthinkable.

Mark stopped running.

Rufus was bounding after the boys, as he always did, and finally Mark had had enough. He stopped.

Rufus, with his brown-and-white coat bouncing in the wind, was running straight toward Mark.

The rest of the boys turned in horror. To their eight-year-old imaginations, the only possible outcome was that Mark would be ripped to shreds, like some cheap plastic chew toy.

In an act of incredible courage, Mark twirled around and threw his backpack on the ground and faced the dog.

"Stop!" Mark yelled at the top of his young lungs.

Rufus stopped. Dead in his tracks. He turned his head sideways.

"No! Go home! Go home, Rufus!" Mark screamed.

Rufus stopped, licked his nose, and then slinked back to his house. Apparently, the fun of chasing the boys was lost now that he'd been scolded.

And that was the last time Rufus chased Jon and his friends.

All because someone had found the courage to face the dog.

FACE THE DOG

Here's what that story reminds me of—when we're afraid of something, we run away. This is just what we do.

We're afraid of not getting a part in the play, so we don't audition.

We're afraid that someone won't like us, so we don't say hi.

We're afraid that class will be too difficult, so we don't sign up for it.

We're afraid of the bully, so we don't stand up for the person who's being picked on.

We're afraid of the test, so we avoid studying.

We're afraid we won't fit in, so we stay silent and don't try to make new friends.

We're afraid someone won't agree with our idea, so we don't share our thoughts.

We're afraid someone will say no, so we don't ask.

We're afraid of the future, so we ignore it and distract ourselves with entertainment.

At some point in life, you have to admit to yourself that you're scared out of your mind and that you don't know what to do.

You have to **face the dog.**[2]

You have to stop giving in to the adrenaline of fear. You have to stop running away. You have to stop and face your fears.

Part of being a young person is that nearly EVERYTHING is new and scary. You've never done ANY of this before. When you were fourteen, it was the very first time you had ever been fourteen. Your first day of physics class was the very first time you've ever been in a physics class. You've never done ANY of this before. It's all new and a little exciting, but also a little scary.

Right?

And if you're like me, you're nearly constantly besieged by a giant and vast list of fears.

You have to turn and face the dog.

And when you do, you realize that things aren't as terrible and awful and hopeless as you initially thought.

In fact, do you know one way people who face real phobias actually get better? They slowly expose themselves to the very thing they're afraid of.

This process of facing fears is called exposure. In this form of therapy, a person faces their fear in a safe environment, so they start to feel a little less afraid and a little more comfortable the longer they face their fear. When exposure is done correctly, that person is eventually able to better deal with the thing they're afraid of because what they were terrified of isn't as scary anymore. For small fears, exposure might be one event; for bigger, deeper fears or issues, it's usually done gradually over time.

So if you're afraid of spiders, you'd hold a tarantula.

If you're afraid of tests, you'd sign up for some practice ones and take them.

If you're afraid of the water, you'd sign up for swimming lessons at the pool and learn how to swim.

Professional counselors and psychologists recommend this to some of their patients. In fact, this is a way you can overcome everyday fears. This is a way you can stop the anxiety.*

You have to turn and face the dog.

---

* Now, if you have severe PTSD or a fear of something that really shakes you, I'm not recommending you try to overcome something like that on your own. Trained counselors and therapists can safely help you through those things.

Because when you do, you'll find out it's not nearly as frightening as you initially thought. You made it out to be FAR WORSE in your head than it was in real life.

The dog will slink home.

And you can walk ahead in peace.

But to do this, you have to stop running.

You gotta face the dog.

———— REHAB TIME ————

COACH PEP TALK

You'll never get traction in your life if your actions and reactions are caused by fear. In the table below, I'm going to ask you some questions about what kinds of things fill you with nervousness or dread. Chances are you avoid those things. Think about what you're avoiding, or running from, and how you can take a step to face the dog.

What is something I am anxious about or afraid of?	How do I avoid or run from this thing?	What small step could I take to face (or get more exposure to) this thing?

FAILURE ISN'T FATAL

I want to talk about failure.

Because I can almost guarantee this: you are walking around right now with a bad definition of failure.

You think that failure is when something doesn't go right, when you don't win, or when you don't succeed at something.

But that's not failure.

True failure is when you stop trying.

True failure is when you quit.

True failure is when you give up.

The main reason why people are afraid to fail is because they're afraid of what comes with it.

Failing is embarrassing. If you have a big dream or a big goal, and you let people know it, and then it doesn't happen, you think you'll look bad. And people might laugh at you. Or people might say, "I told you that you couldn't do it." And you'll feel like you've let yourself down.

But failure is not final. In fact, the opposite is true.

There's no success without failure.

There's nothing great that's been built that didn't involve failure. In fact, some of the most successful people fail quickly and often.

My friend's daughter is in competitive gymnastics and has been since she was five years old. For fifteen hours a week, she trains in a USA Gymnastics gym. And for fifteen hours a week, she's basically failing.

Falling off the beam.

Not making that kip on the bar.

Messing up that tumbling pass on the floor.

Not sticking the landing off the vault.

She's failing constantly. All the time. Pretty much the entire practice. She once estimated that it took her about ten hours of failure to get one new skill down.

Ten.

Hours.

Of failure.

I once watched her at the gym. There was a line of balance beams seven deep, each with a girl in a leotard on it. For an entire hour, the team practiced a new skill—a back handspring with a twist onto the beam. For a solid hour, my buddy's daughter fell off the beam. Every few seconds, she would try the skill, teeter, and then fall off the beam onto the blue mats below. She'd hop back on the beam and try again. And fall. And she wasn't the only girl. This was the same for every single other girl on the team. Just massive failure. Nobody landed it. Not even once.

But the coaches didn't scold them. They didn't fold their arms in disgust. They didn't shout their disapproval. They were cheering and clapping and encouraging the girls. The coaches told the team, "The quicker you fail, the more often you fail, the closer you are to finally getting the skill down."

Wait. Could that be true? Is it possible that failure is actually a good thing?

I think so. In fact (and this is going to sound crazy), I'm learning to love failure. Because it means growth.

If you're failing, then you know that you're pushing yourself beyond your comfort zone. If you don't want to fail, don't try anything new. Don't try to grow or develop in any area of your life.

Any person who we consider great has endured great failure. But instead of letting the failure fold them or break them, they learn from that failure. They fail forward.

Kobe Bryant is the third-highest point scorer in the history of the NBA.[1] He also has the record for the most missed shots in NBA history (he missed more than 14,000 shots).[2] But he's scored more than 33,000 points. Because he understood that the best way to get out of a shooting slump was to keep shooting.

Barry Sanders has the fourth-most yards rushing in the history of the NFL.[3] But he also has the NFL record for most rushing yards lost by one player (he lost 1,114 yards on 336 carries).[4] Those were plays where Sanders was trying to get something going and ran backward to elude defenders, but got tackled. But Sanders also has more than 15,000 rushing yards.

Thomas Edison tested more than six thousand plant materials in order to find the right filament for the light bulb.[5] He finally figured out what to use: carbonized bamboo from Japan could stay lit for more than 1,200 hours when electrified.[6] Edison experimented with six thousand different materials; 5,999 failed. But Edison didn't look at it that way. He told people he'd simply found all the ways that do not work.

Missed shots.

Lost yards.

Busted inventions.

Errors.

Mistakes.

Failures.

The lives of Kobe Bryant and Barry Sanders and Thomas Edison show us that those things don't stop you from being great. Failure doesn't disqualify you from greatness. In fact, if you look at anyone great, failure is often a key component of their growth and success.

In order to be great, you have to be ready to fail.

If you ain't failing big, that means you're not going for anything big.

Failure is just a stepping stone.

Looking back on it now, the largest professional failure of my own life has been getting cut from the NFL. I failed in my dream to make a roster and make it in the NFL. Completely failed. Well, failed at that one tiny aspect of life, in that one narrow career field. Failing in the NFL wasn't the end of my life. It wasn't the end of me. I'm not saying it didn't hurt or wasn't disappointing—I mean it wasn't FINAL. I knew there were lessons in there, and I had to find them.

So I spent a lot of time asking myself (and asking God), "What can and should I learn from this part of my life?" And let me tell you, it didn't take long to realize there were a ton of things I could learn from it.

Failure doesn't mean that it's over. It means you're trying.

So.

Fail quickly.

Fail often.

Fail forward.

And regarding the folks who criticize you because of your failure, I'd like to leave you with some words of encouragement.

Their thoughts don't matter.

They're not for you.

They're not helping you become the best you.

I'll leave you with a quote to chew on, from a man who took a lot of criticism. He was (and is) the youngest president in the history of the US. His name was Teddy Roosevelt, and these are his words:

> It is not the critic who counts; not the man who points out how the strong man stumbles, or where the doer of deeds could have done them better. The credit belongs to the man who is actually in the arena, whose face is marred by dust and sweat and blood; who strives valiantly; who errs, who comes short again and again, because there is no effort without error and shortcoming; but who does actually strive to do the deeds; who

knows great enthusiasms, the great devotions; who spends himself in a worthy cause; who at the best knows in the end the triumph of high achievement, and who at the worst, if he fails, at least fails while daring greatly, so that his place shall never be with those cold and timid souls who neither know victory nor defeat.[7]

That's right.
Now, let's get out there and get our failure on.
Because that's the only way to move things forward.
Let's get it.

————— REHAB TIME —————

COACH PEP TALK

Failure goes hand-in-hand with success. If you want to beat a video game, you will lose a life or two in the process. If you want to lift more weight, you will reach a point where you can't lift more. If you want to get better at math, you'll get some problems wrong. It's how it works. Think about what you want to get better at and how failure will help you along in that process.

QUESTION 1

What's something that you want to get good at?

....

QUESTION 2

In order to get good, you'll have to fail. What does failure look like in this particular area as you work to get better (for example: falling off the beam to get better at gymnastics)?

....
....
....

QUESTION 3

Take a baby step: write out a particular way you want to fail in the next month in order to get better.

....

....

....

HOW TO HACK FEAR

I'm at the local pool, watching a little boy at the top of the high dive. He's maybe seven years old.

The board is about ten feet above the pool, but to him, it might as well be a hundred. He stares at the water below. And what seemed like a good idea a few minutes ago now isn't. His toes instinctively curl around the green fiberglass diving board. His friends cajole him from the ladder below.

But the kid is frozen.

His body is locked up.

Because that's what fear does to you. Fear paralyzes you. There's the good kind of fear that warns you to avoid danger and keeps you alive. That's good fear.

But there's another kind of fear that keeps you frozen. I hate that kind of fear.

Watching this kid, I am reminded of all the times that fear has reared its ugly head in my own life, and how often, like that kid, I've been stuck in life—and I mean I am not moving for *anything*—because of fear.

Fear yells at us. It screams at us. And it's always telling us about the absolute worst-case scenario.

You won't be good at this.
You won't succeed.
You will fall down flat.
You will make a fool of yourself.
Everyone is going to make fun of you.

Here's a definition of fear I have that's helped me.

Fear is creating a known result from a situation you haven't experienced yet.

Fear is basically telling yourself "This is how it's going to be" before you ever go do it. You convince yourself you know the end result—and it's bad.

You don't *know* this.

But you convince yourself of it.

And so of course you don't do it.

I saw this in football all the time. Our team would be playing an opponent that was better or stronger or higher ranked than us. And inevitably, there'd be one guy on the team who would get into his head, "There's no way we can win this game. We're going to lose. And lose badly."

Guess what? That dude always had a terrible game. It's nearly impossible to perform at a high level when you think the only outcome that can happen is bad.

I think of it like this: that frightening situation is like a door. A scary door. And fear is yelling in your mind all the terrible things that are behind that scary door. As a result, you are never going to open the scary door. So you're stuck. Paralyzed. Like the kid on the diving board.

So what gets us to move?

WE HAVE TO HACK FEAR

In order for me to walk through that scary door, I have to think about good reasons why I *should* walk through the door. So I sit for a minute, and instead of using my imagination to think about all the terrible things that might happen, I think instead about all the good that could happen. Instead of saying, "What's the worst that could happen?" I flip it and say to myself:

What's the best that could happen?

I could learn something new.

I could meet someone cool.

Even if I don't win, there will be something in this for me.

It won't be perfect, but it will help me.

I will definitely grow as a person.

So that's a meaningful exercise to do. Tell yourself, "I've used my imagination to think about all the bad things that could happen, but now let me use my imagination to think about all the good, positive things that could result." Brainstorm.

But that's not all I do.

Because I'm going to be honest with you guys, I have a pretty active imagination. I can imagine all sorts of bad things. Ridiculous things. And those things sometimes stop me from trying. They keep me at the threshold of the scary door.

When that happens, I use something I call "leverage statements."

Basically, I try to trick myself into looking at things in a different perspective to coach myself into taking meaningful risks.

And I am extreme about this.

For example, the other day, my friend took me out to run some trails. And it sucked. The incline was way steeper than I thought. I was sucking air. My legs were burning. And I just wanted to stop.

I wanted to quit.

There's nothing for me. There's no reason to keep going.

I could almost hear my old football coaches yelling at me from the bleachers.

"How bad do you want it, Shelton?!"

And the answer was, "Not very much, Coach. I do not want this.

What I want is to stop and sit in the shade and drink some nice cold Arctic Blitz Gatorade."

I was about to stop.

So I began to invent reasons to keep going. Leverage statements. Here's what I told myself.

If I quit on this, then I am letting down all the people who follow me on social media—all my Rehabbers. They're going through really tough stuff all the time, and I tell them to keep going, even when it's hard. Especially when it's hard. If I quit on this trail run just because it's hard, I'm letting them down. And I'm being a hypocrite. If I tell them to push, then I need to push.

That worked a little. So I kept going with this narrative.

If I quit on this trail right now, then I am quitter. I'm putting the mindset of being a quitter into my life. And my son and my daughter will see that. And that will affect them as they grow up. They'll quit when it gets hard, and their potential will be harmed because I quit on this trail run.

Is that a reasonable thing to think? Uh, no. But that's what I did, and it worked. I kept pushing myself so I wouldn't give up.

But here's the thing. Fear has played such a big role in my life, and it's been such a debilitating enemy, that I have to do these mental exercises. I have to force myself into thinking about the positive, because if I do not, fear will stop me.

Maybe you're like me in that way.

Maybe fear is your constant companion.

Whispering words of doubt.

Telling you again and again it won't work.

It will never work.

You'll fail.

You're not good enough.

Fear can do terrible things to a person. I know this full well.

On July 5, 2010, I received one of the worst phone calls of my life, telling me that my college roommate Anthony Arline had committed suicide. Anthony and I were more than teammates. We were friends.

I was wracked with grief. My world turned upside down. I couldn't make sense of any of it.

I still don't know why Anthony chose to take his own life, but he had decided that life was not worth living. The voice of fear won in his life.

I know it might sound morbid, but in trying to process the loss of my good friend, I thought a lot about death. I would go to cemeteries and walk around, staring at the headstones. I stared at the dates, and the dash separating when the person was born and when they died. Some people were eighty years old when they died. Some were five. Adults. Elderly people. Children. Black, white, Asian. Death comes for everyone at some point. And you can't control that.

I realized that tomorrow is never promised.

TOMORROW IS NOT PROMISED

Around 57 million people die each year[1]; that means roughly 150,000 people die each day in the world. That's more than 6,000 every hour. Although this sounds pretty dark, it was actually motivating for me. It reminded me that I should live my life to the fullest.

If I'm not going after the fullest possible life, then I'm going to die incomplete. I am going to die being a person God didn't create me to be, not doing the things that God wanted me to do.

After the death of my friend Anthony, I realized life is a precious gift.

And I don't want to waste my life. So that's why I use those leverage statements. At the end of the day, though, they're just motivation challenges.

What is going to make you move?

What do you need to examine?

What do you need to think about that will allow you to push through crippling and paralyzing fear so that you can move?

What will get you to take the first step?

And the next step?

Because if the reward is big enough, you'll conquer fear.

Think about it. I'm afraid of lions. But if my daughter somehow got trapped in a lion's den, I wouldn't think twice about going in there and facing those lions. Why? Is it because I'm no longer afraid of lions? No. I would overcome that fear because of the potential gain—in this case, the very life of my daughter.

Do you see?

If the reward is big enough, you'll conquer fear. So focus on the reward. It might be the very thing that gets you to take the next step.

The kid looks down at the pool. The lifeguard yells some encouraging words: "You got this!" His dad is in the water, in the deep end: "I'm right here, buddy!" His brother is at the ladder in the water, on the side of the pool: "It's fun! I promise!"

They're painting the positive things that can happen if he goes through the scary door.

The kid jumps.

For a moment, he disappears below the surface of the blue water.

He bobs to the surface.

His dad and brother cheer.

The boy's face is beaming.

"That was awesome," he yells.

It was. It was awesome. But not because a kid jumped off the board.

But because in that moment, fear lost a battle.

REHAB TIME

COACH PEP TALK

It's time to be honest about your fears, and no, I'm not talking about how much you hate clowns. It's deeper than that. These questions will help you process how to get to the bottom of your own fears and make progress in overcoming them.

QUESTION 1

What is something you're afraid of?

....

QUESTION 2

Why are you afraid of this thing? Write out your reasons.

....

....

....

QUESTION 3

What's the best thing that could happen if you tried to do the thing you're afraid of? Try using leverage statements. What's something bad that could happen if you don't do the thing you're afraid of?

....

....

....

QUESTION 4

What would it look like to gain exposure to your fear? How could you practice getting close to what you're afraid of? What would that look like?

....

....

....

XI.

STRAIGHT UP

ABOUT YOUR HEART

YOU ARE PURPOSE

For more than a decade, pretty much every day when I got up in the morning, I was thinking about or training for football.

Then, all of a sudden, it was gone.

And if I'm honest, for a moment, so was my purpose in life.

I remember thinking, "If I don't have football, then who am I?"

One of the questions people most often ask me is, "Trent, how do you find your purpose?", hoping I can help them find theirs.

Or maybe the question is this: "Who am I? And what am I here for?"

And the question I had back when football ended, and that I still have today, is, "Where is a person supposed to go to get that kind of information?"

Because Google sure isn't much help.

I want to start off by saying that for the majority of people who have ever lived in this world, that question of "What is my purpose?" is likely not a question they asked. The vast majority of humans who have ever lived throughout history were handed a life because of where and when they were born. They were born on a farm, and they farmed their entire lives—because that's what they had to do to survive. Or they were born into a family of blacksmiths, and they molded metal their whole lives. They didn't get to choose their profession. Or what they did with their days. They had no say.

Welcome to this world. You're a baker. You will bake all your days. Hope you're not allergic to gluten.

And in some ways, that was a lot easier. There was nothing to figure out. You just did what was handed to you. But in some ways, it would have been terrible. I mean, what if you're born into a fishing village and you don't like fishing?

But now, for many people in our modern world, that's not how things work.

People say all the time, "I'm looking for my purpose."

And the most common advice I hear given to this problem is something like this: "To find purpose, you need to look inside yourself. And then, whatever you want, do that, no matter what anyone says."

You need to look inside yourself.

This sounds good, but it doesn't work.

First off, what we find when we look inside ourselves is that we're a mess.

Think about the kind of things you wanted when you were nine years old. When he was nine, my son came up to me and asked me for ninja throwing knives. Later he asked me how much a flamethrower cost. He indicated that he was intending to save his allowance to buy one. The point is, what my son thinks will make him happy would end up killing him and likely destroying our neighbor's house.

But it's not just nine-year-olds. Imagine if you had gotten everything you really wanted when you were fifteen. I would be driving a Ferrari and married to Mariah Carey with a pet tiger.

I was dazzlingly foolish when I was fifteen. And so were you.

In fact (I'm a little older than you, so trust me on this)—I can look back to when I was seventeen and realize I was dumb.

And that I was also dumb when I was twenty-four.

But going further . . . all of my mentors (all of whom are awesome older men) tell me that when I'm fifty, I'll look back at myself in my current state now and think of myself as ignorant.

The point is—and I hate to say this—you're dumb.

I'm dumb.

We're all dumb.

So, if we're dumb and can't even figure ourselves out correctly now, then we can't rely on looking inside ourselves and trusting ourselves to find purpose.[1]

SO HOW DO YOU FIND PURPOSE?

Here's the thing. I don't know if purpose is something you necessarily *find*.

Where is it at? Who has it? Is it down the street? I think when we believe purpose is something we have to find somewhere, we often end up finding fake purpose, or worse, end up lost.

Here's what I've been thinking about lately.

What if purpose isn't something you find, but something that is given to you?

What if you ARE purpose?

After all, you're born on purpose. And technically, you are a miracle.

Do you think of yourself as a miracle? Well, it's true. The chances of you ending up here on this planet were very, very, small.

I found an article from Dr. Ali Bizinar that laid out the supposed probabilities. He claims the following:

If your dad was born twenty years ago, he theoretically could have met 200 million of the women on the planet.

But your dad couldn't have met all them. He likely only interacted with about 10,000 women at most in his early adult life.

So, the chances of your dad meeting your mom are 1/20,000 (10,000 women actually met divided by 200,000 it would be possible to meet).

But just because they meet, that doesn't mean they wind up dating.

There's probably a 1/10 chance they even talk to each other.

Then another 1/10 chance they go out on a date.

Another 1/10 chance they go out for a second date.

And a 1/10 chance they date for a while.

And then, a 50/50 shot they get married.

(*Right now, just the odds of your specific mom and your specific dad just having children is 1/40,000,000, or roughly the population of California.*)

Now, your mom is born with the approximately 100,000 usable eggs she'll have for her entire lifetime.

And your dad produces about 1 trillion sperm during the years you could have been born.

So, the odds of that ONE egg and that ONE sperm get together is about 1 in 400 quadrillion.

That's 1/400,000,000,000,000,000.[2]

A miracle is an event so unlikely to happen that it's almost impossible. And that's you. So if you're looking for a miracle, you are that miracle.

You're not an accident. I am not an accident. My purpose is that I exist. Or as the Bible says,

I praise you because I am fearfully and wonderfully made;
    your works are wonderful, I know that full well.

PSALM 139:14

God created you on purpose.

The purpose in God creating you was for you to exist. You. So in essence, you are purpose. It's you. Your uniqueness IS the purpose.

So my purpose isn't football.

That is something I do.

But that can be lost.

My purpose isn't RehabTime.

That is something I do.

But that can be lost.

My purpose isn't my awesome physique and killer hair.

That is something I have.

But that can be lost.

(Although not today. I am looking good.)

You get the point.

So the fact that you exist and are not an accident is part of your purpose. It's not something you have to find.

It's something that is given to you.

You are purpose.

Go ahead and think about that for a while.

—————————— REHAB TIME ——————————

COACH PEP TALK

Okay, so we already established that finding your purpose is not something you are going to be any good at. But sometimes other people who know and love you can help. So your assignment is to get their feedback by completing this activity below.

ASSIGNMENT

Think of five family members or friends who are older than you by at least ten years (so basically people who are not your peers) and text them this question: What are three adjectives you think best describe me, and why?

PERSON	WORDS THEY USED TO DESCRIBE ME	HOW I FEEL ABOUT THESE WORDS

QUESTION

What did you learn from this assignment? Were there any themes about you that popped up? Why do you think you have these traits? What purpose could they serve?

....
....
....
....
....
....
....
....

LESSON 44

YOU ARE PURPOSE
FOR A PURPOSE

Here's the straight truth.

You're not an accident.

You're not an act of cosmic chance.

God created you on purpose.

But it's not just that. There's a little bit more to this. The second half of the sentence. The other side of the equation. And that's this.

God created you on purpose *for* a purpose.

I love the way Paul puts it in the book of Ephesians. He writes:

> For we are God's handiwork, created in Christ Jesus to do good works, which God prepared in advance for us to do.
>
> EPHESIANS 2:10

God's got stuff for you to do. He's had it planned. And you're a masterpiece. Not an accident.

And I know you're thinking, "Well, what kind of stuff? Do I get a list of tasks? Is there some sort of manila folder I'm handed that includes my mission, should I choose to accept it?"

No.

But before we get into what your purpose IS, we need to talk about what your purpose is NOT.

It's not going to be like Tony Stark's.

In the Marvel movie universe, Tony Stark is a brilliant man. He invents. He builds. He's a visionary. In short, he's a genius. And that genius nets him billions of dollars.

But the problem with Tony Stark is that he's a self-absorbed, egotistical mess of a human being. When we first meet Tony Stark, he lives in a big tower, drives expensive cars, and does whatever he wants. Tony Stark is about one thing: Tony Stark. Tony Stark lives to make Tony Stark happy.

What if everyone has a little Tony Stark in them? I'm not talking about the genius part. I'm talking about the incredibly selfish part.

What if we're also in danger of living our lives with the primary motivation of simply getting what we want?

What if the real danger is that we will waste our lives on things that don't matter? What if the real danger is if we never use who we are to help other people?

What if we just continue on to live quiet, self-absorbed lives?

You see, Tony Stark becomes a hero when he starts to use his life (his intelligence, his experience, his wit, his planning, his technological genius) to help other people.

That's when Tony Stark turns into Iron Man. That's the moment when he turns into a hero. It's when his focus shifts onto other people.

Another example: Bono has been a rock star with the band U2 since the late 1970s. He is a musical genius. But after performing at the now-famous Live Aid concert in 1985, he traveled to Ethiopia and saw terrible conditions of poverty—poverty that was killing children because they didn't have clean water or medicine. His heart broke. He looked at his own wealth and money and how, because of an accident of being born in a different country, he had so much more than other people. So Bono started using his life to speak up for the world's poor. And in 2002, Bono used his fame to arrange a visit with the sitting US president, George W. Bush.[1] He explained the crisis of AIDS in Africa and that lifesaving drugs were just too expensive for the people who needed them. He urged the president to do something. Bush was moved with compassion and started the President's Emergency Plan for AIDS Relief (PEPFAR) the following year. The program has gone on to treat and save millions of people.[2] Bush started the program, but he thanks Bono.[3]

What makes Bono and Tony Stark interesting is that they're geniuses. But what made them heroes was their decision to make the world a better place and use their lives to help people.

This is really helpful for me because it shifts my focus. Instead of asking the question, "What is my purpose?" and thinking of purpose as some buried treasure that I have to go out and dig up, it reminds me that my very life is the point.

I exist.

You exist.

AND we have some things to do. It isn't about me. It isn't about you.

Everybody's purpose is to help someone else.

One of my favorite authors, Frederick Buechner, once wrote, "The place God calls you to is the place where your deep gladness and the world's deep hunger meet."[4]

Or like Jesus said: "Love the Lord your God . . . Love your neighbor as yourself. There is no commandment greater than these" (Mark 12:30–31).

YOUR PURPOSE IS TO USE YOUR LIFE TO HELP OTHER PEOPLE

People say, "I can't help that many people. I don't have that big of an influence. I don't have thousands of followers on social media." You don't need that. You have people you interact with every day. Your platform is this entire world and whoever you run into.

Find your great passion.

Find the world's great need.

And go.

You are purpose.

I am purpose.

Which means, if we use our lives to help and serve other people, we can literally fulfill our purpose ANYWHERE.

I don't need football.

I don't have to be an athlete.

In fact, if I'm honest, I used to think my purpose in life was to be a football player. Everyone thought my purpose was to be a football player. That's what literally everyone told me.

But that was not my purpose.

Football was, in large part, about me. About me getting drafted. About me making it into the NFL. I had to let go of what I wanted to do in order to grab hold of what I was created to do—which was to help other people.

No matter where I go.

Or who I meet.

Or where I live.

Or happen to be on any given day.

My purpose.

Your purpose.

Is to help other people.

My calling is to use my gifts to help other people.

Everybody's purpose is to help someone else.

Now, you have to work through that process. But if you are purpose, then that means you can be yourself anywhere, and help other people anywhere, and fulfill your purpose anywhere.

I don't need to wait until I get that degree. I can start helping people with my life now.

I don't need to wait until I get that promotion. I can start helping people with my life now.

I don't need to wait until I can afford to move into a better place. I can start helping people with my life now.

I don't need to wait until I have more followers on social media. I can start helping people with my life now.

As Martin Luther King Jr. once said, "Life's most persistent and urgent question is, 'What are you doing for others?'"[5]

God created you on purpose *for* a purpose.

So let's get after it.

——————————— REHAB TIME ———————————

COACH PEP TALK

If your purpose is tied to helping other people, I want you to spend some time brainstorming things you've done in your life (and have enjoyed) that have helped other people.

Thing I love to do (and am good at)	How it helps (or has helped) other people

YOU ARE UNIQUE IN YOUR PURPOSE

For the last two chapters, we've talked about this crucial point. **God created you on purpose *for* a purpose.**

You're a miraculous masterpiece. Not an accident. AND God's got stuff for you to do. He's had it planned.

But here's the thing.

If you don't spend some time figuring this out for yourself, you will be endlessly frustrated. You'll either think you don't have a purpose or you'll be lazy and allow other people (who don't know you well enough or love you well enough) to hand you a counterfeit purpose.

Your life is telling a story. Do you know what it is?

Let me explain how important it is to understand your own story and life. If you don't internalize THAT God has made you, HOW God has made you, and WHY God has made you, you might just die.

Literally die.

Viktor Frankl was an Austrian neurologist and psychologist born in 1905. He was captured by the Nazis and put in a concentration camp during the Holocaust. He survived and later wrote a book called *Man's Search for Meaning*. Frankl's book is one of the most-read books written about the Holocaust, and according to one survey it is one of the top 10 most influential books in America, having sold more than 10 million copies in 24 languages at the time of Frankl's death in 1997.[1,2] It attempted to answer the question, "How can you find a reason to live in the middle of the Holocaust?"

In the book, Frankl wrote, "Man's search for meaning is the primary motivation in his life."[3]

Frankl told a story about a group of prisoners who were assigned to a Nazi work camp. Every day, they had to move a giant pile of rocks from one end of a field to the other. Then, when the pile was moved, they heaved it back to its original location. This was nothing but pointless, meaningless work. And Frankl saw men die. Not because they were killed or malnourished or sick. But because they simply gave up their will to live. Just gave up. Because, as Frankl said, "Without meaning, men will wither and die."

Frankl also once wrote, "Life is never made unbearable by circumstances, but only by lack of meaning and purpose." Which means if you have a purpose, you can deal with almost anything.

So here's a helpful activity that might help you with your purpose.

I said earlier that you are purpose. And that your life is meant to help other people. But how exactly? That's what this chapter will help you figure out.

WHAT IS YOUR LIFE SAYING?

I'm going to show you a Venn diagram. It's three circles, each of which are very important. And where they meet together, that's your sweet spot. That's the place where you will make your greatest impact in the world.

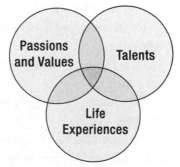

So let's get to it.

Let's get down to the serious business of who you are.

Because if you are purpose, then to find your purpose, you have to do some self-examination.

PASSIONS AND VALUES

Everyone has things they love and personal values they cling to.

For example, my buddy James is driven by justice. When things in life are unfair, it drives him nuts. Now everyone values justice to some degree. Nobody likes when things are unfair. But James is driven by justice. So much so that he went to law school and became an attorney and started working with international governments to use the full force of the law to stop child trafficking. James would never have done that if justice wasn't a core value for him.

I have another friend, Judy, whose core value is diversity. She believes that organizations and teams are better when they are composed of people from different backgrounds, socioeconomic groups, ethnicities, and countries of origin. She works with companies on this, and it is hard work. Companies often believe it's just easier and more efficient if everyone is from the same place with very few differences. But Judy fights this way of thinking. She believes everyone benefits when they build friendships with and learn to value people who are very different from them. Judy fights for this value. And there's no way Judy would do the job she does if she didn't value diversity.

So what are your values?

Maybe it's family. You believe that family can heal people.

Or honesty. You believe truth is the most important thing in every situation.

Or leadership. You believe that everything rises and falls on good leadership.

Or wisdom. You believe that doing the right thing at the right time really matters.

Or creativity. You are endlessly energized by original ideas and want to express them to the world.

ACTIVITY

Read this list of core values. Using a highlighter or pen, mark the ones that jump off the page to you as especially important in your life. Then, choose 3–6 that are the most important to you.

Accountability	Enthusiasm	Joy	Respect
Attitude	Excellence	Justice	Sacrifice
Authenticity	Faith	Kindness	Self-control
Boldness	Faithfulness	Leadership	Self-discipline
Character	Family	Learning	Selflessness
Collaboration	Generosity	Love	Servanthood
Compassion	Gentleness	Loyalty	Steadfastness
Confidence	Goodness	Mercy	Stewardship
Courage	Grace	Obedience	Submission
Creativity	Gratefulness	Openness	Teaching
Dedication	Growth	Order	Teamwork
Devotion	Honesty	Passion	Thankfulness
Discipline	Honor	Patience	Transparency
Discovery	Hope	Peace	Trustworthiness
Diversity	Humility	Perseverance	Truth
Efficiency	Humor	Personal Growth	Unity
Encouragement	Integrity	Relationships	Wisdom
Endurance	Intimacy	Reliability	

TALENTS AND GIFTS

Here's what I believe. Everyone in this world has an "A" gift. Something they're just really, really good at. Exceptional even.

Now, I know that some people have been blessed with an "A+" gift. And some rare individuals have multiple "A+" gifts. But it does no good to compare yourself to other people and their gifts. At the end of my life, God will not ask me, "Why didn't you win *Dancing with the Stars?*" That's not the skill set I have.

Also, because I believe God hates *Dancing with the Stars* . . .

But what if? What if every single person alive has an "A" gift? What if everyone on earth is really skilled at something?

The problem is, in our modern culture, we only measure certain types of gifts and talents.

Lebron James has an "A+" athletic gift.

Beyoncé has an "A+" performance gift.

Ryan Gosling has an "A+" acting gift.

But what if everyone has an "A" gift—it's just that those gifts often are in areas that aren't traditionally measured?

Stay with me.

I have worked with teenagers for a long time. And it has always bothered me that there was no way to reward or formally acknowledge that many of the students I met were extremely gifted at things that didn't show up on a report card.

Like Monica, whose father was severely injured in an accident at work. She went to high school and worked two jobs to help support her family and pay medical bills. And she managed to get into UCLA. I'd like to give her an "A" for resiliency and resourcefulness.

Or Julian, an unstoppable locomotive of laughter and optimism who brightened every class he was in with his sheer joy. He was a "clique-slider"—relating to every sort of student in every social stratum. He made everyone feel better when he was around. I'd like to give him an "A" for relating to people.

Or Brittany, who always seemed to be counseling someone through a tough time. At one point, her friend was dealing with self-harm, so Brittany took a purple Sharpie and drew a butterfly on her wrist and an identical one on her friend's wrist. She told her friend, "Now, when you want to cut, remember, you can't kill the butterfly. Call me instead, and I'll get you help. Let's just take it day by day until this butterfly fades, okay?" I'd like to give Brittany an "A" for creative compassion.

I think those gifts are exceptional. They're not monetized. You don't get rich by being nice to people who are typically ignored in social settings. There's no TV show called "America's Next Top Compassionate Friend." But I think there's a level of exceptional talent in that.

What if every single person has been given an "A" gift? And what if part of our purpose is to discover what that "A" gift is and then use it for the benefit of others?

Everyone has talents and gifts. What do you love to do? What are you good at?

UNIQUE LIFE EXPERIENCES

There's nobody else on this planet who has lived the life you've lived. As we mentioned before, the lessons you've learned from painful experiences can help others. What kinds of things have you been through? What insights do you have because of the way you grew up?

Let me give you an example: Dwight D. Eisenhower, the supreme commander of Allied forces in World War II. At one point, he may have been the singularly most important man in the world because he attempted to defeat Hitler and the Third Reich. How does one handle that kind of responsibility? Well, Eisenhower was the third of seven boys who grew up in a small town. He once explained, "I belong to a family of boys who were raised in meager circumstances in central Kansas, and every one of us earned our way as we went along."[4] So from a young age, he was responsible for making his way in the world and helping his family. Additionally, when he was younger, he was involved in an accident that cost his younger brother an eye. And later, he said that experience taught him the need to be protective of those under him.[5]

It's not a stretch to see how those early experiences shaped Eisenhower to be the man that he was.

What have you been through?

What's your background?

The good.

The bad.

The beautiful.

The ugly.

All of it.

The intersection of these three circles is likely where you're going to make your biggest impact.

Remember.

God created you on purpose *for* a purpose.

So go out there and live it.

REHAB TIME

COACH PEP TALK

Now it's time to go through these three circles and think more deeply about who you are, who God has made you to be, how you're built, and what life experiences you have.

QUESTION 1: *Core Values*

Which core values from the list in this chapter stood out the most to you? Write them down below. What did you learn about yourself in this exercise?

....
....
....
....
....

QUESTION 2: *Gifts and Talents*

What are your unique gifts and talents? What things are you good at that perhaps don't come as easily to other people?

....
....
....
....
....

QUESTION 3: *Life Experiences*

Make a list of five important life experiences you've had. How have these helped to shape who you are?

....

....

....

....

....

MONEY WON'T FILL YOU

Money isn't everything.
But money is *something*.

Money is a reality in this world. You gotta buy food and gas. And have a car to drive (or at least some way to get around) and a place to live. Money is a real thing. It's something.

The problem comes in when people try to make money *everything*.

I put it like this: "If money is in the driver's seat of your life, then it will drive you anywhere it can to get more money." This is why you see so many people losing their minds, losing their morals, and losing their standards to chase more and more money. This is called greed. And it's wildly destructive.

The Bible says, "The love of money is a root of all kinds of evil" (1 Timothy 6:10).

The King James Version actually says, "The love of money is the root of all evil."

This does not mean that the Bible or Jesus is anti-wealth. Some of Jesus's followers, both in the Bible and historically, have been incredibly wealthy. Money is a tool, like words or wood. You can use those tools to make something great and beautiful. Like a song or a home. Or you can use those tools to make something destructive, like a racist manifesto or a guillotine.

Money is a tool. And it takes its form and finds its use in whoever uses it. It exposes us, and a lot of time what's inside us isn't good.

Notice also that this verse doesn't say "money is the root of all evil." It says "the love of money." The lust for more. That's when money is controlling you, and that's when you do whatever it takes to get more money.

So Jesus isn't anti-wealth, but He is absolutely anti-consumerism. Consumerism is when you believe that having more things, having more stuff, will create meaning in your life. That money will give you security. Joy. Peace. Happiness.

Sure, money has to be a part of your life.

Don't let money be in the driver's seat of your life.

I would submit to you that in the US right now, that's what's happened. We have a very unhealthy relationship with money in our country.

An example: Right now, there are around 50,000 self-storage facilities in the US. Have you seen these self-storage garages? Americans have so much stuff that we must rent a mini-garage to store the things that won't fit in our houses. There is more than 1.7 billion square feet of self-storage space in the US. And the storage industry is a 38 billion-dollar industry.[1]

I think we might be letting money drive the car.

There was a show on Netflix in 2019 called *Tidying Up with Marie Kondo* that became a phenomenon. Her message in every show was basically "you have too much stuff." She encouraged people to get rid of their extra stuff. Her big question regarding people's stuff was "Does it spark joy?" The idea is that Americans simply accumulate too much stuff—and it doesn't bring joy.

I gotta be straight up.

Stuff won't make you happy.

Money won't make you happy.

Here's the problem, though. And here's where we get it twisted. Money can solve lots of problems.

It can pay your rent.

And help you go on vacations.

And pay for your school.

And help you get a good job.

But the most important problems in life, money can't solve.

Money can't buy deeply devoted friendships.

Money can't buy a stable and loving family.

Money can't cure terminal diseases.

Money can't give you purpose.

Money can solve a lot of problems. But the biggest problems in life—well, it can't touch them. In the words of the late American philosopher and poet The Notorious B.I.G., "Mo' money, mo' problems."

I know some of you are skeptical right now. You're thinking I'm lying. You're saying to yourself: "Well, if money doesn't buy happiness, then why is everyone in the entire world chasing after it, Trent?"

I get it.

But if money is really a cure-all for happiness, then that means that the lives of the richest people in the world should be the very best lives.

But that's simply not true. You see so many celebrities who look like they are all put-together but have lives that are falling apart. You see so many ultra-rich athletes and entertainment stars who have money but are a hot mess in their personal lives. They can buy a Bugatti but can't get along with their kids or love their spouse well.

Or how about these stats? About 70 percent of people who win the lottery lose all of it within a few years. In 2016, *Time* Magazine wrote an article about four people who had won several million dollars in the lottery. Every single one of them said they wished they had never won the lotto.[2]

This is something I know a *little* bit about.

The moment in my life when I was making the MOST money was when I was the LEAST happy. And I talked to tons of athletes and former athletes who were absolutely loaded, but whose lives were a wreck. They misunderstood something. I misunderstood something.

I bought into the lie that money buys happiness. It doesn't.

True riches come from who you are, not what you have.

Financial freedom is good, but what good is that freedom if your soul is still chained up on the inside? In fact, here's the honest truth: money can mess you up whether you have it or you don't. It can corrupt you whether you have it or you don't. I'll show you.

If you have money, you can be corrupted.

- Money can lead you to be arrogant, thinking you're better than other people, especially people who don't have as much money as you.
- Money can lead you toward pride, thinking you are the source of all your money. There's no such thing as a self-made man. God causes it to rain.
- Money can make you self-reliant, thinking you can solve all of life's problems on your own. News flash: you can't.
- Money can give you control issues. You think you have peace, but really what you're trusting in is your own bank account.
- Money can lead to an insatiable lust for more. America's first billionaire, John D. Rockefeller, was once asked, "How much money is enough?" His answer reportedly was, "Just a little bit more."

So money can destroy you if it's in the driver's seat. But it's darker than that. Even if you DON'T have money, it can still corrupt you if you let it have too much control.

- Not having money can lead you to be deeply jealous and envious of other people, wishing you had their possessions or bank account. This can lead you deep dissatisfaction with your own life.

- Not having money can lead to murderous envy. People have literally killed other people for money.
- Not having money can lead to bitterness. Perhaps toward rich people, but also toward God Himself, because in your own mind, He hasn't taken good enough care of you.
- Not having money can lead to worry, when you are constantly wondering if you'll have enough to make ends meet. This can lead to the destruction of your own peace and the invasion of anxiety.
- And not having money can lead to overworking, where you hustle and kill yourself to get more. This can cause you to sacrifice important things, even vital things, for the sake of money. This leads to an unbalanced life.

So that's the honest truth. Beware. Be on guard. Loving money will get you nowhere fast. Money makes lots of promises that it can never deliver. It can solve some problems, but not the biggest problems. And it can never deliver what it says it can: lasting happiness.

Money needs to be in your life, but it can't be in the driver's seat.

REHAB TIME

COACH PEP TALK

Timothy Keller once wrote, "An idol is something we cannot live without. We must have it. Therefore, it drives us to break rules we once honored to harm others, even ourselves, in order to get it."[3] Money is a common idol in our world. I want you to complete this activity to see that the best things in life are things money can't buy.

QUESTION 1

It's been said that the most important things in life can't be bought with money. For you, what are those things?

....
....
....

QUESTION 2

How could you move toward getting the things on that list?

....
....
....

QUESTION 3

It's also been said that the biggest problems in life can't be solved with money. What are the biggest problems you're facing right now? How could you move toward solving those problems without money?

....
....
....

LESSON 47

PLEASURE ISN'T HAPPINESS

Every year in May, there are high school graduations across the country. They all look pretty much the same. Rows of students in caps and gowns. Diplomas. The song "Pomp and Circumstance" played on loop.

And every year in May, this milestone moment causes parents to ponder about the future and the unknown road that lies ahead for their children.

And because the future can't be known, almost all parents say the exact same thing.

I don't really care what so-and-so does after graduation. I just want them to be _____.

What's the word that parents always say there?

I just want them to be . . . happy.

Man. This makes me want to scream. Here's why. I have seen so many people use their life to go after what makes them happy—and it has destroyed them and deeply hurt the people around them.

Just because it feels good doesn't mean it's good for you.

You can find pleasure in toxic things.

For example, to the parent that says, "I just want my son/daughter to be happy," well, what if your son or daughter is happy cheating and defrauding elderly people out of their life savings?

What if your son or daughter is happy writing racist columns online that stir up violent emotions?

What if your son or daughter is happy being a trafficker, promising people from other countries a chance to "make it" in the United States, while in reality they are forced to work endlessly for impossibly low wages?

Do you see?

The whole "I want my kid to be happy" is a dangerous thing to say.

Because what if they're happy doing something terrible?

Something destructive?

And this is the problem I have with the word *happiness* and why I don't use it. For me, the word *happiness* is a little too close to the word *pleasure*.

For me, those are shallow words. Happiness is a good feeling. Pleasure is a good feeling. And I will say it again, this time for the people in the back of the room.

Just because it feels good doesn't mean it's good for you.

You can find pleasure in toxic things.

You know this.

I know this.

I have friends who have chased the good feeling—the pleasure—of what it feels like to be high on drugs. I've watched them destroy their own lives, throw their potential down the drain, and deeply hurt the people around them. That's an extreme example. Let's go with some others that are less dramatic.

I have friends who have chased the good feeling—the pleasure—of video games. They've spent dozens, perhaps hundreds, of hours playing on the console. And it was fun in the moment, but it definitely wasn't good for them. It got them quite literally nowhere.

I have friends who have chased the good feeling of romance. They get a new boyfriend or a girlfriend, and there is this instant high because someone attractive likes them. It feels good to be liked.

But sometimes people go to such lengths just to get a boyfriend or a girlfriend that they end up losing themselves. Instead of asking, "Is this person right for me?" they ask, "How can I make myself right for this person?" And that's a recipe for misery.

In the end, happiness and pleasure are asking the wrong questions.

Pleasure asks, "What do I want?" instead of "What do I need?"

There's a difference between want and need. For example, when she was a teenager, my friend Frances begged her parents to let her get a tattoo. She really, really wanted a tattoo. Her parents were averse to the idea, but asked their daughter anyway, "If you could get a tattoo, what would it be of?"

Frances then proceeded to describe her dream tattoo. First, it would pay homage to the band Green Day. Frances adored this band, listening to their music every chance she got. But she didn't want to simply get the band's name inked on her arm, or something mainstream lamestream like that. Frances, like Green Day, was not conventional. So naturally, she thought a perfectly punk idea would be to get a tattoo of an elf, only the elf would have the face of Green Day's lead singer, Billie Joe Armstrong.

That's right.

A Green Day Keebler Elf tattoo.

Billie Joe Legolas.

Her parents said no.

Sometimes what you want isn't good.

And just because you want it doesn't mean you should grab for it. But that's not the only problem with pleasure.

Pleasure asks, "What can I get?" but ignores "What can I give?"

One of the most famous one-liners ever uttered by Jesus is "It is more blessed to give than to receive" (Acts 20:35). For the longest time, I thought this was nonsense. I remember Christmas morning, with all the presents around the tree for me. Man. That was the greatest feeling. But then I had kids. And you know what, I get to buy awesome presents for them and wrap them up. And I get to sit on the couch with my wife, and we watch them gleefully tear into the gifts we know they'll love. And I'm telling you, somehow, it's *better*.

Do you hear what I'm saying? I am NOT anti-pleasure. I am not saying, "The goal of life is to be miserable."

I want everyone reading this to be deeply happy.

But pleasure isn't going to fill your tank. I say that all the time to people.

The way to happiness is to seek purpose over pleasure.

In the end, happiness is never found by trying to get happiness. Happiness is a vapor. It's a momentary sense of deep well-being. But what happens when that feeling goes away? I think a better goal is to run after a happiness that doesn't easily float away. For me, I'm all about joy and peace. Those two things are really what you're after.

Joy is happiness on steroids.

And peace is a deep sense that all is okay, and that I'm going to be okay, no matter what.

Those two things cannot be taken away. It doesn't matter if there's chaos. It doesn't matter if things go wrong. Joy and peace will always be there.

Thousands of years ago, people were trying to figure all of this out too. A famous philosopher named Aristotle said that the goal of life is *eudaimonia*. It's a Greek word that means "living well" or "living and flourishing."

Aristotle wondered how humans could live the best possible life. And Aristotle said something controversial that folks are still talking about in universities today. He said this state of *eudaimonia* is a combination of what you do (if you do good things) and who you are (if you're becoming a good person).

I agree with my man Aristotle. Here's how I'd say what he said:

Seek purpose over pleasure.

Your purpose is to find the thing that you're good at, that makes you come alive, and use it in your life to help other people. That's what will bring you the most pleasure.

So, in the end, at my son's or daughter's graduation, I know what I won't be saying.

I won't be saying, "I don't care what they end up doing as long as they're happy."

I know that goal is far too low.

I think I'll say, "I don't want my kids to be happy. I want them to be good."

Because if they live that out, you know what?

They'll get happiness thrown in.

REHAB TIME

COACH PEP TALK

There's a difference between pleasure and joy. Here's a chance to really think about that truth. Complete the questions below to see how you can move toward joy.

QUESTION 1

Has there ever been a time when you did something fun, but it turned out to be a toxic activity that hurt your life a bit?

....
....
....

QUESTION 2

What's the difference between pleasure and joy? Has there ever been a time when you felt deep joy? What was going on?

....
....
....

THAT BLUE CHECK WON'T FILL YOU

This is the thing about social media.

Social media has connected us more than ever. But at the same time, it's disconnected us. I like to put it like this:

Social media has connected us to the world, but it's disconnected us from our world.

Next time you're out and about at a restaurant or coffee shop, look at people. Everyone has their heads down, staring at a screen. We're no longer looking up. We're no longer observing our world.

I grew up in a generation where we had conversations when we were driving. Now I'll see a car with a family in it, and every single person—sometimes even the driver—is on their own device.

Research shows that teenagers spend more than seven hours a day looking at screens.[1] But why? Why are so many people hunkered down over their phones and laptops?

Part of the reason is that we're addicted to the affirmation.

A new study shows that receiving "likes" on social media activates the same circuits in the teenage brain that are activated by eating chocolate or winning money.[2] Your brain releases a chemical called dopamine, which creates a feeling of pleasure in the brain.

So when you post something online on Snapchat or Instagram and positive comments or likes or shares come in from your friends, it's a little bit like a drug. It's a drug of connection that says, "I am liked."

A 2017 study of more than 500,000 teenagers found that the number of eighth through twelfth graders exhibiting high levels of depressive symptoms increased by 33 percent between 2010 and 2015. In the same period, the suicide rate for girls in that age group increased by 65 percent.[3] It's important to remember that smartphones were introduced in 2007. And in the coming years, teenagers and young adults scrambled to own them. According to a 2019 survey by Common Sense Media, 81 percent of fourteen-year-olds own a smartphone—a number that climbs to 91 percent for eighteen-year-olds.[4]

Social media has now become the driver of people's self-esteem.

When I was a kid in high school, we knew who the most popular people were. We knew who was and wasn't cool. But we didn't have numbers assigned to everyone's names on a daily basis.

Now there's a scorecard. You know exactly how many followers. How many likes. How many shares. How popular you are.

So many people will do anything to gain a following. Because if you have a following, that means you're somebody. If I have a blue check by your name, you're successful.

And this puts so much pressure on you. In fact, CNN did a story that Snapchat-filtered selfies are putting so much pressure on beauty standards it's driving many young people to seek cosmetic procedures to look more like the filters on their social media posts.[5]

So many people are afraid they won't measure up, so afraid that people won't like them. They wear so many masks that it's like Halloween every single day. I've seen people do really dumb stuff on purpose in hopes of going viral.

I've seen people lose scholarships because of what they posted.

One guy I knew had a full Division I scholarship to play soccer at a major school and posted "Marijuana is my favorite." He lost his scholarship and so couldn't afford to attend that college. I've known folks who were well on their way to getting full scholarships who posted idiotic stuff on social media, and the coaches saw it and literally stopped recruiting them.

I've seen people get fired from their jobs because of what they put on social media. One of my favorite stories was about a guy who worked at a cell phone store in the mall and posted that he wanted to go home and play Minecraft and create this cell phone store in the virtual land, and slowly burn it to the ground. He posted that at 9 a.m. By 11 a.m., he didn't have a job.

The desire to get "likes" can have a really high cost. This all goes to show an important point.

You can lose yourself pleasing other people.

I know quite a few people in the fitness industry. And I've seen this thing happen (especially with women). They post a picture of their face—just a beautiful picture—and they get a few likes. But if they post a picture that shows more of their body, shows some skin, shows their butt, suddenly the likes go through the roof.

So they learn the lesson.

I am not enough. I have to show more of my body. I have to turn myself into an object to get approval and attention.

And that's not only wrong, it's crazy. And I've watched this phenomenon change the way people think about themselves.

It's dangerous to judge your value by the number of likes you get.

Your value is not in how many likes you get on social media sites. If you base your worth on likes, you're in trouble.

You'll never have enough followers.

You'll never get enough affirmation.

It's an exhausting hamster wheel.

Your life is already difficult enough, and then you add to it an incredible social pressure and repeated (almost daily) messages that you're "not enough."

So what is the solution? Well, I know part of it. Here are two things:

You need to be connected to real people in way where you truly share and are truly known.

We are social creatures. Even as babies, we need connection with other people. We need community. You might even say we're hardwired for it.

And real human interaction, that's what validates us.

Not clicks.

Not likes.

In fact, the amount of connection formed by a click is actually very, very, very low. It's the equivalent of being hungry and someone giving you a Skittle.

But you know what works way better?

Hanging out with a friend.

Getting a hug.

Sharing a meal.

Those things dramatically increase your connection. They remind you that you're a real person (not just a profile online) and that real people really like you. So go out and do that. Focus on real time with real people.

Don't focus on followers. Focus on impact.

I remember around 2013, social media likes were controlling me. I was chasing the numbers, constantly trying to get likes. I had to get the numbers up. Then I had a bit of a revelation. I asked myself a question.

Trent, would you rather have a million followers and get that blue check mark on Twitter? Or would you rather make a legitimate impact in the lives of a thousand people?

The answer to this is easy. Fame is deeply overrated. People try to go for fame in this day and age. But fame isn't the point of life.

Impact is.

You and I both could name five people who have millions of followers on Instagram or Twitter—but they are absolutely not making any impact on the people's lives who follow them. They're not.

And you and I could also name five people who maybe aren't even on social media who have made a gigantic impact on our lives.

Fame doesn't matter in the end. Followers don't matter in the end. What matters is what you choose to do with those. How you leverage that for impact. And in the end—if you think about that—helping a thousand people would be incredible.

You are enough.

Use social media. Don't let it use you.

REHAB TIME

COACH PEP TALK

You and I both need to be thoughtful about the role of technology and smartphones and social media in our lives. Here are four questions that I ask myself to help me analyze whether I'm using my phone or my phone is using me. Answer these honestly and see what answers you come up with.

QUESTION 1

Is your phone crowding out your time for silence, solitude, and contemplation? What steps should you take to ensure that you have time with yourself?

....

....

....

QUESTION 2

Is your phone more addictive than it should be? What steps could you take to decrease its control over your behavior?

....

....

....

QUESTION 3

Is your phone distracting you from doing your best creative work and/or thinking deep thoughts? What steps could you take to limit distractions?

....

....

....

QUESTION 4

Is your phone stealing your attention from the most important people in your life? What steps could you take to make sure this doesn't happen?

....

....

....

XII.

STRAIGHT UP

ABOUT MAKING AN IMPACT

BUILD YOUR LEGACY

Your legacy is what you leave when you die.

When you die, people will talk about who you were, what you did, and what you left here. This is great, especially if what you leave behind is positive.

But here's the thing: even though your legacy is what you leave when you die, you actually build it when you're alive.

Your legacy is built every single day.

You build it now.

Today.

Right now.

You have a chance to build your legacy every single day. Put another brick in the wall of what you leave. And I know I've talked a lot about the future in this book—and that's good because it's important to be future-focused—but it's also just as important to focus on the day we have right in front of us. The Roman poet Horace penned a Latin phrase you're probably familiar with: *carpe diem*, which means "seize the day." Horace was trying to get his countrymen to realize an important idea: this day is too important to let slip by. This day.

Right here.

Right now.

So I like to ask myself, "What is my legacy going to be *today*?"

- Can I make or create something on social media that will encourage people?
- Can I coach my son's football team and encourage those young guys?
- Can I do something for my family to make them feel secure and loved?

LEAVING A LEGACY IS ABOUT MAKING TODAY BETTER FOR SOMEONE ELSE

Think about the people in history who have made the greatest impact on this world. Almost always, they're people who used their lives every day to make life better for someone else.

A while ago, I had a chance to go to Washington, D.C. and walk around all the monuments. And I was struck by the reality that every single monument was basically a story of someone (or a whole group of someones) who used their lives to help other people.

The monument that affected me the most was the Martin Luther King Jr. Memorial.

Standing on the bank of the Tidal Basin, Dr. King's figure is carved in granite; the statue is titled the *Stone of Hope*. It towers. It should. In his hand, Dr. King is holding a rolled-up script, the draft of his "I Have a Dream" speech, according to the sculptor.[1]

Around the statue is a marble wall featuring quotes from Dr. King, appropriate since words were his primary weapon of peace. Some of the quotes are beautiful and poetic. Some are soothing. Some ring like a bell of truth in your mind. And others are prophetic and bound to make some folks wildly uncomfortable.

Just like Dr. King himself.

As I stood at the base of the monument, looking up at the statue, I thought to myself, "Is it possible that Dr. King was the American in the last one hundred years who left the largest legacy?"

Think about what King left behind.

A change of laws.

A change of heart.

Love conquering hate.

What a legacy. He dedicated his life to the nonviolent struggle for equality. He dedicated his life to the idea that people of all races could not only coexist but be brothers and sisters. He dedicated his life to the service to others. And King's dream, his legacy, marches on today.

That's a legacy.

But even if you don't wind up with a statue of yourself in our nation's capital, you can still have a meaningful legacy.

YOU CAN'T CHANGE THE WORLD . . . BUT YOU CAN CHANGE THOSE IN YOUR WORLD

Leaving a legacy doesn't always mean something big. It's about leaving your mark on every single day.

How can I show up?

How can I make today better for somebody else?

You can choose that.

When you interact with people, there are basically three things you can do.

1. You can make their life worse.
2. You can do absolutely nothing for them.
3. You can make their life better.

And let me tell you, it doesn't take a whole lot of effort or cost a bunch of money to make people's lives better.

People walk around every day, wanting to be seen and wanting to be heard. We're desperate for meaningful connection. And you and I can give that to people. There are so many ways that you can add value to people's lives.

The other day, I was out running the trails in the foothills around my house. Side note: I don't think I've ever encountered a negative person out running on the trails. I only encounter positive people. In fact, I've been looking for a negative person out there, just to prove myself wrong, but I haven't found one yet.

Anyway, I was running, and it was an off day. I was being pretty hard on myself, and this guy ran by me, and must have seen something in my face, because he said, "You're doing a great job, man. Keep pushing."

What is that? Eight words? I'm telling you, it lifted my spirits. This tiny interaction made me feel good about life and about people.

Is that a dumb example? Maybe you're sitting there thinking, "Trent. Are you honestly suggesting that the world can be made better with eight words? You are dumb."

Maybe. Maybe not.

Listen to this story.

I have a friend, James, who is a high school teacher, and every day, as his students file into his classroom, he greets them by name. He tries to notice if they're wearing something new, or if they have a fresh haircut, or if there's something different about them. And he doles out compliments like McDonald's doles out fries.

One of his favorite students to do this with was Monica, a senior. Whenever she rounded the corner and came into the hallway, my buddy would say, "Maaaaaaaaahnica!" in his booming voice and give her a high five. She'd always smile.

He did that pretty much every single day.

At graduation, Monica found him and told him that the thing she most looked forward to in the day was coming to his class.

"At home, things were always tense, and I was frequently getting yelled at by my mom because she was stressed," she told him. "'Monica, do this. Monica, you forgot that. Monica.' Most days, the only time I heard my name was when I was being told to do something, or that I forgot something, or that I did something wrong. But I knew that when I came to your class, I knew I'd hear my name said different."

I knew I'd hear my name said different.

Okay, first off, it should be "I knew I'd hear my name said differently." But man, what a sentiment. My buddy told me that interaction really affected him.

So if we're keeping track, my day was made better by eight words.

And Monica's day was made better by ONE word.

So yeah. I would say that it doesn't take a whole lot to change someone's day.

But here's the thing.

ADDING VALUE TO OTHER PEOPLE'S LIVES REVEALS YOUR VALUE

When my teacher buddy James realized how much value he had (almost accidentally) added to Monica's life, he was deeply affected. He had NO IDEA how much power his words had. He had no idea how much VALUE he could add to other people's lives just by doing something small.

When you realize how much you can help people, you start to see how much VALUE you can pour into the world, how much power you have to change things in this world. And that makes you feel really good about yourself. In fact, it fills you with hope.

It makes you feel hope about the day, because you can make a real impact.

It makes you feel hope about yourself, because your words and life matter.

It makes you feel hope about your future, because you'll never run out of ways to make a difference.

Your legacy starts today.

Go out there and show up.

Your fullest you.

Your truest you.

Help other people. Make today better for someone else. Add value to people's lives.

Your legacy is what you leave after you die.
But you build your legacy today.
Get to it.

REHAB TIME

COACH PEP TALK

Leaving a legacy starts today. And it doesn't have to be a big thing. Think through these questions about leaving a legacy, and then jump into action. Change starts with you!

QUESTION 1

Who is someone who absolutely made your day a little better today? What did they do? How did this make you feel?

....
....
....

QUESTION 2

What is a little act of service that you can do today for the people you live with to make their lives better?

....
....
....

QUESTION 3

Think about someone you will see tomorrow. What could you do to help that person have a better day?

....
....
....

WRITE A BRAND-NEW STORY

Just because you've had some bad chapters in your life doesn't mean your story can't end well.

That's just facts.

In fact, if you listen to those bad chapters, they can help you as you move forward to create an amazing ending.

There are some folks who are reading this who have a pretty good family life. Sure, they have challenges—but overall, they've been lucky. This was my experience. I grew up with two parents who were married and middle-class, and I went to a school that had good teachers who helped me go to college and follow my dream of playing football. That's a pretty solid base to start from.

But not everyone is that lucky, and I know it.

A while ago, I was at a leadership conference with a bunch of teenagers, and the facilitator put a giant line of masking tape on the floor. People stood on either side of the line, about three feet back on either side. The facilitator then asked a series of questions to everyone, asking students to step forward to the line if the statement applied to them.

There were about forty statements. After each one, students would step to the line. That facilitator would say, "Look around you. Look who's with you. Look who's not."

- Step to the line if your parents were not born in the United States.
- Step to the line if your grandparents were not born in the United States.
- Step to the line if you've ever been to a funeral of someone you love very much.
- Step to the line if your parents are divorced.
- Step to the line if your family ever received government assistance, like food stamps to buy food.
- Step to the line if drug addiction has been part of your family's story.
- Step to the line if alcoholism has been a part of your family's story.
- Step to the line if you've ever seen violence in your house.
- Step to the line if you've ever been made fun of or had hurtful statements made about you because of your race.

The whole experience was very powerful and eye-opening. It made the students realize that some of their friends had been through some tough times that they had never been through.

Maybe that's you.

Maybe you've been through things that many of your friends don't understand.

I know that might not seem fair, but because you've had bad chapters in your life, it's your duty and obligation to yourself (and everyone you love) to try to write a different ending.

You have the chance to write a brand-new story.

Maybe you recall a video that recently surfaced of LeBron James.

He was in a high school gym in Nevada, cheering on his son in an AAU championship game. His son made a great play, and LeBron jumped up and ran around the baseline, cheering. He was jumping and celebrating so hard, he even lost a shoe.

Some of the folks who saw that video said that LeBron just

wanted to draw attention to himself. That he's a fame junkie addicted to attention and media coverage and he needed another hit.[1]

I don't see it like that at all.

Now, I don't know LeBron James. So I don't know what he was thinking. But when I watched that video, this is what I saw: I saw someone rewriting his own story.

You see, LeBron grew up without a father. But he says that the experience inspires him to be a good father to his own kids.[2]

So when LeBron shows up at his son's game, he's doing something. He's changing the story. He is literally giving his kids something that he never had growing up.

A present, active, involved father cheering from the stands.

Was his cheering a bit over the top?

I don't know. I happen to sympathize with LeBron. As an athlete, I've had some big moments, but I'm telling you there is NOTHING more exciting than watching your kid do something well. It really is exhilarating. I think James lost himself in the excitement of watching his son play well in a sport he adores.

I think he's celebrating as a proud father.

And I bet when his son sees that clip, he sees that love.

WRITING A BRAND-NEW STORY MEANS WRITING IN WHAT WAS MISSING

Instead of focusing on what you didn't have, use that as motivation to say, "I'm going to be sure to give what I never had to other people."

What didn't you have?

You never had a good coach who truly cared about you? Become that coach.

What is your wound?

Your father left your family? Be the dad who always shows up for your kids.

What do you wish you had?

You grew up without stability because of your parent's bad financial decisions? Be the parents who give their kids financial stability.

What is the number one thing you would give to your younger self if you could?

Go out and give that to someone else.

Become the person that you needed when you were younger.

The cards that you were dealt might not have been fair, but you can still turn them into a winning hand. And you're strongest when you stand up and say, "My circumstances don't define my life. What defines my life is what I do with my circumstances."

The things that were supposed to break you can make you.

Nobody wants to read a story where everything is sunshine and rainbows. Is that interesting? No. So instead of sitting there and making a list of all the things you DON'T have or DIDN'T have growing up, go out there and make a list of all the things you want to make sure you add them into your life going forward.

I have a friend, Nicole, whose parents got divorced before she was even born. She has literally never known a moment when her parents were together. She counted once, and between her mom's four brothers and her dad's four brothers (and her parents), there were nineteen divorces in her family tree.

Nineteen divorces.

From ten people.

Nicole grew up as a child of a divorce. And she always told herself, "I'll probably get divorced too. Maybe my second marriage will be a happy one."

That was literally what she thought. Until a mentor came along and said, "No, girl, you're going to break the cycle. The line of divorce ends with you."

That mentor helped Nicole see that instead of rehearsing the same old story, she could write a brand-new one. Nicole stopped dating guys who weren't serious about commitment. She started talking to her cousins about what it might look like for them to build families that were stable. She took herself and her future seriously.

"What if," she said, "all of our kids grow up and never have to experience divorce firsthand? What if we all grow up and reverse this trend and we all stay married?"

She wanted to write a brand-new story.

As of right now, Nicole has six cousins who are married. No divorce, or even a hint of divorce, in any of their marriages. And Nicole's two kids are now twelve and fourteen, and they've experienced the home that Nicole never had. They are writing a new story with a much better ending.

WRITE A BETTER ENDING

We've been programmed to focus on what we don't have, but progress comes when you fight to give other people something that they don't have.

You're one choice away from a new beginning. Say to yourself, "Where I'm at may suck, but it's not where I'm going to stay." Remind yourself of this:

My current situation isn't my final destination.

You have to use that as your motivation. It's like a cake. If you eat each the ingredients of a cake separately, they taste terrible (Anyone up for a nice cup of sifted flour?). But when you put them all together, something pretty delicious can happen.

So.

This chapter in your life isn't great.

That's okay.

Go out there and write a new ending to your story.

Do it for the world's sake.

Do it for the sake of the people around you.

And do it for your own sake.

REHAB TIME

COACH PEP TALK

I believe that you can use the pain of your past to help guide you to build a strong future. I also believe that you can become the person that you needed when you were younger. As you think about what kind of life you want to lead, fill out and think about this chart. It might be a little painful to think about (or a LOT painful) but that's okay. Use that to guide your future.

WRITING A BRAND-NEW STORY

What didn't you have in your life growing up that you wish you did?	
As you think about the time when you have your own family, what is the number one thing you will do differently for them?	
What is the number one thing you would give your younger self if you could?	

DON'T MAKE THE SEQUEL SUCK

True facts. I had a pretty darn good childhood.

My parents were awesome. I lived in a solidly middle-class neighborhood. I had brothers to play with. I had awesome grandparents. My schools and teachers were good.

All things considered, I was dealt a pretty good hand.

I mean, I wasn't like Carlton from *The Fresh Prince of Bel-Air*. I didn't live in a mansion with a butler or nothing. But I had it pretty good.

Maybe you're like me.

Maybe you identify.

Here's the thing that scares me: I almost messed it all up. I almost blew it.

I think about it like this: my parents and grandparents were the first two legs in an Olympic 4x400 meter relay. They ran their hearts out, giving me a substantial lead.

And I dropped the baton.

All their work and effort to help make sure I got the best head start possible—so that I could win the race of life—and I dropped the baton.

Man.

So if you're like me, and you had a pretty good childhood and upbringing, I'm begging you, learn from me. Here are the two things that I desperately wish I would've done. Learn from me, and don't make the same mistakes I made.

LISTEN TO YOUR PARENTS

I did not have toxic parents. I didn't have abusive or manipulative parents. My parents had earned the right to have me listen to them. They had proven, a thousand times over, that they were for me and loved me and my brothers.

But I still disregarded them.

You know, as kids, I think we all secretly believe our parents aren't actually that smart. We forget they've already been through (pretty much) all the stuff that we've been through. We forget they have a lot of knowledge about how to live.

There was a time there when I just decided I needed to do things my own way. I had gotten distracted. If I had just listened to what my parents had said, instead of trying to do things my own way, I would have saved myself a lot of heartache and trouble. Just that simple move—listening to my parents—would have gotten me out of situations I should never have been in.

It's like that toddler who smells the burger and wants to put his hand up on the grill, and his dad says, "No, don't touch that. It will burn your hand!"

Well, let's just say I grabbed the hamburger, and I got the burn to show for it.

In other words, I was kind of stupid there for a while.

For me, the second I realized that my parents knew more than I did (and I started listening to them)—things got better.

REALIZE THAT LIFE IS BIGGER THAN YOU

The second thing that got me back into the relay was the birth of my son. My son helped me realize that my life is a lot bigger than just me. Now, I know you don't have kids yet, but this is the life event that grabbed me by the collar and shook me like a rag doll. It was like this life lesson that was screaming at me:

"IT'S NOT JUST ABOUT YOU, TRENT!"

We all have people we influence. Every day that you walk out of your house, you're going to be influencing people. And you're either going to make their lives better or make their lives worse.

In this relay race of life, my parents had given me a head start when they handed off the baton. And I'd almost bungled it by not listening to them and focusing on myself. And I didn't want to make my son have to sprint his whole life because I'd made some bad decisions.

I didn't want to be the reason my child was left behind.

So I said to myself, "I have got to pick up the pace."

I had to ask myself some hard questions: What path did my parents show me? What path am I really following? What path am I leading my family down? Is this the right path? Am I honoring my parents' legacy with my decisions? Am I honoring my grandparents' sacrifice and love with my decisions?

It's like those movies where the first one is so good, but then the sequel comes out and it's terrible. Just hot garbage. And you're like, "Why? Why is this so bad?"

That's where my life was heading. I was writing the sequel to my parents' and grandparents' story, and it was starting to suck.

I had to make some changes.

If I didn't get this right, I was going to set my kids up to follow in my footsteps, and at that time, I knew I was heading for destruction.

I was leading them toward destruction.

And I made a vow. I refused to give my son that.

He didn't deserve that. He deserved better.

I refused to live that way. I was determined not to drop the baton.

I want my ceiling to be my children's floor.

My wife and I had this conversation. We realized as parents, our child's definitions of the world would be based on our example.

The word *faith* was going to be defined by what they saw in my life.

The word *family* was going to be defined by what they saw us trying to build.

The word *love* was going to be defined by what they saw in our actions.

We were going to pass on the definition of nearly everything to our kids. But then we also realized that because of our upbringings, we had a head start. My parents had already shown me what a good marriage could be. They showed me how to argue while still being kind and loving. They showed me what a home filled with unconditional love looked like.

I just had to keep it going.

And maybe try to make it a little bit better.

I don't know what my kids are going to end up doing. Frankly, I don't really care. I just want them to grow and become whoever God created them to be. I want them to be the best versions of themselves.

And I want their sequel to be even better than mine.

That's the goal.

REHAB TIME

COACH PEP TALK

Figuring out what went wrong in a plane crash is usually pretty easy. What's far more difficult is figuring out what went RIGHT. If you are part of a pretty good family (as I was), sometimes it's hard to put your finger on why it's a good family. These questions might help you put it into words.

QUESTION 1

What are some of your favorite memories with your family? Write out as many as you can think of.

....
....
....

QUESTION 2

When you think about raising your own family, what kinds of things will you absolutely continue to do that your family does now? What do those things build in your family?

....
....
....

QUESTION 3

What are three adjectives that describe your father? Do you have those same qualities? What aspects of your father do you most admire?

....
....
....

QUESTION 4

What are three adjectives that describe your mother? Do you have those same qualities? What aspects of your mother do you most admire?

....
....
....

TWO WORDS YOU HATE (BUT REALLY NEED)

When I was little, my grandmother used to say to me, "Always leave a place better than you found it."

I think she was trying to get me to quit leaving my toys all over her house.

But it was also a statement she wanted me to live by.

Make the world better.

Don't leave a mess.

Before you go, look around and see what you can do to clean things up.

What my grandmother was trying to communicate is a word that isn't used much or talked about much. It's the word *responsibility*, and I believe it's critically important. Responsibility is the first stop on the road to maturity. If you aren't responsible, you aren't mature. So let's take some time to talk through this concept.

Responsibility means realizing you affect other people.

One of the great transitions in life is to move from being a child to being an adult. Do you know what one of the major differences is between immature people and mature people? Mature people don't believe they are the center of the world.

There's a famous poem by John Donne where he writes that "No man is an island."[1] The point Donne is making is that we're connected to each other, like clumps of dirt on the mainland. As Martin Luther King, Jr. once said:

> We are tied together in the single garment of destiny, caught in an inescapable web of mutuality. And whatever affects one directly affects all indirectly. For some strange reason I can never be what I ought to be until you are what you ought to be. And you can never be what you ought to be until I am what I ought to be. This is the way God's universe is made; this is the way it is constructed.[2]

In that speech, King is making the point that the way to find purpose and meaning in life is to recognize that life is not about only you. That you and I were made to help and serve and love one another. That you and I are tied to one another.

Immature people pretend like their actions don't affect other people. This ranges from basic things, like leaving dirty dishes in the sink (who exactly do you think is going to clean those?) to far more extreme examples, like getting a girl pregnant and then walking away from the situation.

Mature people think about the effect their actions have on others.[3]

Responsibility is cleaning up messes you didn't make.

One of the surest signs of maturity is when someone takes responsibility for cleaning up a mess they did not create.

Like when I ask my kids to pick up the living room, and they'll only pick up their toys. And I'll say, "Put *everything* away," and they will fall on the floor and moan and complain and say, "But I didn't play with that game! Why do I have to put it away?"

And then these words come out of their mouth.

"It's not fair!"

You're right. It's not fair. It's absolutely not. But do you know what else is not fair?

A lot of things.

It's not fair that my wife had to endure nine months of dramatic changes in her body, including some that were very uncomfortable and downright painful, just to bring kids into this world. Do you know what I had to do during those nine months? Do you know what happened to my body?

Nothing.

How is that fair?

Or think about Thanksgiving. When I was little, I absolutely LOVED Thanksgiving. It was one of my favorite holidays.

Do you know how long that single meal takes to prepare?

Do the potatoes mash themselves?

Does the turkey stuff itself?

Do those pies bake themselves?

No. Oftentimes in our family, multiple family members would be up early in the morning, chopping and dicing and cooking and stirring. For hours.

Do you know what I was doing on Thanksgiving morning with the rest of the kids?

Playing football outside.

Did I help prepare ANY of the food when I was a kid?

No.

Did I eat the food?

Oh heck to the yes. I ate it all.

Is that fair? No. It's not.

This is how life works. When you're young, you think things just happen. That Thanksgiving meals just appear. But it's always a mature and dedicated adult who has stepped up to say, "I'm going to take responsibility for this." It's always a mature adult who says, "I'm going to make this my job."

Don't ask, "Is this fair?" Fair is overrated. Life is very often not fair. Instead say, "What's the right thing to do?"

Responsibility means using your life to make the world better.

Almost every day, I drive over a bridge. There are forty-three different bridges in the city where I live. Now I don't think about bridges. I just drive over them.

But I'd like to stop and think about them for a second. The West Fork of the Trinity River runs through Fort Worth. It's not little. So I went online and looked when all these bridges were built to deal with that waterway. I was shocked at the years. 1925. 1903. 1954. 1936.

Which means that dozens of decades before I was born, a group of engineers and city planners said, "Look, people in this city need a way to get around town. And this river is preventing movement. Let's build a bridge."

So they did.

They used steel.

And wood.

They had to build columns out of concrete.

They had to make sure the bridge was safe and would last.

They had to make sure it could support all that weight.

That's a lot of work. A lot.

And I never once think about the men and women who spent a lot of time making sure the bridges I drive over were not only built, but were safe. I don't.

But maybe I should.

Because without them, my car would be very wet right now. And I wouldn't be able to get home.

I feel like in life, there are a lot of people who have built bridges in my life who I never think about. Think about where you are right now and all the people who came before you. There are people who sacrificed so much just to get you where you are.

I think about this a lot because I'm black and live in Texas. My hometown saw a triple lynching of black men in Dealey Plaza in 1860. Brave civil rights leaders were literally killed by members of the KKK for standing up for things like the right to vote. In 1954, after *Brown v. Board of Education* made segregation illegal, the governor of Texas dispatched the Texas Rangers to prevent black kids from going to a newly desegregated school. This happened in my hometown.

The generation before me had to endure all this and fight for things as simple as the right to vote, the right to go to a good school, and even the right to choose where they lived.

I take all this for granted. But it didn't just happen. It happened because people stood up and made it happen. They put their lives on the line to build a better future for me.

They built that bridge that I drive over every day.

So. Here's what I want you to do.

I want you to build a bridge.

Heck, I want you to build a couple of bridges, because some of you have it in you.

Think about how you can use your life to make things better for the people who will come after you. Think about what they need (what you wish you had right now), and then go out and get that done.

Build a bridge.

Even if you yourself never get to drive across it.

Do it anyway.

REHAB TIME

COACH PEP TALK

When I was little, I loved Thanksgiving. Still do, but when I was little, I thought that the food just magically appeared. But now that I'm older, I see how much work it takes from adults to make Thanksgiving happen. They spend hours cooking the meal, and then they spend hours cleaning up afterwards. This is what service and duty and obligation look like. This is what adulting looks like. Answer these questions to see who has served you, and what that's meant to you—and how you can take steps to serve others.

QUESTION 1

Who are the two people in your life who have served you the best? Who has been dedicated to making sure you were okay and had what you needed?

....

....

QUESTION 2

Take some time and try to make a list of the "messes" that they cleaned up that they did not make. This can be literal or figurative.

....

....

....

....

QUESTION 3

Going forward, what is a mess that you see that needs cleaning up (that perhaps you didn't cause)? What would cleaning up that mess yourself look like?

....

....

....

Notes

LESSON 02

1. Fred Rogers, interview by Karen Herman, *The Interviews*, Television Academy Foundation, July 22, 1999, https://interviews.televisionacademy.com/interviews/fred-rogers.

LESSON 03

1. Names have been changed for this story.

LESSON 04

1. "Oprah Winfrey: Media Pioneer," The Academy of Achievement biography, accessed January 14, 2020, https://www.achievement.org/achiever/oprah-winfrey/.
2. Jill Nelson, "The Man Who Saved Oprah Winfrey," *The Washington Post*, December 14, 1986, https://www.washingtonpost.com/archive/lifestyle/magazine/1986/12/14/the-man-who-saved-oprah-winfrey/66d7b7b3–98af-4495–82a7–6b04827f1bd6/.
3. Peter Jones, "How Oprah Winfrey Overcame Failure," *The Job Network*, https://www.thejobnetwork.com/how-oprah-winfrey-overcame-failure/.

LESSON 05

1. Lewis Carroll, *Alice's Adventures in Wonderland* (London: Macmillan, 1865), chapter 6.

LESSON 06

1. President John F. Kennedy, "Special Message to the Congress on Urgent National Needs" (presidential address, joint session of 87th United States Congress, Washington, DC, May 25, 1961).
2. "10 Things You May Not Know About the Apollo Program," History.com, accessed January 6, 2020, https://www.history.com /news/10-things-you-may-not-know-about-the-apollo-program.
3. "Apollo in 50 Numbers: The Workers," BBC Future, The British Broadcasting Corporation, last modified June 19, 2019, https://www.bbc.com/future/article/20190617-apollo -in-50-numbers-the-workers.
4. "Empire State Building Fast Facts," CNN, updated July 29, 2019, https://www.cnn.com/2013/07/11/us/empire-state -building-fast-facts/index.html.
5. 157 Cong. Rec. H9265 (June 17, 2013) (statement of Rep. Barr).

LESSON 07

1. Juliana Menasce Horowitz and Nikki Graf, "Most U.S. Teens See Anxiety and Depression as a Major Problem Among Their Peers," Pew Research Center, February 20, 2019, https://www .pewsocialtrends.org/2019/02/20/most-u-s-teens-see-anxiety -and-depression-as-a-major-problem-among-their-peers/.
2. Christopher James, "NYU Study Examines Top High School Students' Stress and Coping Mechanisms," New York University news release, August 11, 2015, www.nyu.edu/about /news-publications/news/2015/august/nyu-study-examines-top -high-school-students-stress-and-coping-mechanisms.html.

3. Christina Veiga, "Students Feel the Pressure of More Work, Expectations—and So Do Their Teachers," *The Miami Herald*, August 6, 2016, www.miamiherald.com/news/local/education/article94124892.html.

4. Kyle Spencer, "Taking Summer School to Get Ahead, Not Catch Up," *The New York Times*, August 16, 2016, www.nytimes.com/2016/08/17/nyregion/taking-summer-school-to-get-ahead-not-catch-up.html.

5. "Asian Grading Scale," r/asianpeopletwitter, reddit.com, accessed January 7, 2020, https://www.reddit.com/r/AsianPeopleTwitter/comments/9tolst/asian_grading_scale/.

6. Julie Scelfo, "Suicide on Campus and the Pressure of Perfection," *The New York Times*, July 27, 2015, www.nytimes.com/2015/08/02/education/edlife/stress-social-media-and-suicide-on-campus.html.

7. Steven Reinberg, "1 In 5 College Students So Stressed They Consider Suicide," *HealthDay News*, September 10, 2018, consumer.healthday.com/general-health-information-16/suicide-health-news-646/1-in-5-college-students-so-stressed-they-consider-suicide-737502.html.

Lesson 08

1. Rev. Dr. Martin Luther King, Jr., *A Gift of Love: Sermons from "Strength to Love" and Other Preachings* (Boston: Beacon Press, 2012), 46–47.

Lesson 09

1. Bill Gaultiere, "Dallas Willard's Definitions," *Soul Shepherding*, November 25, 2016, www.soulshepherding.org/dallas-willards-definitions/.

2. Mahatma Gandhi, *Young India*, April 2, 1931.

LESSON 11

1. *Spider-Man*, directed by Sam Raimi (Culver City, CA; Columbia Pictures, 2002).

LESSON 12

1. Brené Brown, *Braving the Wilderness: The Quest for True Belonging and the Courage to Stand Alone* (New York: Random House, 2017), 157.
2. Alexander Tuerk, "Eliud Kipchoge Dashes Past 2-Hour Marathon Barrier in Assisted Event," National Public Radio, October 12, 2019, https://www.npr.org/2019/10/12/769732863 /eliud-kipchoge-dashes-past-2-hour-marathon-barrier-in -assisted-event.

LESSON 14

1. J. M. Twenge, et al., "Decreases in Psychological Well-Being among American Adolescents after 2012 and Links to Screen Time During the Rise of Smartphone Technology," *Emotion* 18, no. 6 (September 2018): 765–780, https://psycnet.apa.org /record/2018–02758–001.

LESSON 16

1. "Fast Facts," Smoking & Tobacco Use, Centers for Disease Control and Prevention, last modified November 15, 2019, https://www.cdc.gov/tobacco/data_statistics/fact_sheets/fast _facts/index.htm.
2. S. C. Hitchman, et al., "The Relation Between Number of Smoking Friends, and Quit Intentions, Attempts, and Success: Findings from the International Tobacco Control (ITC) Four Country Survey," *Psychology of Addictive Behaviors* 28, no. 4 (December 2014): 1144–1152, https://www.ncbi.nlm.nih.gov /pmc/articles/PMC4266625/.

LESSON 17

1. "NFL Receptions Career Leaders," Leaders Index, Pro Football Reference, last modified January 8, 2020, https://www.pro
-football-reference.com/leaders/rec_career.htm.

LESSON 19

1. If you'd like to watch the documentary as well, it's called *Touching the Void*, and retells the story of Joe Simpson and Simon Yate's near-fatal climb of the Suila Grande in the Peruvian Andes in 1985. The story is also a book of the same name by Joe Simpson.

LESSON 21

1. Okay, to be honest, the letter already existed, but my friend was definitely the reason they had to send it out that day.

LESSON 23

1. Her name was changed here, but I definitely see the woman as a Glo.

LESSON 26

1. C. S. Lewis, *The Four Loves* (New York: Harcourt Brace Jovanovich, 1960), 169.
2. John Stott, *The Cross of Christ* (Downers Grove, IL: InterVarsity Press, 2006), 326.

LESSON 27

1. Joe Berkowitz, "Infographic: This Is How Your relationship Will Likely End," *Fast Company*, accessed January 20, 2020, https://www.fastcompany.com/3024299/infographic
-this-is-how-your-relationship-will-likely-end.
2. Ibid.
3. "Peak Breakup Times on Facebook," *Information Is Beautiful*,

accessed January 20, 2020, https://informationisbeautiful
.net/2010/peak-break-up-times-on-facebook/.

4. Elizabeth Svoboda, "The Thoroughly Modern Guide to
Breakups," *Psychology Today,* last modified June 9, 2016,
https://www.psychologytoday.com/us/articles/201101
/the-thoroughly-modern-guide-breakups.

LESSON 28

1. Dr. Henry Cloud is—in my opinion—about as good as it
gets when it comes to relationship advice, and he talks about
similar topics in his work, including this article: https://www
.boundaries.me/blog/the-7-warning-signs-of-a-bad-relationship.

2. Henry Cloud, *Changes that Heal: Four Practical Steps to a
Happier, Healthier You* (Grand Rapids, MI: Zondervan, 1990),
22.

3. If you want to watch the movie, it's called *Gaslight,* directed
by George Cukor (Culver City, CA: Metro-Goldwyn-Mayer,
1944).

4. "Median Age at First Marriage, 1890–2010," Infoplease,
accessed January 8, 2020, https://www.infoplease.com/us
/marital-status/median-age-first-marriage-1890–2010.

5. "Historical Marital Status Tables," United States Census
Bureau, updated November 2019, https://www.census.gov/data
/tables/time-series/demo/families/marital.html.

LESSON 29

1. This story is based on an old fable, but Timothy Keller also
inspired the idea in his book *The Reason for God: Belief in an
Age of Skepticism* (Penguin Books, 2018), 46.

2. This "I give up being able to do anything in order to accomplish
something I want more" is tied to the idea of negative and
positive freedoms, first proposed by Kant and developed
by philosophers like Isaiah Berlin, Thomas Hobbes, and

John Locke. If you want to dive into the theories, this is a great site to check out: https://plato.stanford.edu/entries /liberty-positive-negative/.

LESSON 31

1. *Merriam-Webster*, s.v. "lazy (adj.)," accessed December 19, 2019, https://www.merriam-webster.com/dictionary/lazy.
2. Vikas Jha, "Oprah Winfrey's 13 Empowering Quotes on Self-Leadership," Medium, August 11, 2015, https://medium.com /productivity-revolution/oprah-winfrey-s-13-empowering-quotes -on-self-leadership-8a8b89ee34b6.

LESSON 32

1. Darren Rovell, "Muhammad Ali's 10 Best Quotes," ESPN, June 3, 2016, https://www.espn.com/boxing/story/_/id/15930888 /muhammad-ali-10-best-quotes.
2. Robert M. Yerkes and John D. Dodson, "The Relation of Strength of Stimulus to Rapidity of Habit-Formation," *Journal of Comparative Neurology and Psychology* 18, no. 5 (November 1908): 459–482, http://psychclassics.yorku.ca/Yerkes/Law/.
3. *The Lord of the Rings: The Fellowship of the Ring*, directed by Peter Jackson (Los Angeles, CA: New Line Cinema, 2001), 178 min.
4. "Estimated Probability of Competing in College Athletics," Research, National College Athletic Association, updated April 3, 2019, http://www.ncaa.org/about/resources/research /estimated-probability-competing-college-athletics.
5. *Braveheart*, directed by Mel Gibson (Santa Monica, CA: Icon Productions, 1995), 178 min.

LESSON 33

1. There are several versions of this story in books and online, but the closest version I found to the one I've often heard told is in

Terry Hershey's *Sacred Necessities: Gifts for Living with Passion, Purpose, and Grace* (Ava Maria Press, 2005), 68–69.

2. "Sleep in Adolescents," Sleep Disorder Center, Nationwide Children's Hospital, accessed January 8, 2020, https://www .nationwidechildrens.org/specialties/sleep-disorder-center /sleep-in-adolescents.

3. I ran across Tim Ferriss's *The 4-hour Workweek* (Crown, 2007) after I wrote this section of the book, and he goes into much more depth on this idea if you want to dive in further.

Lesson 34

1. "Why the Family Meal Is Important," Stanford Children's Health, accessed August 10, 2019, https://www.stanfordchildrens .org/en/topic/default?id=why-the-family-meal-is-important-1–701.

2. Wasantha P. Jayawardene, MD, PhD, et al., "Exercise in Young Adulthood with Simultaneous and Future Changes in Fruit and Vegetable Intake," *Journal of the American College of Nutrition* 35, no. 1 (2016): 59–67, https://www.tandfonline .com/doi/abs/10.1080/07315724.2015.1022268#.Vcreq5Oqqkp.

3. "5 Friends Purchase First Property after Saving $50 per Week for 2 Years," Philadelphia, Fox29 Philadelphia, last modified August 6, 2019, https://www.fox29.com/news/5-friends -purchase-first-property-after-saving-50-per-week-for-2-years.

4. I ran across this same "sink-cleaning" advice after my friend told me about her new habit, which apparently is a "spillover habit" since it gets you started on other habits—Marla Cilley, aka the FlyLady, is a big proponent of the clean sink: www .flylady.net/d/getting-started/flying-lessons/shine-sink/.

5. Admiral William H. McRaven, "Commencement Address" (speech), University of Texas at Austin, May 17, 2014, Austin, TX, video, 19:26, https://www.youtube.com /watch?v=pxBQLFLei70.

Lesson 35

1. Thomas Aquinas, *Summa Theologica*, and specifically his treatises on Temperance (*Summa Theologica* IIaIIae 141–154). https://books.google.com/books?id=E2JAkRmPWosC&pg =PA255&dq=Thomas+Aquinas,+Summa+Theologica,+and+his +treatises+on+Temperance&hl=en&newbks=1&newbks_redir =0&sa=X&ved=2ahUKEwjcx5ux4KTnAhXWU80KHWw WBSYQ6AEwAnoECAIQAg#v=onepage&q=Thomas %20Aquinas%2C%20Summa%20Theologica%2C%20and %20his%20treatises%20on%20Temperance&f=false.

2. His book is also what got me thinking about Aquinas's cardinal virtues and temperance, so I'm very thankful.

3. *Encyclopædia Britannica Online*, s.v. "Michael Phelps: American Swimmer," accessed January 9, 2020, https://www .britannica.com/biography/Michael-Phelps.

4. Julian Linden, "Insight: The Greatest Olympian and His Coach," Reuters, August 12, 2012, https://www.reuters.com /article/us-oly-end-phelps/insight-the-greatest-olympian-and -his-coach-idUSBRE87B06N20120812.

5. Carmine Gallo, "3 Daily Habits of Peak Performers, According to Michael Phelps' Coach," *Forbes*, May 24, 2016, https://www .forbes.com/sites/carminegallo/2016/05/24/3-daily-habits-of-peak -performers-according-to-michael-phelps-coach/#fbd9306102cc.

6. Katie McLaughlin, "Michael Phelps: 'I Consider Myself Normal,'" CNN, August 1, 2012, https://www.cnn.com/2012 /07/30/us/michael-phelps-on-pmt/index.html.

7. https://www.reference.com/world-view/michael-phelps-training -schedule-778a242121006858.

Lesson 36

1. Tremper Longman III, *Proverbs* (Baker Academic, 2006), 131.

2. Bruce K. Waltke, *The Book of Proverbs, Chapters 1–15* (Grand Rapids, MI: Eerdmans, 2005), 90–91.

Lesson 37

1. Mark Medina, "Kobe Bryant Credited with Reshaping Culture of USA Basketball, Helping Lead Team to 2008, 2012 Gold Medals," *The Orange County Register*, August 12, 2016, www.ocregister.com/2016/08/12/kobe-bryant-credited-with-reshaping-culture-of-usa-basketball-helping-lead-team-to-2008–2012-gold-medals/.

2. Jim Collins, *Great by Choice* (New York: HarperCollins, 2011), chapter 2. Also: "Great by Choice: How to Manage Through Chaos," Articles, JimCollins.com, October 2011, https://www.jimcollins.com/article_topics/articles/how-to-manage-through-chaos.html.

Lesson 38

1. Andy Crouch also addressed this issue, among many others, in a poignant and important article in *Christianity Today*: www.christianitytoday.com/ct/2015/december-web-only/thoughts-and-prayers-after-san-bernardino-shooting.html.

2. If you want to see all the stories, a handy list of all of Jesus's miracles can be found here: http://blog.adw.org/wp-content/uploads/2018/03/37-Miracles-of-Jesus-in-Chronological-Order.pdf.

Lesson 39

1. His name has been changed.

Lesson 40

1. I swore this story my friend told me about himself was true, but I later learned it happened a completely different way. But to me, it still holds a little truth.

2. Special thanks to Jon Fortt and Mark Cornelison for the ideas, themes, and lesson of this fictitious story. Jon and Mark started a band called Face the Dog, which played in quite a lot of local

bars in Lexington, KY, at the turn of the century. Sadly, there is
no record of this, and the band's music has been lost to history.

LESSON 41

1. "All Time Leaders," NBA Advanced Stats, National Basketball
   Association, accessed January 10, 2020, https://stats.nba.com
   /alltime-leaders/.
2. Chris Johnson, "Kobe Bryant Breaks NBA Record for Missed
   Shots," *Sports Illustrated*, November 11, 2014, https://www.si.com
   /nba/2014/11/12/kobe-bryant-lakers-missed-shots-nba-record.
3. "NFL Rushing Yards Career Leaders," Leaders Index, Pro
   Football Reference, accessed January 10, 2020, https://www
   .pro-football-reference.com/leaders/rush_yds_career.htm.
4. Eric Edholm, "Team for the Ages—Barry Sanders," Pro
   Football Weekly, July 11, 2018, https://www.profootballweekly
   .com/2018/07/09/team-for-the-ages-barry-sanders/ag3sbhv/.
5. "Edison's Lightbulb," History of Science and Technology, The
   Franklin Institute, accessed January 10, 2020, https://www
   .fi.edu/history-resources/edisons-lightbulb.
6. "The Practical Incandescent Light Bulb," Edison Files, Edison
   Museum, accessed January 10, 2020, http://edisonmuseum
   .org/content3399.html.
7. Theodore Roosevelt, "Citizenship in a Republic" (speech,
   Université Paris-Sorbonne, Paris, France, April 23, 1910).

LESSON 42

1. Hannah Ritchie, "How Many People Die and How Many
   People Are Born Each Year?", Our World in Data, September
   11, 2019, https://ourworldindata.org/births-and-deaths.

LESSON 43

1. Someone who really helped inspire my line of reasoning here
   is Tim Keller, specifically a sermon called "Your Plans: God's

Plans," where he said: "Look, when I was twenty-two, twenty-three—I use this illustration for other things, it's very helpful in many ways—I did everything I possibly could, everything I possibly could, like Oedipus, you know, everything I possibly could to get married to a woman who if I had gotten married to her, would've been the wrong woman. And as I look back at my twenty-two-year-old self, I now think that probably about two-thirds of the things I wanted were wrong or bad, bad things, and if I gotten them, they have been very bad—two-thirds! Now here's the thing that scares me. What's my percentage now?" You can listen to the sermon here: https://www.youtube.com /watch?v=3OXaJPiov5E

2. Dr. Ali Bizinar, "Are You a Miracle? On the Probability of Your Being Born," *Huffington Post*, June 6, 2011, https://www.huffpost .com/entry/probability-being-born_b_877853?guccounter =1&guce_referrer=aHR0cHM6Ly93d3cuYmluZy5jb20vc2Vhcm NoP3E9Y2hhbmNlIcytvZit5b3UrYmVpbmcrYm9ybiZzcm M9SUUtU2VhcmNoQm94JkZPUk09SUVOQUUx&guce _referrer_sig=AQAAAGEHlv6qDD_M-XML8lrVN2 -LYaIuKnhIFn8KDzc8opNfojLc8cgir5ERFQjJBmYLLVdcHtBUT _jxB02QpGkevQ4RU_ovVDIM8EVQHlMtumElhlmmu M2oGLeofdEpQcDIA_8g4fXVBMplsgwUI7FqYWI4_ NcgQetyLFPr1xF6sL5e.

Lesson 44

1. Christina Saraceno, "Bono Meets Bush," *Rolling Stone*, March 15, 2002, https://www.rollingstone.com/politics/politics-news /bono-meets-bush-194801/.

2. Simon Vozick-Levinson, "Bono: 'I've Grown Very Fond' of George W. Bush," *Rolling Stone*, November 30, 2018, https://www.rollingstone.com/music/music-news/bono -george-w-bush-world-aids-day-761747/.

3. George W. Bush (@georgewbush), Instagram post, May 26, 2017, https://www.instagram.com/p/BUkZ3WKBfXD/.
4. Frederick Buechner, *Wishful Thinking: A Seeker's ABC* (New York: HarperCollins, 1993), 119.
5. Rev. Dr. Martin Luther King, Jr., "Three Dimensions of the Complete Life," in *Strength to Love* (New York: Harper and Row, 1963), 72.

LESSON 45

1. Esther B. Fein, "Book Notes," *The New York Times*, November 20, 1991, Section C, Page 26, accessed January 18, 2020 via https://www.nytimes.com/1991/11/20/books/book-notes-059091.html
2. Holcomb B. Noble, "Dr. Viktor E. Frankl of Vienna, Psychiatrist of the Search for Meaning, Dies at 92," *The New York Times*, September 4, 1997, Section B, Page 7, accessed January 18, 2020 via https://www.nytimes.com/1997/09/04/world/dr-viktor-e-frankl-of-vienna-psychiatrist-of-the-search-for-meaning-dies-at-92.html.
3. Viktor Frankl, *Man's Search for Meaning* (Boston, MA: Beacon Press, 1992), 105.
4. Dwight D. Eisenhower, "Television Broadcast: 'The People Ask the President,' October 12, 1956" in *Public Papers of the Presidents of the United States: Dwight D. Eisenhower, 1956, January 1–December 31, 1956*, 906 (Washington, DC: Government Printing Office, 1956).
5. Robert Sullivan, "Ike: The Indispensable Man," in *LIFE D-Day 70 Years Later*, ed. *LIFE* Magazine editors (New York: LIFE Books, 2014).

LESSON 46

1. Alexander Harris, "U.S. self-storage industry statistics," SpareFoot Storage Beat, updated March 11, 2019, https

://www.sparefoot.com/self-storage/news/1432-self-storage
-industry-statistics/.

2. Melissa Chan, "Here's How Winning the Lottery Makes You
Miserable," *Time*, January 12, 2016, https://time.com/4176128
/powerball-jackpot-lottery-winners/.

3. Timothy Keller, *Counterfeit Gods: The Empty Promises of
Money, Sex, and Power, and the Only Hope that Matters* (New
York: Penguin Random House, 2009), xvii.

LESSON 48

1. Rachel Siegel, "Tweens, Teens, and Screens: The Average
Time Kids Spend Watching Online Videos Has Doubled in 4
Years," *The Washington Post*, October 29, 2019, https://www
.washingtonpost.com/technology/2019/10/29/survey-average
-time-young-people-spend-watching-videos-mostly-youtube
-has-doubled-since/.

2. "Social Media 'Likes' Impact Teens' Brains and Behavior,"
News, Association for Psychological Science, published May
31, 2016, https://www.psychologicalscience.org/news/releases
/social-media-likes-impact-teens-brains-and-behavior.html.

3. Jean M. Twenge et. al., "Increases in Depressive Symptoms,
Suicide-Related Outcomes, and Suicide Rates among
U.S. Adolescents after 2010 and Links to Increased New
Media Screen Time," *Clinical Psychological Science* 6, no.
1 (November 2017): 3–17, https://journals.sagepub.com/doi
/10.1177/2167702617723376.

4. "Media Use by Tweens and Teens 2019: Infographic,"
Common Sense Media, updated October 28, 2019,
https://www.commonsensemedia.org/Media-use-by
-tweens-and-teens-2019-infographic.

5. "Influencer: I Want to Look Like I Do on Instagram," interview
by Hala Gorani, CNN Business, May 14, 2019, video, 3:25,

https://www.cnn.com/videos/business/2019/05/14/instagram
-influencers-selfie-plastic-surgery-gorani-pkg-vpx.cnn.

LESSON 49

1. Molly O'Toole, "Martin Luther King Memorial Unveiled on National Mall," Reuters, August 22, 2011, https://www.reuters .com/article/us-king-memorial/martin-luther-king-memorial -unveiled-on-national-mall-idUSTRE77L5HJ20110822.

LESSON 50

1. Tzvi Machlin, "LeBron James Is Getting Crushed for How He Celebrated His Son's Dunk Saturday Night," *The Spun*, July 29, 2019, https://thespun.com/nba/los-angeles-lakers/lebron -james-is-getting-crushed-for-how-he-celebrated-his-sons-dunk -saturday-night.
2. Des Bieler, "The Latest LeBron James Debate Isn't About Basketball. It's About His Parenting Skills," *The Washington Post*, July 31, 2019, https://www.washingtonpost.com/sports /2019/07/31/latest-lebron-james-debate-isnt-about-basketball -its-about-his-parenting-skills/.

LESSON 52

1. John Donne, "No Man Is an Island" (London: Souvenir Press, 1988), 3.
2. Rev. Dr. Martin Luther King, Jr., "Remaining Awake Through a Great Revolution," in *A Knock at Midnight: Inspiration from the Great Sermons of Reverend Martin Luther King, Jr.*, ed. Clayborne Carson and Peter Holloran (New York: Warner Books, Inc., 1998).
3. I happened to listen to an audiobook of *Extreme Ownership* by Jocko Willink before I started writing this book, and his idea of "take full responsibility for what is happening or has happened" was likely still partly lodged in my brain as I put my thoughts together here. So I have to credit Jocko for the great idea.

The Greatest You

Face Reality, Release Negativity,
and Live Your Purpose

Trent Shelton with Lou Aronica

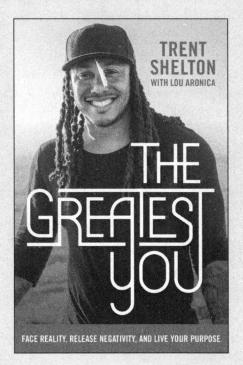

"If you want to become the best you, but
are unsure how to get there, start here."

RACHEL HOLLIS, #1 *New York Times* bestselling author of
Girl, Wash Your Face and *Girl, Stop Apologizing*

In this remarkable, life-changing new book, renowned inspirational speaker Trent Shelton shares his revolutionary tool kit for transforming your life and reaching your goals.

Trent Shelton seemed to have it all together—until everything fell apart. A college football standout, his NFL dreams died when he was cut from multiple teams. With no job and no prospects, learning he had a child on the way and numbing himself with whatever he could find, Trent then found out one of his closest friends had killed himself. Life seemed without hope—until Trent discovered the secret to finding promise in the darkest of times. And now he shares that secret with you.

Writing from deep, been-there experience, Trent walks you on a journey to become the best hope-filled version of yourself. In *The Greatest You*, Trent takes you through the necessary steps to become everything you are meant to be, helping you to:

    face the reality of your circumstances
    realize your purpose in life
    break free from toxic environments
    forgive those—including yourself—who've harmed you
    learn how to guard yourself against the pitfalls of life

Weaving together personal stories from his own life and from others who have also gone through hard times, Trent reveals how you can bring out the best in yourself and establish a happier, more fulfilled future for generations to come.

Available in stores and online!

Connect with Trent Shelton!

On Instagram: @trentshelton

On Snapchat: @rehabtime

On Facebook: www.facebook.com/LikeTrentShelton/

Website: www.trentshelton.com